John Reed

John Reed

Radical Journalist, 1887–1920

Kenneth Z. Chutchian

McFarland & Company, Inc., Publishers
Jefferson, North Carolina

LIBRARY OF CONGRESS CATALOGUING-IN-PUBLICATION DATA

Names: Chutchian, Kenneth Z., 1957– author.
Title: John Reed : radical journalist, 1887–1920 / Kenneth Z. Chutchian.
Description: Jefferson, North Carolina : McFarland & Company, Inc., Publishers, 2019. | Includes bibliographical references and index.
Identifiers: LCCN 2019039486 | ISBN 9781476676975 (paperback) ∞ | ISBN 9781476637945 (ebook)
Subjects: LCSH: Reed, John, 1887–1920. | Revolutionaries—United States—Biography. | Journalists—United States—Biography. | Communists—United States—Biography.
Classification: LCC HX84.R4 C44 2019 | DDC 070.92 [B]—dc23
LC record available at https://lccn.loc.gov/2019039486

BRITISH LIBRARY CATALOGUING DATA ARE AVAILABLE

ISBN (print) 978-1-4766-7697-5
ISBN (ebook) 978-1-4766-3794-5

© 2019 Kenneth Z. Chutchian. All rights reserved

No part of this book may be reproduced or transmitted in any form or by any means, electronic or mechanical, including photocopying or recording, or by any information storage and retrieval system, without permission in writing from the publisher.

Front cover: John Reed (Library of Congress)

Printed in the United States of America

McFarland & Company, Inc., Publishers
 Box 611, Jefferson, North Carolina 28640
 www.mcfarlandpub.com

This book is dedicated to CAROL COULTAS.
In 1983, after midnight in the *Lowell Sun* newsroom,
she named the entire starting lineup for the 1967 Boston Red Sox.
A year later she invited me to a conference in New York City
that Jack Reed would have attended.
She still surprises and inspires me.

Acknowledgments

My list of thanks begins with Martina Duncan for the welcoming environment she created in the Maine Humanities Council's Teaching American History Through Biography program, which was directly responsible for me believing I could pull off this book idea. Martina had some help dealing with our unwieldy group of 30–35 teachers reading and discussing more than 25 biographies over a three-year period, but she set the tone for humor and appreciation of the fact that we were trying to become better teachers by improving our content knowledge. I am thankful for support from Patrick Rael, Anne Schlitt, Libby Bischof and Charles C. Calhoun during the TAH program. In recent years Patrick has listened patiently to this first-time author during several meetings at Byrnes Irish Pub in Brunswick, Maine. He directed me to conferences and the academic publishing field. He called me indefatigable, which is one of my favorite words.

I am grateful for the access and assistance extended to me by the good people at Bowdoin College Library, ten miles from my house in Harpswell and a cool place to kill a few hours in the winter, spring, summer and fall. I am probably the only person who has checked out John Reed books from Bowdoin in the last ten years. I used them often enough to require rebinding for the Gelb, O'Connor and Rosenstone volumes.

I am indebted to the staff at Harvard University's Houghton Library, home of John Reed's collection of personal papers, photographs and manuscripts. Staff members reassured me that their library's online search aids are not necessarily intuitive.

Thank you, Carol, for wanting me to do my thing. And thank you, Maria and Jack, just because your magic can help me do anything.

Table of Contents

Acknowledgments	vi
Preface	1
One. You Can't Go Home Again, Part I	5
Two. Three Men: Copeland, Steffens, Eastman	26
Three. Endless Storm: Harvard to Mexico	43
Four. Two Women: Mabel Dodge and Louise Bryant	63
Five. Crossing Borders and Boundaries	75
Six. The Retreat of American Journalism	98
Seven. The Classic and the End Game	105
Eight. Radicals, Revolutionaries and Reed: Berkman, Goldman, Haywood, Debs	123
Nine. You Can't Go Home Again, Part II	135
Ten. Revolution: The Day After	152
Chapter Notes	165
Bibliography	177
Index	179

Preface

John Reed did not lead a linear life. For that reason and others (including the way my brain works), this is not a linear book. We begin in 1912, when he was 24, take a brief step backwards into the history of his family and hometown, and then strap ourselves in for the wild ride of Jack Reed the man, also known as John Reed the journalist, along with a dozen or so labels from people who tried in vain to categorize him. (For the most part, "John" was his professional writer's name, while "Jack" was how everyone addressed him.) The story I tell does move forward, from 1912 in Chapter One to 1920 in Chapter Ten, but there are strategic detours along the way. Chapters two, four, six and eight attempt to put Reed in the context of people who shaped him as well as people who shaped one of the most remarkable decades in American history. These chapters contain mini-profiles of individuals who worked directly with Reed as he crammed an impossible amount of life in nine years. Until 1912, his life was nothing remarkable. Eccentric relatives, some inherited privilege, a lot more misdirected rebellion in college than most undergraduates ... but nothing remarkable. Nothing to hinder construction of a linear and successful life. The rest of his life appears (to anyone who studies it) chaotic, perhaps random, possibly schizophrenic, with a few threads holding the story together. A romance with the working class that became sustained anger at the power of big business and all three branches of our government—especially the military. An over-the-top need to make people laugh and stop taking themselves too seriously. And movement. From rally to rally, story to story, city to city, border to border, nation to nation, woman to woman.

In some respects, John Reed's life does not make sense. Historians have been trying to string together linear biographical sketches and full-length linear biographies since Granville Hick's excellent *The Making of a Revolutionary* in 1936, but they pretty much stopped after the release of Warren Beatty's film *Reds* in 1982. Although books published in 1987, 1992 and 2002 have analyzed his writing in one context or another, the last true biography of Reed, by Robert Rosenstone, was published in 1975, more than forty years ago. That followed a mini-burst of interest in Reed with biographies written in 1973 (Barbara Gelb) and 1967 (Richard O'Connor and Dale L. Walker). Historians were trying to make sense out of Reed's life in the sixties and seventies, turbulent times when the most extreme left-wing activists in America spoke openly of socialism and, yes, revolution. Just as they did in the 1930s. Just as they have 1910–1920. Each Reed biographer faced the same problem. Connecting dots for cause and effect seems futile as you try to follow Reed splattering himself against the canvas of a decade that shook the identities of nations and cultures.

The parallels between Reed's decade of work-write-play-romance-revolt and the decade of 2010–2019 are not perfectly aligned. But they can be discomforting. Concerns and hysteria over national security. Challenging the patriotism of those who disagree with us. Hostility toward immigrants. Pushback against labor unions. Advances in technology compelling us to move faster for more production and "a better life." More leisure time for some, and fewer wage increases for many more. Gender roles challenged. Women refusing to be defined, let alone bullied, by men. Check, check, check. And nationalism.

When my 11th- and 12th-grade students tell me history repeats itself, I say to them we're all too busy or tired or entertained to give history the respect it deserves. Jack Reed has re-emerged from time to time in op-ed columns a century after the anniversary of one of many historical events that he jumped into with both feet. Then he disappears, like a Snapchat photo. History evaporates unless we keep checking in. This books tries to remind us that history always needs revisiting. The book tries to put the S word (socialism) into historical context that my students understand without losing their minds over the possibility that the old guy at the front of the classroom is recruiting for party membership. You can find the word "socialism" in a lot of headlines and news stories in 2019. And you can hear the word misused, intentionally and unintentionally, every day from people with or without post-secondary degrees.

Jack Reed had conversations with a lot of people from all walks of life, from many places around the world. He never got over his exasperation with the American inclination to oversimplify complex issues or to deny fundamental economic truths. Most of the writing he produced has direct application to our world in 2019. Observer, listener and wordsmith that he was, his character sketches may be relevant and beautiful to read for a long time. He said he loved people, which may not be technically true. He loved people who told stories with their faces, their walks, their actions at work and play, and their spoken word. These are all good reasons for the first biography of John Reed in 44 years. One more reason: the guy was just plain crazy fun.

CHAPTER ONE

You Can't Go Home Again, Part I

He had not really attained grown-up status at the age of 24. He held a degree from Harvard and counted among his undergraduate peers a number of young men who would do impressive things with their writing talents, including Walter Lippmann, T.S. Eliot, and Hans V. Kaltenborn. At 24, John Reed—known as "Jack" to friends and acquaintances, as "John" to those who only knew his writings and bylines—would soon attain stardom in his chosen career, journalism. But the nicknames he acquired along the way ("Storm Boy," "Playboy", "Wonder Boy," and "the Golden Boy of Greenwich Village")[1] revealed popular perceptions of him as a man-child. By age 24, "he was one of those boy-men that America seems to produce on an assembly line," wrote one historian. "And like so many recent American writers—Jack London, Stephen Crane, Scott Fitzgerald, Thomas Wolfe, Ernest Hemingway—he was a combination of explosive vitality and sustained immaturity."[2] Less than two years after becoming a working journalist in New York, John Reed needn't worry about his professional reputation. His reporting, short stories and poetry were in demand, published in *Collier's*, *The Saturday Evening Post*, *Forum*, *Century*, *Metropolitan Magazine* and *Smart Set*. He could write, he could get anyone to tell their story, and he could work without sleep. He did not spend much time concerned about how he came across to serious-minded people. "Little given to introspection, he rarely probed the wellsprings of his actions and desires," wrote another historian.[3] Having already been exposed to the heroic and the tragic, the whimsical and the reckless, he had been impressed with few elders in his young life. By the summer of 1912, Jack Reed was known as much for laughing, pulling pranks, calling attention to himself or thrill-seeking as he was for his writing.

The real story of Jack Reed begins in the late summer and early fall of 1912, as he approached his 25th birthday, and after the death of his father, when Reed spent four months at his childhood home in Portland, Oregon. Out of necessity, Reed was forced to spend quiet time alone with his mother, Margaret Green Reed, and take stock. At this point in his life, reflection was out of character for Reed. He was a gifted writer, but he always seemed more interested in action.[4] Four months thinking about his father's life helped him come to terms with ambition beyond the confines of his Oregon upbringing, beyond the stifling confines of Harvard—even past the glory and grotesqueness of New York. A four-month pause helped Reed wrap his brain around what it meant to be a transplanted Westerner. Four months—mid–July to mid–October 1912—sent Reed on a collision course with history, an astonishing eight years during which his brand of reporting and writing marked him as a top-rate journalist while his political activism branded him as a revolutionary—and possibly the most dangerous American rebel of the 20th century.

His rise and fall between 1910 and 1920 gets lost in the fog of history. The decade produced some of the most astonishing upheavals in American life. Day after day, week after week, newspaper readers learned of labor strikes, anarchists, violence and death at political rallies, revolutions real and threatened. They read about government crackdowns on immigration, free speech restrictions, national security threats from within our borders, and the European War (or was it the Great War?). Americans opposed the war, re-elected a president who promised peace, and then blinked, embracing nationalism and militarism. They read about indefatigable suffragettes losing their patience as they demanded the same reforms that had been called for since the women's movement began 60 years earlier in Seneca Falls, New York. Already slipping away by 1912 were the noble efforts of progressive politicians and investigative journalists in the previous two decades as they exposed corporate and government corruption. Americans turned on each other between 1910 and 1920. Civility in political discourse evaporated.

John Reed—journalist, poet, ladies' man, revolutionary, early 20th-century rock star—had been groomed for American greatness before he set out to expose America's dark side. He targeted the middle class and the wealthy with his scorn. He could write like nobody else, capturing the sound of unfiltered conversation, possessed with an unnerving gift to get anyone to expose their thoughts and feelings. "In his time, no one ever thought of defending John Reed's writing," wrote scholar Daniel Lehman. "Some things—like Ty Cobb's hitting or Jack Dempsey's two-fisted fury or John Reed's genius for the descriptive sentence—simply held true without debate."[5] He could mingle among the privileged with ease, but he often chose to immerse himself with people who had no money or choices in life, people who didn't know or care who he was as they spoke freely about the hard reality of living poor in the world's wealthiest nation. Powerful men could not shut him down with censorship, threats, violence or imprisonment. They were dealing with the son of a fighter, C.J. Reed, a Progressive who had investigated corruption and did not back down until he died. John Reed had the looks and pedigree of a glamorous American success story, but he would not stop writing about America's horrific treatment of its own people. In 1919, at a time when the U.S. government exiled 249 political radicals to Russia on a ship nicknamed *The Soviet Ark*,[6] Reed may have been considered more politically dangerous, peaking as one of the best reporters of his generation, bypassing Progressivism in his march to socialism and then communism. Who would follow him? The Feds did not know. With his passion and playfulness, he made political rebellion look cool.

For ten years, Reed moved with such speed and ferocity that it doesn't seem possible he had time to write. He raced from one episode to the next, one explosive story to another, jumping into an endless series of political and social conflicts and extracting himself from tumultuous love affairs with high-profile women. In the summer and fall of 1912, however, Reed had time to think about who he really was and what he wanted to do with his life. He had traveled through Europe and the Middle East after graduating from Harvard, and he had spent a year devouring life in New York City. Pausing as he approached his 25th birthday, Reed tried to comfort his mother, who had exposed him to the world through globe-trotting relatives, Chinese servants, and lots of books while protecting him from the rougher sides of Portland life. From mid–July to mid–October 1912, Reed wrote letters, newspaper articles, poems, personal essays and fiction. He reflected on the wealth he had seen abroad and in New York while at the same time it became apparent that his family's inherited wealth was evaporating. He brooded over his father's rise and fall in business and politics. He thought about the awe-inspiring hope of the doomed underclass in New York—and in Lawrence, Massachusetts, where in June he had seen the Industrial Workers of the World help striking factory workers win a labor dispute against textile mill owners.[7]

Getting a fresh perspective on his hometown and upbringing after storming through Europe and New York for 18 months, Reed knew he wanted to be a writer, but decided, in the summer and fall of 1912, that his heroes were not Mark Twain or other favorite childhood authors. His heroes were not the captains of industry who built his hometown (whom his father had admired), or the future leaders groomed at Harvard, or Theodore Roosevelt (who loved Reed's father), or even Charles Copeland or Lincoln Steffens, his beloved mentors in college and journalism. His heroes were now the uneducated laborers who had made the Industrial Revolution possible and who had made the United States an economic giant. They were exploited, he realized, just as American Indians had been exploited by his maternal grandfather, Henry Green.[8] Reed's father, C.J. Reed, had pushed back against corporate exploitation of land, legal loopholes and political corruption, but he couldn't push hard enough because he was a self-made businessman without a college degree who desperately wanted to send his boys to Harvard and who always spoke the unfiltered truth. Young John Reed had attended Socialist Club meetings at Harvard, but within two years after graduation his ravenous appetite for adventure gave him reason to believe that mistreatment of workers was the only way that capitalism could work. C.J. Reed had been collateral damage in the corporate pushback against progressive reforms. In the summer and fall of 1912, John Reed realized that his father, too, was a hero (he wrote about this in an unpublished autobiographical essay, "Almost Thirty," in 1917).[9] Jack Reed would pick up where his father left off to resume C.J. Reed's fight with vengeance—the fight for equality under the law, the fight for human dignity regardless of social class, the fight that killed both father and son.

* * *

The impulsive young man who could not sit for long had often fancied himself a poet, playwright and artist, but now he had a writer's most valuable commodity—time—and he barely knew what to do with it. At 24, John Reed had seen much. Immigrant families dreaming the American dream alongside bankers, bohemians, bums and prostitutes of New York. Striking mill workers, among them pre-adolescent girls, in Lawrence, Massachusetts. Reed understood that two years of post-college adventures were not unusual in the big picture. True, they contained hilarious moments that would live forever, including a charge of manslaughter that disappeared when his friend and alleged victim appeared in court to offer himself as a witness.[10] True, in 1911–1912 he had already established himself as a player on the Greenwich Village literary scene. But Reed knew some history. He had already seen stars of various kinds rise and fall. For perhaps the first time, he began to think about what is important beyond fame, fun and adventure.[11]

He had been a sickly child fiercely protected by his mother. He had been an introvert and a mama's boy mocked by the neighborhood kids in Portland. He was a child of the still-untamed West, then a prep school boy and a lost freshman at Harvard before morphing into a campus celebrity with a big mouth and a contagious sense of mischievous humor.[12] He developed his own insights about people and cultures in foreign lands while suspecting that his fascination and empathy did not jive with the views of his family, his hometown or his college classmates. In 1912, he started to become John Reed on John Reed's terms.

Reed had been exposed to careless wealth, beginning with his grandmother and uncle, and again at Harvard. His family had a name worth protecting. "The son of C.J. Reed, the famous wit," wrote Granville Hicks in 1932. "The son of Margaret Reed, one of Portland's accomplished hostesses.... The grandson of old Mrs. Green, who still gave hilarious dances and was always traveling the world. Everybody knew him, and knew he was going away to school. Good Portlanders always sent their children east for their education."[13]

A similar message came from other sources, including friends who missed him. They offered advice as well as condolences. Reed read their letters, churned them over in his head and heart, and, for the most part, rejected suggestions that he start acting like a Harvard man or that he meet anyone's expectations except his own.

"The very conception of losing one's father is ghastly, yet it is always simply a matter of time," read one letter from old friend Joseph W. Adams in July of 1912.

> Knowing this, the thing to do is think as little about it as possible. Looking backward in contemplation of the loss helps matters very little; and looking ahead may help a great deal in bridging the gap.... If I were in your place, I think my dominant idea would be best expressed by the following algebraic expression:
>
> *Father's attainment = own attainment*
>
> *Father's preparation for life = own preparation for life*
>
> I don't know whether you catch the idea or not. By attainment, I mean how big a man is in the final analysis after throwing out the superficial elements. Where the start was with from advantages, and your own preparation was of the best, the equation for X (your own attainment) shows that you have a mighty high mark to reach in order to keep the family up to standard. If a man doesn't maintain or exceed his father's ratio of attainments to preparation, things are going backward.[14]

Two months later, in September 1912, with Reed still in Portland, Adams sent him another letter that included this line: "Tell the boys that I'm getting fat (which is the truth), and as soon as you make up your mind, let me know whether you're going to be a perfect stinker, just a dub, or a good kid."[15]

At 24, Reed had plenty of friends who were not shy about offering advice. He admitted, in "Almost Thirty," that he often had no idea what the road ahead of him looked like. But he was working on it during the late summer of 1912. From his mother's home he wrote a poem about his past year in New York, "The Day in Bohemia or Life Among the Artists," paying homage to his new friends while satirizing their futile efforts to make art meaningful in a crass, capitalistic world. It began:

> Muse, you have got a job before you, —
> Come, buckle to it, I implore you.
> I would embalm in deathless rhyme
> The great souls of our little time:
> Inglorious Miltons by the score, —
> Mute Wagners, —Rembrandts, ten or more, —
> And Rodins, one to every floor.
> In short, those unknown men of genius
> Who dwell in third-floor-rears gangreeneous,
> Reft of their rightful heritage
> By a commercial, soulless age.
> Unwept, I might add, —and unsung,
> Insolvent, but entirely young.
>
> ❧ ❧ ❧
>
> Twixt Broadway and Sixth Avenue,
> And West perhaps a block or two, —
>
> ❧ ❧ ❧
>
> From Third Street up, and Ninth Street down,
> Between Fifth Avenue and the Town, —
> Policemen walk as free as air,
> With nothing on their minds but hair,
> And life is very, very fair
> In Washington Square.
>
> ❧ ❧ ❧
>
> Bohemia! Where dwell the Sacred Nine,
> Who landed, steerage from the White Star Line, —
> (For, when the Sacred Springs dried up in Italy
> They packed their duds and emigrated prettily,
> And all the Ladies, donning virile jeans,
> Became the Editors of Magazines.)[16]

From Portland, Reed wrote letters to Harvard classmate Robert Canby Hallowell (former editor of *Harvard Lampoon*), one of which said, "I'm quite crazy to live here,"[17] meaning he understood the appeal of the West, the place that had drawn his father, his maternal grandfather, and other Easterners of the previous 100 years pursuing gold, land, space and riches. He recognized the West's ability to mesmerize Americans. Having split two years between European and New York adventures, in Oregon he felt the geographical contrast rock his soul as if he were discovering his home state for the first time while reminding himself that this is where he came from. He was Oregon at the core.

He had already expressed love for his home state in a letter to Hallowell a few days before his third year at Harvard in August 1909. By that time Reed had earned a reputation as a grandstanding boy from the West with no chance of acceptance among the Harvard elites.

> I received your letter ... just before my departure on a 200-mile walking trip down the Oregon Coast.... Four of us went, carrying blankets and grub on our backs, sleeping in the open, and bathing in the surf three or four times a day. We would travel from seven in the morning to five at night and then catch a mess of trout for dinner. At one beautiful beach we stayed three days and held Olympic games.... The nearest house was 30 miles off, and we remained naked for most of the time on the beach. You really ought to see Oregon country.... I am still in favor of starting the Western "life," and will jump in with any of you who want to do it, but I have my doubts as to whether it won't peter out with you fellows.[18]

He was torn about his beautiful hometown that had betrayed his father. "There is no one to talk to, and I'd go mad in a year," he told Hallowell in the July 1912 letter. In October he told Hallowell, "I am half dead for New York.... I am engaged now in a newspaper controversy that I started in order to stir up a little excitement, but it's not much fun. Besides that I don't do anything much but write."[19]

He was being honest, but he was wrong. In addition to writing, Reed was creating a bridge between his past and his unknown future. Although five years later he would claim, in his autobiographical essay "Almost Thirty," that he never had a life plan, he was wrong about that as well. In the summer and fall of 1912, Reed hatched a plan to make his father's death mean something.[20] He did not want to be the Golden Boy or Storm Boy that friend and peers called him or that crazy court jester from Harvard. He wanted to be a man of action and principle, a man who would fight to preserve what is decent, honest, fair and beautiful. And he insisted on having fun doing it.

* * *

A century later, Reed would not recognize Portland, Oregon, which took a long time to shift from suffocating conservatism to liberal playground.

Barack Obama won 82 percent of the city's vote in the 2008 presidential election; in subsequent years Portlanders elected a gay mayor and 60 percent of the voters rejected a referendum ballot question to ban gay marriages; the city hosts an organized naked bicycle ride every year and has the highest number of strip clubs per capita in the United States; beginning in 1992, the *Oregonian* newspaper stopped using sports team names considered offensive to members of racial, religious or ethnic groups.

Portland has produced other radicals besides John Reed, many of them chronicled by home-grown socialist professor Michael Munk. But for most of the century following his death in 1920, Portland did not embrace its connection with John Reed, the native son and journalist known for getting arrested at labor rallies, riding with Pancho Villa in Mexico, embracing Bohemian free love, and aligning himself with the Communist Party after writing *Ten Days That Shook the World*, the definitive American account of the Bolshevik Revolution. The city of Portland had no public memorial to Reed until 2001. MacCormac Snow, one of Reed's few boyhood friends, said, "Portland was generally horrified by him."[21] Biographer Richard O'Connor wrote that "John Reed would never be a hometown hero."[22] Reed College, founded in 1911 by Portland pioneer Simeon C. Reed, had no connection to John Reed but endured a false reputation for training young Communists—a myth reinforced by a seemingly impossible second coincidence: Reed College's first president was William T. Foster. Years later, the leader of the American Communist Party was a man named William Z. Foster. While *World Almanac* has called John Reed one of Portland's "best-known natives," his name does not make the cut in a list of notable Portland authors on Wikipedia's Portland page. Readers of the *Oregonian* website responded to a Labor Day column about Reed in September 2011 with classic 21st-century online venom:

> "A kissy-face column about a Communist who was buried close to Stalin?"
> "Good gawd, the gibbering sphincter Socialists are out in force today."
> "Had Reed lived, he'd doubtless have joined Times reporter and Pulitzer Prize winner Walter Purany in simply denying Stalin's mass starvations, shameful show trials and prison gulags."[23]

* * *

Its colorful beginnings and secure place in Wild West lore, complete with a story of two settlers naming the new town via a coin flip,[24] did not stop Portland from taking itself very seriously while Margaret and Charles Jerome Reed were raising their son John (also known as "Jack," "Caleb" and "Colby"). Outside their home in downtown Portland in the 1890s, American entrepreneurs jockeyed to be in the right place at the right time in a raw timber city that aspired to be "sober, public spirited and virtuous,"[25] all while keeping an eye on who was associating with whom, what they were wearing, and how they carried themselves. "Respectability was the essential quality for social acceptance; gaiety was suspect and nonconformity unheard of," historian Richard O'Connor wrote in 1967.[26] "It was and is one of the stodgiest port cities in the world." At the end of the 19th century, two generations after the Gold Rush and more than a decade after Reconstruction, America positioned itself to be an economic power with no limits. Portland was all business, all the time. "In public life, the businessmen who controlled the community upheld the stern and frugal virtues of their New England ancestors," wrote historian Robert A. Rosenstone in 1975. "For them work was life and life was work. The poetry they knew was confined to the Bible, music to the plain and simple hymns of Protestant churches, imagination to the opportunities for economic development of the abundant Northwest."[27] You were not supposed to succeed in this arena—competing against savvy businessmen migrating from the East—by being rebellious or weird.

John Reed's family had plenty of room for the serious, the rebellious, and the weird.

Margaret Green Reed was born into money. Her father, Henry Green, landed in Portland in 1853, ten years after the city was founded. As a capitalist and adventurer who had sailed around the world, he flourished in the new city, purchasing control of Portland's gaslight, water works and ironworks systems. He built an estate in the Cedar Hills section of Portland, where Jack Reed was born on October 22, 1887. Green's backstory, the way he was able to begin building his wealth, foreshadowed John's later contempt for the underpinnings of capitalistic society. Henry Green and his brother had established a trading post at the mouth of the Columbia River in upstate New York and had scant competition. "The method was simply a swindle based on the Indians' ignorance on what their furs were worth in the Eastern markets," according to O'Connor.[28]

"I still remember my grandfather's house where I was born—a lordly gray mansion modelled on a French chateau, with its immense park, its formal gardens, lawns, stables, green-houses and glass grape-arbor, the tame deer among the trees," John Reed recalled in "Almost Thirty," an unpublished, 8,000-word autobiographical essay.

> All that remains to me of my grandfather is his majestic height, his long slim fingers, and the polished courtesy of his manners.
> He had come around the Horn in a sailing ship when the West Coast was the wild frontier, made his pile, and lived with Russian lavishness. Portland was less than 30

> years old, a little town carved out of the Oregon forests, with streets steeped in mud and the wilderness coming down close around it. Through this my grandfather drove his blooded horses to his smart carriages, imported from the East—and from Europe—with liveried coachmen and footmen on the box!
>
> The lawn terrace below the house was surrounded on three sides by great fir trees, up whose sides ran gas-pipes grown over with bark; on summer evenings canvas was laid on the turf, and people danced, illuminated by flaming jets of gas which seemed to spout from the trees. There was something fantastic in all that.[29]

John's recall of his grandfather's appearance had to come from stories and photographs handed down, because Henry Green died in 1885, two years before John was born. In 1890, Henry Green's land was valued at $28,000—one of only two dozen properties in the city valued at more than $10,000. That year Charlotte Green sold the entire estate.[30] She continued to live large, dressing in a style considered flamboyant by Portland's standards and making friends with whomever she chose. She would leave the country periodically whenever she grew tired of Portland's "infamous political and artistic conservatism."[31]

Charlotte's brother, Ray, was a piece of work. Reed recalled,

> And there was my uncle, a romantic figure, who played at coffee-planting in Central America, mixed in revolutions, and sometimes blew in, tanned and bearded and speaking in "spigotty" like a mestizo. Once the tale ran that he had helped to lead a revolution that captured Guatemala for a few brief days, and was made Secretary of State; the first thing he did was to appropriate the funds of the National Treasury to give a grand state ball, and then he declared war on the German Empire—because he had flunked his German course in college! Later he went out to the Philippines as a volunteer in the Spanish War—and the tale of how he was made King of Guam is still told with shouts of mirth by the veterans of the Second Oregon.[32]

John Reed's mother, Margaret, understood the family's place among Portland's wealthy and prominent families. She was more socially conservative than the man she married—Charles Jerome Reed, an agriculture equipment dealer who had migrated from upstate New York. C.J. Reed arrived in Portland without a college education but in strong possession of political and business savvy as well a sharp wit and a sharper tongue.

The Reeds threw large parties, which John recalled as "a crowd of gay young people around my gay young father and mother." The Reeds had moved from the estate that Henry Green built to a modest downtown home, probably because grandma Charlotte was busy spending "the pile" that her husband had made. "Then we were poor," Reed wrote—perhaps an overstatement, perhaps not. He grew to not only appreciate the financial sacrifice his father made to send him to Harvard but also to be overwhelmed by the personal price he paid.[33]

When they lived with Jack's grandparents, the family could afford servants—a strange and fascinating collection of individuals who introduced to young John the power of travel and imagination that uncle Ray had introduced. "Almost all the servants in those days were Chinamen, who staid [sic] for years, at last getting to be almost members of the family," Reed wrote. "They brought ghosts and superstitions into the house, and the tang of bloody feuds among themselves, idols and feeds and drink, strange customs and ceremonies; half affectionate, half contemptuous, wholly independent, withal outlandish, they have left me a memory of pigtails and gongs and fluttering red paper."[34]

* * *

Beyond the eclectic cocoon of the Reed homestead, however, Portland did not have much tolerance for free spirits, as historians O'Connor and Rosenstone noted. The city had an inferiority complex. Back when it known simply as "The Clearing," one of its early pioneers, Tennessee native William Overton, quickly grew tired of clearing trees and building roads, and within two years of filing a land claim with Oregon's provisional government, he sold his rights to Francis W. Pettygrove of Portland, Maine, in 1845. At that point, Pettygrove and Asa Lovejoy of Boston, Massachusetts, owned all the important land in The Clearing, along with nearby waterfront and timberland. Both Pettygrove and Lovejoy wanted to name the area after their hometowns. They flipped a coin to decide, and Portland, Maine's Pettygrove won. A year later, in 1846, Lovejoy sold his half of the land. Two years after that, Pettygrove found the California Gold Rush far more interesting than Portland, so he sold nearly all of the townsite to Daniel H. Lownsdale, a tanner who paid him $5,000 in leather. Pettygrove reportedly made a handsome profit by selling Lownsdale's leather in San Francisco.[35]

Portland was never going to be another San Francisco; by the 1890s Seattle had surpassed Portland as the major port in the Pacific Northwest. While Portland had established itself as a major settlement in that region, its leaders during the early growth period bristled from derogatory assessments of the city from outsiders and the local press. It was known as "Stumptown" and "Mudtown." Historian Kimbark E. MacColl called it a city where "stumps from fallen firs lay scattered dangerously about Front and First Streets ... humans and animals, carts and wagons slogged through a sludge of mud and water ... sidewalks often disappeared during spring floods." The *Oregonian* called Portland "the most filthy city in the Northern States."[36]

That was one layer of the world beyond John Reed's childhood cocoon.

Closer to home lay toughies, bullies and gangs, the children of laborers and dockside workers on Portland's waterfront. His mother tried to protect him, screening his social contacts as best she could, even scolding a houseguest whose daughter had kissed John; Margaret Reed believed the family, although welcome in her home, had crossed social boundaries. Her son recalls hiding in a fantasy world fueled by books on the one hand and stories from the cast of characters in his home on the other.[37] Between his early bookishness and constant illness (mostly a weak kidney condition that would return later in life) that kept him indoors far more than most children his age, John came across as an easy target for neighborhood boys to push around for fun. He paid a nickel to one boy to not beat him up. Scraps were unavoidable. He fought back well enough to avoid being completely ignored, which would have been worse than the physical altercations he detested, as he noted in "Almost Thirty":

> I wasn't much good at the things other boys were, and their codes of honor and conduct didn't hold me. They felt it, too, and had sort of good natured contempt for me. I was neither one thing nor the other, neither altogether coward nor brave, neither manly nor sissified, neither ashamed nor unashamed. I think that is why my impression of my boyhood is an unhappy one, and why I have so few close friends in Portland, and why I don't ever want to live there again.
>
> It must have disappointed my father that I was like that, though he never said much about it.[38]

Anger and melancholy surfaced in his writings about Portland after Reed became an established journalist. Of his schooling at Portland Academy, he wrote, "Why should I have been interested in the stupid education of our time? We take young soaring imaginations, consumed with curiosity about the life they see all around, and feed them with dead technique.... And the teachers, men and women—usually women—whose chief qualification is that they plough steadily through a dull round of dates, acts, half-truths and rules for style, without questioning, without interrupting, and without seeing how ridiculously unlike the world their teachings are."[39]

Nevertheless, his 1912 interlude wasn't the last time Reed warmed up to his hometown—although the landscape seemed to impress him more than the people. He took time during a 1914 visit to Portland to write newspaper reviews of local artists. At that time he wrote: "Portlanders understand and appreciate how differently beautiful is this part of the world—the white city against the deep evergreen of the hills, the snow mountains in the east, the ever changing river and its boat life—and the grays, blues and greens, the smoke dimmed sunsets and the pearly hazes of August, so characteristic of the Pacific Northwest.... You don't have to point out those things to our people."[40]

It was a multi-dimensional world where John Reed spent the first 16 years of his life—the comfortable yet fragile lifestyle and social status built on a dwindling supply of inherited wealth; the firsthand tales of world adventures from his elders; the boy's imagination ignited by reading Mark Twain, humorist Bill Nye, the stories of King Arthur, history and poetry; and the working class neighborhoods where he claimed membership in the Fourteenth Street Gang (led by an Irish boy who later became a cop). He could have turned into his uncle Ray, a raconteur devoting his life to world travel for the sake of pleasure and pranks.[41] As it was, John Reed channeled enough of uncle Ray to do what historian Howard Zinn had suggested a century later—he made rebellion look like a lot of fun. He could have emulated his maternal grandmother, remaining in Portland while offending local sensibilities with a raucous social life. He could have shaken off the bruises inflicted upon his father's name by re-establishing the family's place in Portland's social order, a respectability highly valued by his mother.

Instead, John Reed became a louder, angrier, funnier and more artistic version of his father, a young man of conviction and ambition whose vision for social justice was often compromised by his penchant for laughing at people who took themselves too seriously. The relentless search for new people and places ... the annoying but entertaining way he called attention to himself ... these were adornments, outer layers that became associated with Jack Reed as much as if not more than his true character. C.J. Reed, in fact, was the template and the model of what Jack Reed would become.

There is no evidence to suggest that C.J. Reed gave his sons, John and Harry, a lot of attention or affection when they were young. That, of course, was not the way fatherhood worked in those days. Trying to work out his childhood memories, John would not describe himself as a happy boy, but he recalled many stories from a family environment that seemed almost too colorful for him to comprehend as an adult. Although he did not say as much, it becomes clear that C.J. Reed was the indispensable component, without which the family history did not make a lot of sense.[42]

C.J. Reed knew a lot of people in business and politics. He befriended one of the great journalistic muckrakers of his time, Lincoln Steffens, as well as President Theodore Roosevelt. At home, C.J. rolled his eyes at the antics of his in-laws, who unwittingly made great fodder for his dark sense of humor. He may have demonstrated his appreciation for their worldly sensibilities by fostering a domestic environment where Chinese servants felt free to express their culture with the Green-Reed home—even when that expression included mockery of their employers.[43]

For many of the people who knew C.J. Reed, his defining moment of truth arrived when a U.S. district attorney from San Francisco, acting on behalf of President Roosevelt, asked him to serve as a U.S. marshal to investigate widespread corruption in what came to be known as the Oregon Land Fraud. C.J. Reed could have said no, as most people with his community stature would have done, given the obsession Portland had with social order and conformity. Had he turned down the job, Jack Reed may have developed a different approach to power and politics. He probably would not have written these words from "Almost Thirty":

> He was a great fighter, one of the first of the little band of political insurgents who were afterwards, as the Progressive Party, to give expression to the new social consciousness of the American middle class. His terrible slashing wit, his fine scorn of stupidity and cowardice and littleness, made him many enemies, who never dared attack him to his face, but fought him secretly, and were glad when he died.
>
> As United States Marshal under Roosevelt, it was he who with Francis J. Heney and Lincoln Steffens smashed the Oregon Land Fraud Ring; which was a brave thing to do in Oregon back then. I remember him and Heney in the Marshal's office guying William J. Burns, the detective on the case, for his Hawkshaw make-up and his ridiculous melodramatics.
>
> In 1910 a man came around to browbeat my father into contributing to the Republican campaign fund, and he kicked the collector down the courthouse stairs—and was removed from the Marshalship by President Taft. Afterward he ran for Congress but lost out by a slim margin, mainly because he came East to see me graduate from college instead of stumping the State.[44]

* * *

The Oregon Land Fraud involved "great tracts of valuable timber and grazing land ... stolen from the American public."[45] It began with the U.S. government issuing three million acres of land to the Oregon and California Railroad company to build a rail line from Portland to California. The grants stipulated that parcels of 160 acres would be sold to settlers for a low price to encourage economic development. Because the land was heavily forested, there weren't many interested buyers. Timber companies were interested in the land, but their aims did not meet the requirements of the land grants. So Edward Harriman, president of the South Pacific Railroad (owner of the Oregon and California RR company), hired a surveyor to round up people from saloons in Portland's waterfront district to act as proxy purchasers of O & C parcels, after which they transferred their new property to the surveyor, Stephen A. Douglas Puter. The parcels were then sold in bulk for timber harvest to the highest bidders.

The scandal, which also involved bribing the Oregon General Land Office to accept fictitious names of homesteaders, spread rapidly. The point man leading the federal government's investigation, U.S. District Attorney Francis J. Heney, narrowed down an initial list of 1,000 indictments issued by his predecessor to 35 of the worst offenders. Heney's investigation eventually led to the conviction of surveyor Puter for conspiracy to defraud the U.S. government through the fraudulent acquisition of timberlands from the public domain. Three of Oregon's four congressional delegates were indicted for their roles in the scandal, including U.S. Senator John H. Mitchell and U.S. Representatives John N. Williamson and Binger Hermann. Mitchell was convicted of using his position to help others commit fraud. He was sentenced to six months in prison and a $1,000 fine, but he died before his appeal could be heard. Williamson was convicted for subornation of perjury in 1905, but the Supreme Court overturned the verdict due to jury intimidation. Hermann was found not guilty of destroying public documents; a second charge of collusion ended in a hung jury.

Francis Joseph Heney was the star and villain of the story, prosecuting the biggest names in Oregon business and politics. He replaced the initial lead prosecutor, John Hicklin Hall, who was removed from the case by President Roosevelt for dragging his feet on the case; Heney also successfully prosecuted Hall for his role in the land swindle. A year after he gained national attention for his role in the Oregon Land Fraud trials, Heney prosecuted San Francisco mayor Eugene Schmitz and political boss Abe Ruef for rigging city contracts in the aftermath of the 1906 earthquake. During that trial Heney was shot in open court, recovered, and later took on more Oregon Land Fraud cases.[46]

Given his tenacity, adversarial relationships with the power elite, and the adventures of his life, it makes perfect sense that Francis Heney would develop a bond with C.J. Reed while working on the same case. Heney, a native upstate New Yorker (as was C.J. Reed), moved to San Francisco with his family at the age of four. He was expelled from the Hastings College of Law in his first year for fighting with another student, but he recovered to pass the California Bar examination in 1883. Eight years later, Heney shot and killed a man whose wife he was representing in a divorce case. An investigation concluded that Heney acted in self defense.[47]

It was Heney who encouraged President Roosevelt to appoint Reed as a U.S. marshal to investigate the movers and shakers in Portland. The backlash directed at Reed was swift and harsh. C.J.'s motives for taking on the job seem above reproach; his politics were not only in step with the Progressive Party's push for government to rein in the excesses of big business—he may have been ahead of his time as well as more wedded to social justice than most men of his position, given the culture he was taking on in Portland—but it is also true that he needed the modest salary that the government position presented. His high-profile job with an agriculture equipment company had evaporated when the firm was sold. The bank panic and economic depression of 1893 made work hard to find. He sold insurance for awhile, taking a few years to draw a decent income. He was involved in city and state politics, serving as U.S. jury commissioner and in other roles. By the time his son John entered Portland Academy for his secondary education, however, C.J.'s star was already falling. Men of wealth who had set the rules for Portland's social decorum—men with long memories of "his fine scorn for stupidity and cowardness and littleness"—found his role in the investigation of their business climate reprehensible.[48]

Although he had reached the rarefied air of Portland elite with his membership in the Arlington Club, C.J. Reed did not hide his disdain for entitlement. He had never sugar-coated his commentary about his wife's side of the family, and he would not (or could not) pretend he held the same values as his peers at Portland's elite social club that, well into the 21st century, considered itself the paternal guardian of the city.[49] In 2015, the Arlington Club's website reported on the possible origins of its name: "Perhaps it was derived from old English nomenclature in which 'Arlington' signified the 'finest' or 'highest.'"

"Thirty-five leading businessmen met in December 1867 and agreed to found *a club where they could fraternize for mutual enjoyment and relaxation, and to provide a meeting place for discussing their own and Portland's destiny,*" the website states, providing its own italics. "Today, the Arlington Club, true to its original purpose, continues to welcome civic minded leaders from all walks of life to continue those discussions in their clubhouse comfortably nestled in the center of Portland's cultural district."[50]

C.J.'s politics tanked his social standing in Portland; his choice of friends did not help. He had developed a bond with Theodore Roosevelt that held strong years after his death. The former president showed his loyalty by helping C.J.'s eldest son when John's antics in Germany during the Great War threatened his journalistic credibility; at the same time, Roosevelt made it clear that his motives for helping the young man did not change his desire to apply his proverbial "big stick" to the man-child.[51]

C.J. also had a close friendship with Lincoln Steffens, whose investigative journalism compelled the federal government to get serious about the Oregon Land Fraud. Steffens later became C.J.'s eyes and ears for the purpose of keeping John both grounded and receptive to all opportunities that New York City had to offer a young journalist. C.J. died during his son's first year in New York; Steffens, who had already set up Jack with a magazine job while listening to endless stories about his discoveries, filled a huge void. Steffens became a surrogate father for the untamed adult son of C.J., doing exactly what C.J. wanted him to do.

Steffens visited the Arlington Club with C.J. Reed one day and later reported these words from his friend: "That's the crowd that got the timber and tried to get me. And there, at the head of the table, that vacant chair, that's my place. That's where I sat. That's where I stood them off, for fun for years and then for months in deadly earnest; but gaily, always gaily. I haven't sat in that place since the day I rose and left it, saying I'd never come back to it and saying that I would like to see which one of them would have the nerve to think that he could take and hold and fill my place. I have heard, and I am glad to see that it is vacant yet, my vacant chair."[52]

In his investigative role, C.J. Reed was essentially picking fights with the locals. He fought corruption and the power structure of his adopted home state in the name of fundamental fairness. He never said that he wanted his sons to fight, but he fought to earn enough income—after the family wealth evaporated—to send them to Harvard. From there his sons would receive a better education than he had, whereupon they would, presumably, have more options when considering what was worth fighting for.

* * *

Jack Reed was angry as he considered what his father had sacrificed while he played at Harvard, in Europe and New York. C.J. had scraped together $100 for his son's travels through England, France and Spain.[53] Skeptics have assumed that wild-child John received some funding from his grandmother, but in fact Reed had to work on a transatlantic cattle ship in order to finance the trip. Soon the family's wealth would morph into crushing debt and humiliation. At Harvard, Jack had noticed how routine it was for some of his classmates to receive yearly allowances of $15,000 for leisure and recreation.[54] The Green side of his family had shown him the darkness as well as the dazzling opportunities brought forth by money.

The family money was just about gone by the time C.J. Reed passed away, according to letters Jack received from his brother Harry in 1911, 1913 and 1915. In December 1911 Harry wrote, "I can't afford to buy you a Christmas present, and I don't want one from you." In March 1913 Harry said he was trying to sell family properties to pay off interest on loans and bank notes. In October 1915 Harry reported that the family was borrowing more money for basic living expenses and that their properties were not selling.[55]

Jack worked hard at maintaining his Harvard contacts after graduation; given his ambition, he would have been a fool not to do that. On the other hand, he never lost his zeal for pulling back the curtain to expose his alma mater as a house full of flawed individuals—just like any other group, community or organization. He felt he owed that to Harvard, and that the institution needed his jabs. Consider his impassioned defense of a satirical essay he had written about Harvard in a 1912 letter to Robert Hallowell: "And as for the Alumni, there will be two classes who will criticize: Old Farts, who once laughed at that very thing themselves, or wrote about it in [the *Harvard Lampoon*], or Young Farts who take themselves too seriously.... Harvard is a public institution ... a maker of citizens, existing [taxes, etc.] by permission of the state. No aspect of it should be private or secret. No aspect of it can be so, without doing the University an injustice."[56]

In the spirit of uncle Ray, Jack had looked for and found adventure in Europe in 1910; sometimes adventure found him. From the get-go, his travel companion, Waldo Peirce of Maine, provided Reed with a sensational story that made it into print in the *Boston Post* daily newspaper. Shortly after their cattle ship left its U.S. port, Pierce jumped off and swam to shore because he realized he was going to miss his girlfriend. When Reed reached the shores of England, he was charged with manslaughter. The case ended when Pierce showed up in court during a pretrial hearing, cracking jokes and proving beyond a reasonable doubt that Reed did not—and had no intention to—kill anyone.[57] The Pierce story is one of many sprinkling Reed's life that seem to have been written for a screenplay comedy. Reed was fascinated by people and curious about the way the world worked, but he was serious about the need for laughter, and he rarely took himself seriously.

"The Day in Bohemia," written during the summer and fall of 1912, does not read like the words of a writer ready to transition from starving artist to serious career man. In fact, he was evolving into something else. He did not love being broke because it made him look cool in Greenwich Village. He loved the way poverty liberated his art.[58]

> Lives there a man with soul so dead, I ask,
> Who in an attic would not rather bask
> On the South Side, in lofty-thinking splendor,
> Than on the North Side grow obese and tender?

> The North Side, to the golden ladle born,
> Philistine, suckled at a creed outworn!
> Unnumbered Jasons in their motor cars
> Pass fleeceward, mornings, puffing black cigars—
> We smoke Fatimas, but we ride the stars!
>
> ❧ ❧ ❧
>
> True to our Art, still there are variations,
> Art cannot flourish on infrequent rations;
> We condescend to work in humbler sort,
> For Art is long and money very short.
> Hence it is not so terribly surprising
> That ANDREWS deigns to scribble advertising;
> ROGERS, whose talent is of epic cast,
> at Sunday-paper stuff is unsurpassed.
> LEE teaches in an Art School he abhors,
> and LEWIS tries to please the editors;
> BOB EDWARDS, when he needs some other togs,
> Draws pictures for the clothing catalogues.
> And I, myself, when no one wants my rhymes,
> Yes, even I relax a bit at times.
>
> ❧ ❧ ❧
>
> Yet we are free who live in Washington Square,
> We dare to think as Uptown wouldn't dare,
> Blazing our nights with arguments uproarious;
> What care we for a cull old world censorious
> When each is sure he'll fashion something glorious?
> Blessed art thou, Anarchic Liberty
> Who asketh nought but joy of such as we![59]

* * *

Charles Jerome Reed died of heart attack on July 1, 1912. John had been in Cambridge to attend his brother Harry's graduation from Harvard; they both rushed home to witness their father's final days. John spent the entire night of July 1 and and early morning of July 2 walking the streets of Portland alone. And then the riches-to-rags story of his family hit him hard: "So badly tangled were financial affairs that he was forced to linger in Portland for weeks, then months, helping to settle a pitiful estate consisting of a few thousand worthless shares in gold and silver mines, debts totaling many thousands of dollars, and a single tangible item, a gold watch, willed to Jack," wrote Robert A. Rosenstone.

He indulged in some self-incrimination over his rowdy, rule-breaking ways at prep school, Harvard, Europe, and New York, but he did not beat himself up for very long. Instead, as Zinn and Rosenstone have noted, he decided to use his father's death as motivation to lead a more meaningful life, totally and unequivocally on his terms, without suffering fools gladly.

"He never let any of us know, but he was harassed into the grave," Jack wrote. "Money!"[60]

He would return to New York, but he would go with more on his plate than poetry, parties, women, and the pursuit of literary fame. He became a fighter—one who could write and laugh, but a fighter nonetheless who would shake the world with tales of what he saw, touched and felt.

Zinn wrote:

> In New York in 1912, for anyone who looked around as sharply as John Reed, the contrasts of wealth and poverty stunned the senses. John Reed could not be forgiven by the Establishment (nor even by some of its critics, like Walter Lippmann and Eugene O'Neill) for refusing to separate art and insurgency, for being not only rebellious in his prose but imaginative in his activism. He saw revolt as not mere fulmination, but fun, not just analysis but adventure. This caused some of his liberal friends to take him less seriously ... not understanding that, to the power elite of the country, protest joined to imagination was dangerous, courage combined with wit was no joke. Grim rebels can be jailed, but the highest treason, for which there is no adequate punishment, is to make rebellion attractive.[61]

Jack Reed took his father's fighting spirit with him to New York, Mexico, Colorado, France, Germany, the Western Front in the European War, the Baltic states, St. Petersburg, Moscow, and to his grave in Russia. C.J. Reed was a hero to John, but the father was frozen in time, leaving the world before he grew old, leaving before his oldest son could develop a nuanced understanding of him. By comparison, Margaret Reed did not fare as well in Jack's eyes. Even though he dutifully kept in touch his mother, her open disapproval of his radical politics prompted him to lash out at her on more than a few occasions. His brother Harry, the family diplomat, finally explained to Jack in 1915 the raw suffering of a family that had lost its patriarch as well as its social and financial bearings while the oldest son chased his dreams.

> Dear Jack:
>
> When I got home last night I found mother in tears over your letter, which she had just received, and she wept openly all night. I know what she said to you in the letter at which you took offense, and I don't see how you could have misunderstood her meaning, as she meant nothing that could have possibly offended you. Now I have only this to say to you—Mother doesn't lead a very happy life, and you and I are all that she has in the world. Anything possible that you can do to make her happier should be more than worthwhile, it seems to me, and it is in your power to do a great deal. Your long silence and then this letter have affected her more than you think.... I *must* feel as if I can count on you to help, and you can do it by writing to her often and affectionately and in general backing me up. Be honest and admit one thing—there has never been a time when either Mother or myself has not had the utmost respect for your views and opinions, even if we haven't always agreed. She thinks now that she has lost you, that you don't love her any more or have any interest in her....

You have done more than your share—I know that, but you've got to do more and back me up in keeping our family together, and you can by taking a lot of things into consideration that don't always appear on the surface. I haven't kicked or belly-ached to you before, and things have been hopeless enough for me. I have practically had to give up all idea of getting married or amounting to anything because I have had to make a choice. I have done it gladly knowing what we owe Mother and Pa. But of course don't mention to Mother I feel this way, and after all things may turn out all right.[62]

Postcards that John sent to Margaret from Europe and the Middle East in 1910–1911 bear the markings of a devoted son keeping his mother up to date on his latest adventures, trying to share his discoveries. Four months at home with her in 1912, however, did not strengthen their relationship. As he began to construct a serious, specific purpose for his adult life, he often hurt his mother, and she let him know it.

Some of the material he wrote during these four months became published, but most of it served the purpose of finding out who the hell John Reed really was and what he wanted to do with his life. He had to address the contradictions of American life, some of which contributed to his father's downfall, and some of which were seared in his memory of the New York streets. Without New York's noise, friends and adventures that he had courted, Reed wrote notes for future essays: "We are a conquering, gross, dull Roman race.... We have banded together to crush sensitiveness and fineness." The quest for individual success, as America defined it in 1912, made men "intent upon merely making a little money for himself, without any thought of the ... incongruity of his plan with the immutable rhythm of nature." The American obsession with facts, pragmatism and conformity were killing intelligence and imagination, according to Reed. He brainstormed topics for future essays: Individualism, Why I Hate My Government, Newspapers as Disseminators of Misunderstanding, The Senility of God, Labor, Radicals.[63]

And yet, until he returned from his reporting on the Bolshevik Revolution in 1918, Jack Reed did not often look or sound like the proverbial Angry Young Man. For a rebel who loved the heat of battle, Reed seemed to love laughter just as much. Lincoln Steffens, Max Eastman, the women he loved, Harvard classmates and historians all agreed that Reed was a romantic with a constant need to find wonderment and beauty. He was indeed that, but between 1912 and 1918 nobody was ready for the other side of a reinvented Jack Reed, a man always under construction.

Chapter Two

Three Men: Copeland, Steffens, Eastman

"Get in, get wise, and get out."—Harvard professor Charles Copeland, advising Jack Reed as his student considered a career in journalism

Given the energy, money and social capital he had invested to send his sons to an elite Eastern school, C.J. Reed didn't have a lot of time to counsel his boys on how to be a man. "Get him a job, let him see everything, but don't let him be anything for a while," the elder Reed told his friend, journalist Lincoln Steffens, when John first landed in New York in 1911. "Don't let him get a conviction right away or a business or a career, like me. Let him play."[1]

Charles Copeland, Lincoln Steffens and Max Eastman did a lot of the heavy lifting in the construction of John Reed the man, as Reed made history while reporting it. Neither Copeland, a Harvard professor, nor Steffens, a prominent journalist, could possibly know that in a few short years Reed—despite their wisdom and love—would become a threat to the U.S. government after he had established himself as one of the most accomplished reporters of his time. Eastman, on the other hand, gave Reed a visible platform for his radicalism along with brotherly advice. He sat in the same courtroom with Reed as both faced charges of obstructing the military draft. He embraced Reed's virtues and flaws before realizing how dangerous Reed had become to himself.

* * *

Charles Copeland showed Reed how to dream big on paper. He taught

Reed how words matter, how they should be cherished, cultivated, nurtured, chosen, edited, stirred, blended and presented in a display of undeniable uniqueness. The Copeland mantra: write what you see, write what you feel, write about what you read, and express it in your own way. Without Copeland's indulgence, prodding and occasional criticism, Jack Reed may not have taken himself seriously enough to become John Reed, world-famous writer. Reed had too much to do and see to seclude himself for extended periods, as writers must do. Reed was unsure of himself at Harvard, where he developed an oversized personality to compensate for insecurity and to let people know how angry he was. "Rejection made him so pushy and aggressive that social leaders recoiled even more," wrote historian Robert Rosenstone.[2] Copeland, in some ways, rescued Reed, convincing his student that he was special before Reed was ready to show the world.

Copeland had already earned fame within the confines of Harvard College when Reed began his freshman year in 1906. Copeland was a rare Harvard specimen in that he had almost no aspirations in his field other than to maintain his popularity among students, keep his writing course exclusive, and find the writers with a chance to make literary impact.[3] He showed no interest in publishing for academic journals and thus did not qualify for promotions at Harvard. He had his niche, and he stuck to it, honestly and without temptation to diversify or climb the professional ladder in higher academia. The college allowed Copeland to hand-pick his students, whom he selected after sizing up their potential for greatness and willingness to placate his ego. He had no system other than his intuition.

"Once upon a time, Professor Charles Townsend Copeland went to a particularly dull house party," wrote Stephen C. Clapp for *The Harvard Crimson* in 1958.

> Conversation dragged and the afternoon appeared to be a total loss. When he returned, some friends asked him whether or not he had enjoyed himself. "I should have been bored," Professor Copeland replied, "had I not been there myself."
> Professor Copeland, "Copey," was witty and knew it. Harvard anecdotes about him, like Lincoln stories, are legion and legendary. But the reason for the stories, both true and apocryphal, is that they perpetuate the personality of a truly unique teacher who left no other significant relics. As an English instructor, and later as Boston Professor of Rhetoric and Oratory, he taught two famous courses.... He wrote only one book, compiled two anthologies, and allowed a short moving picture to be filmed of himself reading aloud. Since he left few tangible achievements, there is little solid for biographers to fall back on.[4]

The Copeland aura was such that his chambers at 15 Hollis Hall—the location of his Saturday night free-wheeling gab sessions with favored students—

was known as Copeland's Castle. There he held court on a wide range of cultural issues. Sitting at Copey's feet, sometimes literally, were students who were on their way to distinguished writing careers, such as Maxwell Perkins, Hermann Hagedorn, Robert E. Rogers, Edward Sheldon, H. V. Kaltenborn and Lee Simonson.

In *Fifty Fabulous Years,* H.V. Kaltenborn wrote, "In selecting men for his English 12, Copey sought the well rounded man rather than the industrious grind. I once asked him why he had admitted a certain man whose intellectual virtues were not readily apparent to me. 'Oh, he just looked so healthy,' Copy replied." The young man, Kaltenborn noted, flourished under Copeland's instruction.

"Copeland insisted that his students express themselves with vigor and force, that they appreciate and emulate the sinewy quality that was the glory of American prose," wrote Richard O'Connor in *Lost Revolutionary.*[5]

Copeland rejected Jack Reed's initial application to join English 12, Advanced Composition. He later consented because Reed was persistent, passionate, and charming—and he promised to behave himself, something he was not known for doing or even trying to do. In his autobiographical essay "Almost Thirty," Reed credited Copeland with driving him to "find color and strength and beauty in books and in the world, and to express it again."[6]

Copeland wrote dozens of letters to Reed between Jack's graduation in 1910 and his reporting on World War I in 1916, when their relationship suffered from building tension between the professor's unabashed patriotism and his former student's unapologetic radicalism. As Reed's anti-war writings and activism morphed into a crusade, both Copeland and Lincoln Steffens warned their protégé about the inevitable consequences of turning political convictions into published words and turning either words or convictions into action. "Professor Copeland, though still friendly, was in a frame of mind that thinks no one is a he-man who hasn't gone into naval aviation."[7] Nevertheless, many of Copeland's letters to Reed reflect a yearning for face-to-face contact with one of his brightest stars.

Their mutual admiration was undeniable in 1914, when Reed became a celebrated journalist on an international level with the publishing of *Insurgent Mexico,* his account of the Mexican Revolution. Reed dedicated the book to Copeland. "It is all good, and more than good," Copeland told Reed in a letter, before adding, "You are a born writer—I discovered long ago. But I think you don't work hard enough at writing."[8]

At times they seemed smitten with each other. During his senior year at Harvard, Reed published this poem, teasing Copeland about his bachelorhood:

> Chamber'd Nautilus of Hollis
> When you'd play the lover's part,
> Do you find sufficient solace
> For your heart?
>
> ❧ ❧ ❧
>
> Don't your acolytes distress you,
> In their circle Johnsonese?
> Vying which shall cry "God bless you!"
> When you sneeze?
>
> ❧ ❧ ❧
>
> Does your fancy score the Present
> When your chorus leaves at last?
> Do you flirt with ladies pleasant
> From the past?...
>
> ❧ ❧ ❧
>
> Show some living maid your pity,
> Make her happy past her hope;
> Here's health—the lovely, witty
> Mrs. Cope![9]

Fittingly, Copeland and Steffens (who did not travel in the same circles) played indispensable roles helping Reed cross an important threshold as a young journalist—publishing his first article in *American Magazine*, the home for many of muckraking writers in the early 1900s. Steffens helped Reed land a full-time job at the *American*. Copeland was the subject of Reed's profile for the magazine's "Department of Interesting People" section. There he described Copey's "castle" on those Saturday nights at Harvard:

> It is a wonderful room, lined from floor to low ceiling with books. The broad mantel and little wall space are covered up with signed pictures of great people that you have read about and all the long generation of boys whose friend he has been. Over the door is a horseshoe and bunch of rowan berries. The only light is from the fire, perhaps a candle on the mantelpiece, and the reading light to the left of the fire, where sits the little man, interminably smoking an infamous brand of cigarettes. Everyone talks of the thing nearest to his heart; everyone finds himself alert, quick, almost brilliant.[10]

Reed had not yet developed what writer Barbara Gelb called "the kind of spontaneous, enthusiastic description that later became his hallmark—a style of personal journalism that had immediacy and intimacy, that put his readers on the scene, compelling them to share (if not always approve of) Reed's own passionate involvement with his subject. When he wrote cleanly and simply, as he soon realized, he was at his best."[11]

The writing itself was a function of Copeland's inspiration, not his instruction. Copeland did not actually teach the art of writing.[12] He found potential writers and compelled them, through the sheer force of his personality, to reach for the moon while appreciating every breath on Earth. After his post-college, almost penniless tour of Europe, and before the Portland interlude from July through October 1912, Reed spent most of 1911 and the first half of 1912 finding "color and strength and beauty" in New York, just as Copeland had instructed him to do.

Not long after his flattering but mechanical profile of Copeland in *American Magazine*, Reed began to find his writing voice in an article about New York's Bowery neighborhood, where he reported on a dinner handout for the homeless and the unemployed:

> They began to gather—the diners—at half past six on the morning. It was clear and keenly cold. I came upon them about half past ten, a thousand bent and haggard creatures in a single line that stretched five blocks along the Bowery. Flowed by the holiday crowd, some sodden and old, drifting and seemingly lost because the work that occupied their fingers and soothed their brins had stopped; some dull and old who worked not but mostly youth, hard faced and young faced, animated, happily filthy of tongue, harshly singing touched as by the bizarre slip of a painter's brush, with garish bits of color. A peddler stood on the corner with trayful of brooches—imitations of precious stones, such as the dark, foreign sweat shop girls love to clasp at their throats. He cried monotonously, "Come git your genuyne Brazil di'monds"—A cop tried to Nicolo the bootblack into believing his license was void; after he had gone, Nicolo told me cynically, "He try-a graft da Chreestamus presunt."[13]

Years later, in "Almost Thirty," Reed wrote, "In New York I first loved, and first wrote of the things I saw, with a fierce joy of creation—and knew at last that I could write. There I got my first perceptions of the life of my time. The city and its people were an open book to me; everything had its story, dramatic, full of ironic tragedy and terrible humor. There I first saw that reality transcended all the fine poetic inventions of fastidiousness and medievalism. I was not happy or well long away from New York."[14]

Reed had read a lot of books before he entered secondary school as a teenager, but, after he entered Harvard, books could not compete with the intensity of interacting with the world at full speed. "On the whole, ideas do not mean that much to me," Reed wrote. "I had to see. In my rambles about the city I couldn't help but observe the ugliness of poverty and all its train of evils, the cruel inequality between the rich people who had too many motor cars and the poor people who didn't have enough to eat. It didn't come to me from books that the workers produced all the wealth of the world, which went to those who did not earn it."

Although he later cringed at his former student's radicalism, Copeland had much to do with Reed's developing worldview. "Hardly a theorist, [Reed] knew from the relationship with Copey that education was not a matter of requirements—it was more the magic of two individuals coming together in some affable manner and winging into unchartered realms," wrote Robert Rosenstone.[15]

The impact that Copeland had on Reed emerges in the student's carefully crafted tribute to his professor in the *American Magazine* profile and in an unfiltered rant that the world-famous journalist wrote to his old professor.

From Reed's note to Copeland, in the dedication of *Insurgent Mexico*: "As I write these impressions of Mexico I couldn't help but think that I never would have seen what I did see had it not been for your teaching me.... To listen to you is to learn how to see the hidden beauty of the visible world ... to be your friend is to try to be intellectually honest."[16]

From a letter to Copeland as Reed despaired over the horrors and hypocrisy that he found while trying to write about the European War in 1915:

> Circumstances of mailing—convenience, neutrality and so forth, force me always to return to Roumania and the "Paris of the Balkans," though I detest the country and its people.
>
> Imagine a small Paris in every essential respect—cafes, kiosks, pissoirs, and Academy occupied with producing a dictionary, Futurist painters and poets who are pederasts ... politicians who are known by their mistresses they keep, craven newspapers, bawdy weeklies....
>
> Your true Roumanian boasts that there are more cocottes in Bucharest in proportion to the population than in any two cities of the world. No one does anything except screw, drink and gamble....
>
> Officers in salmon-pink and baby-blue uniforms ... sit at cafes sipping ices and eating tartlets all day long or drive up and down the Calea Victoriei in cabs, winking at the throngs of women.... There is a dinky Hohenzollern king, a dinky throne and court, a dinky aristocracy of fake Byzantine Emperor's spawn. Everyone is crooked.... It reeks with millionaires, grown rich by hogging the oil wells or by the absentee ownership of vast lands where the peasants sweat out their lives for a franc a day....
>
> Their politics is as mean as anything about them. They persecute the Jews with petty police tyranny; they sell the military secrets and the Cabinet to Germany and the Entente ... and now, they are trying to sell the lives of the peasant-soldiers to whichever side will be the most cash to the capitalist class.
>
> If I ever saw a place ripe for revolution, this country is ripe. The peasants are very fine and poetic people, but they are cowed.
>
> I hate old Europe more every day. America's the place?[17]

Despite the appeal to Copeland's patriotism in the final three words of his letter, Reed's take on the First World War's core issue—a war to protect capitalists, a "war of traders," as he called it—undoubtedly pinged another dent into the relationship with his mentor, who already had misgivings about his star pupil's openly anti-war rhetoric. "Copeland always praised Reed's achievements as a writer but detested the 'Bolsheviks' who, as he believed, seduced Reed from his true vocation," wrote Richard O'Connor.[18] By the middle of the decade, Reed was coming out of the professor's spell. There was no beauty to be found in the War to End All Wars.

"Copeland had a great deal to do with the making of John Reed," wrote Heywood Broun, one of Reed's Harvard's classmates. "Copey did not know, and no one of us knew, that this humorous, light-hearted youngster would burn himself up in a fever of revolution. We believe only a few things which Reed believed. As a political economist he did not inspire admiration, but he stuck closely to the creed which an artist ought to have as any man we have ever known. He wrote what he felt. Copey did not groan in vain for this pupil."[19]

* * *

Lincoln Steffens served Reed first as a professional contact, then as a surrogate father, a close friend, and always as an ambassador for the best of American journalism—particularly the kind of journalism that aimed for the highest levels of reporting while acting as an agent for social change. With impeccable credentials as a muckraker and investigative reporter, and with a never-ending devotion to the memory of his good friend C.J. Reed, Steffens was a human bridge between Jack Reed, the unleashed manboy romping through Greenwich Village, and John Reed, the relentless journalist who had to be taken seriously by serious people.

Steffens was among the most accomplished reporters of the early 1900s. President Theodore Roosevelt famously labeled this crowd "muckrakers" with a typically Rooseveltian double-sided edge; Roosevelt loved newspaper reporters and often cajoled them to get better at their government watchdog role, but when the questions hit too close to home, he lashed out. It was a matter of no harm, no foul; a reporter facing a tonguelashing from TDR owned a badge of honor not held by a reporter ignored by the blustery president.

What distinguished Steffens' relationship with Jack Reed was the unbridled joy that Lincoln himself expressed as Reed the protégé made one discovery after another about New York and its human drama. C.J. Reed had asked Steffens to keep an eye on his son in New York. Steffens took this role seriously, but he had no idea how much fun he would have on the job, watching Jack pace around Lincoln's apartment, rambling like a lunatic about the scenes and people he had seen, the conversations he had stumbled into, the raw beauty and ugliness of the greatest city in America.[20] Whereas Charles Copeland unabashedly showed his need for Reed's company to reassure himself that this rising star was a product of his unorthodox teaching, Steffens required no such validation. He had been around the block a few times as a reporter. Although a generation older than Jack Reed, Steffens was still a professional peer, a working journalist writing about serious public policy issues. Years later, after the Bolshevik Revolution, Steffens traveled to the new Soviet Union (on assignment from the U.S. government) and declared the revolution a success. A decade after Reed's death, Steffens acknowledged that the Soviet political system was not working, but that did not stop him from supporting socialist causes. Steffens was a tireless critic of government corruption on any level, and he often used morality as the measuring stick between corruption and incompetence. He called himself a Christian anarchist.[21]

In 1911 and 1912, whenever Jack Reed burst into Steffens' Greenwich Village apartment to give him a play-by-play of his adventures after staying up all night walking the streets of New York, the young journalist was preaching to the choir. Steffens had been there and done that, but he maintained an impish quality, a wink and smile that some of his literary peers— notably Max Eastman—interpreted as a sign of weakness.[22] Quite simply, Steffens did not take himself seriously enough for the Bohemians. Eastman said Steffens would rather sound clever than extend an intellectual argument. This may have been true by the time Eastman and Steffens began traveling in the same circles—at socialite Mabel Dodge's salon parties, at McSorley's tavern, at any of a number of gathering and drinking spots where Greenwich Village artists, radicals and writers gathered to tackle the world's problems through rambling dialogue. Reed's return to New York in October 1912 occurred when the Golden Age of the village was flourishing, at about the same time investigative journalism was falling out of fashion. Progressivist reforms in local, state and federal levels of government—while often reactionary and bereft of long-term planning— placated many Americans who had been outraged by the muckrakers' exposés. Steffens, for his part, professed to prefer revolution over reform as a viable solution to problems in American society (until Palmer raids on radicals and the U.S. government's mass deportations and jailings of 1919). But Steffens was not interested in arguing all night about making the world a better place. He was in his mid-forties at the beginning of the 20th century's second decade. His wife had recently passed away, and one of the reasons he moved into the same apartment building as Reed on Washington Square was to feel the energy exuded by Reed and his young friends. He advised many young journalists who went on to accomplished careers, but none of them gave him the joy that Reed offered.[23]

"I used to go early to bed and to sleep, but I liked it when Jack, a big, growing, happy being, would slam into my room and wake me up to tell me about the 'most wonderful thing in the world' that he had seen, been or done that night," Steffens wrote in his autobiography. "Girls, plays, bums, I.W.W.'s strikers—each experience was vivid in him, a story, which he often wrote; every person, every idea; Bill Haywood, some prostitute down and out on a park bench, a vaudeville dancer; socialism; the I.W.W. program—all were on a level with him. Everything was the most wonderful thing in the world. Jack and his crazy young friends were indeed the most wonderful thing in the world."[24]

Steffens and Reed bonded on several levels. Each man used humor as a weapon to soften their anger over the world's relentless injustices. They used journalism as a tool for calling attention to these same injustices. But it was the personal history, above all else, that compelled Reed to seek Steffens' counsel, and, if possible, his approval (Reed rarely took anyone's disapproval personally or as the final say in his decision-making). Although there is no tangible evidence that the great muckraking stories in the first decade of the 20th century—including Steffens' *Shame of the Cities* and Upton Sinclair's *Jungle*—had major impact on Reed's decision to become a journalist, Steffens' professional credentials and the role he played as a C.J. Reed advocate during the Oregon Land Fraud scandal left an indelible mark on Jack.

In "Almost Thirty," written in 1916, Reed may overstate Steffens' role in busting up the scheme involving large transfers of public lands in Oregon into private hands for profit. Much of the wealth found within Portland's social, cultural and business elite could be directly traced to the scandal, which was made possible through bribes, forged signatures, falsified records, and good old-fashioned Wild West opportunism as government regulators looked the other way. Steffens did write about the issue for *American Magazine*, but only after the investigation had begun. He did recommend C.J. Reed for service as a U.S. marshal to participate in the investigation, which occurred on President Roosevelt's watch (thus leading to future explosions between combustible personalities—TDR and Jack Reed). C.J. Reed accepted the federal post in 1905 and dove into his role with a vigor that set up his own downfall, as he alienated nearly everyone with any influence in the Portland business-power-social hierarchy. Steffens stood by as a loyal friend reassuring the devastated C.J. that he did the right thing.

Steffens never took credit for unraveling the Oregon land scandal, only for informing the American public about what was going on. He did, however, take credit for steering the future author of *Insurgent Mexico* and *Ten Days That Shook the World* away from an engagement to a French woman, Madeleine Filon, that could have altered Jack Reed's history. The romance and engagement occurred during Reed's travels around Europe following his Harvard graduation. The commitment was still semi-official when Reed landed in New York in 1911. "I got Jack clear; by insisting only that he not marry unless he loved the girl," Steffens told his sister in a letter. "He didn't really love her. So it was called off and no harm done."[25]

The Madeleine Filon affair was not the only time Steffens stepped in to help with Reed's romantic problems. Steffens was a frequent guest at Mabel Dodge's parties, where the conversation often turned to free love, art and "parlor socialism." Dodge, absurdly wealthy, self-conscious and a bore, seduced Reed and took him in as her lover, even though she was married (this was considered somewhat hip by Greenwich Village standards, although nobody would ever label Dodge as hip). She smothered Reed and tried to own his time. When Reed walked out on her and announced the end of the relationship, she took morphine in an apparent suicide attempt. Steffens was on hand to get her medical attention and clean her up after Reed had left the apartment. A few years later, when Reed broke up with writer Louise Bryant (one of their many break-ups), Steffens called Reed "a cad and a fool." Reed eventually admitted that his only true love in life was Bryant, who was at his deathbed in Russia in 1920.[26]

In the summer and fall of 1912, as Reed took stock of where he was and what was next, Steffens' impact on his life over the previous year resonated as much as anything. The Portland interlude did not stop their communications. If anything, it fortified the bond while Reed hit the reset button for the first time in his adventure-hunting adult life.

During his junior year at Harvard, Reed had written a letter to Steffens, seeking advice on how to go about assembling a journalistic philosophy for *Harvard Monthly*. Steffens was more than happy to write a long reply. The exchange occurred just a few years after C.J.'s fall from grace in the Portland community, and it laid the foundation for Reed's journalistic identity. Steffens wrote:

> The way to go about your job is to sit down together, you and your crowd, and together perceive what the Harvard Monthly should be. I think its function is to express Harvard, and all that Harvard stands for in the world—to the world. That's a large order, and I submit it in all its might, not because I think you can achieve it in one year, but because with that end in view, you will begin to clear your minds....

> Magazine editors commonly err [by trying] to "make" a magazine. They think up what will be a good article or story; then they set about getting some writer to write it up. Some of that has to be done, of course, and sometimes a writer will do pretty well with an order like. But we all hate it. We all do our best work when we are permitted to write that which it is in our minds to tell.... As an editor I found ... it was hard very often to make the man understand that what I wanted was what he cared most to say. But when the right man once got that into his head something good came out of it....
>
> Everyone [who can write] has some pet thought or theme or feeling. When you have found out what it is, consider whether it would be suitable for the Monthly, and if it is—order it. And anything is suitable for the Monthly that is interesting to the world; and each editor is to regard himself as the whole world; whatever will interest him involuntarily (not as an editor, but as a human being) will interest the rest of us human beings.... It's all a matter of expression, which is journalism and which may be literature—if the writer is striving not to make a work of art, but simply to tell his story for you and me and the man on the street.[27]

Steffens also wrote a touching letter while Reed was grieving in Portland, offering his support in any way imaginable. By itself, the letter may not have been special, but it was something Reed could hold that represented his recent past—the correspondence during his Harvard years, daily discoveries in New York, advice on women—and a vision of what he might become. To Steffens, Jack was a younger fusion of himself and his dear friend C.J. The younger Reed had been dabbling in journalism during his first few months in New York; he wasn't supposed to get conviction, according to the message his late father had relayed to Steffens. But there was C.J.'s wild son, producing work that impressed editors in New York while almost living with a journalistic giant. The impact was powerful.

In the summer of 1912, Reed wrote a poem about Steffens. He meant to create a tribute, but he misjudged the nation's political climate badly (it wouldn't be the last time). "Sangar," published in *Poetry* magazine, was widely praised by respected writers who did not consider themselves political radicals. For the pro–labor union, socialist crowd, however, "Sangar" was an amusing mockery of Lincoln Steffens' attempt to broker a settlement between J.B. McNamara and 11 defendants who had dynamited the anti-union *Los Angeles Times* office, killing 21 people. Steffens, the self-described "Christian anarchist," heard, perhaps for the first time, that many of his friends felt his sanctimony was over the top. Steffens was extremely hurt by their reaction to his efforts in the McNamara case and then crushed by the popular perception that Reed's "Sangar" validated their judgement.[28]

"Sangar" was a romantic allegory, with Steffens as Sangar, a soldier-hero acting as peacemaker between two armies, before his own son kills him while shouting:

> Father no more of mine
> Shameful old man—abhorr'd
> First traitor of all our line

As the poem develops, Sangar's soul ascends, Christ-like, and the poem ends with

> Oh there was joy in heaven when Sangar came
> Sweet Mary wept and bathed and bound his wounds
> And God the father healed him of despair
> And Jesus gripped his hand, and laughed and laughed.[29]

Reed had great difficulty wrapping his brain around the fact that his good intentions—especially for someone he revered—had been distorted and had backfired. Their relationship survived, nonetheless. Steffens had Reed's back when Reed suffered his own public humiliation covering the Western Front in the European War in 1915. He and another correspondent found their way into German trenches, where officers got them drunk and goaded them into firing rifles in the direction of the French army. While Reed faced widespread scorn back home, Steffens wrote that the episode simply proved that war turns all men into killers.[30]

In 1918, at the height of American hysteria toward everything labeled "red" or "socialist," Steffens stuck his neck out for Reed—and in doing so may have changed the history of American journalism. Reed's *Ten Days That Shook the World*, published in early 1919, ranks seventh in New York University's list of top 100 works of journalism in the 20th century, but Reed may not have been able to write the book had not Steffens persuaded Woodrow Wilson's top advisor to return Reed's notebooks from Russia; they had been confiscated by the government for national security reasons. Every important piece of information about the Bolshevik Revolution that Reed gathered had wound up in the hands of U.S. federal authorities. He was openly despondent to friends and associates, less concerned about his fate as a feared Communist than he was about having his life's most important work stolen by his own hostile government. Steffens, the former muckraker sometimes criticized for acquiescent journalism, called in a huge favor and cleared a path for Reed to retrieve his research.[31]

* * *

Almost from the moment they first met, Eastman and Jack Reed became the perfect storm. Eastman's radical politics and intellectual intensity intersected with Reed's journey of self-discovery, adventure hunting, opportunism, and social crusading. The final leg of that journey—Reed's embracement of the Bolshevik Revolution—created distance between Reed and Steffens and between Reed and Copeland. Both Steffens and Copeland loved Reed the man, but they loathed Reed the radical and his uncompromising vision of a global dismantling of capitalism. ("Jack you do wrong to buck this thing.... It is wrong to try to tell the truth now," Steffens told Reed in 1918).[32] Eastman, himself charged with conspiracy to overthrow the U.S. government, watched with pain as his reporter and good friend became tragically misguided. The revolutionary storm in America may have been moving out by 1918, but Eastman could not get that message across to the man who went from Storm Boy to great journalist to uncompromising revolutionary. Trying to explain John Reed to a jury when the two men were on trial in 1918, Eastman said, "Some people, you look in their eyes and you say 'This man is honest and kind,' and you feel that no further questions need be asked. Jack had such eyes."[33]

Neither Max Eastman's first impression of Jack Reed, toward the end of 1912, nor one of his final encounters with Reed, in 1918, were favorable. In the beginning, the audacious young writer forced his way into an appointment that Eastman didn't want to have. Reed paced the office where Eastman worked, rambled incoherently, and didn't make much eye contact. He was trying to get a story published in *The Masses*, Eastman's new magazine. He not only succeeded, but he also astonished Eastman with the beauty of his writing and the sharpness of his reporting. Six years later, on the streets of Manhattan, Eastman ran into a ravaged and rapidly aging Reed while he was in the midst of writing *Ten Days That Shook the World*. Reed looked like hell, not having left his apartment for weeks, barely taking time to eat, bathe or shave.[34] The product of his efforts was a world-famous book that has stood the test of time for a century. Two years later, Reed would be dead.

In between these encounters, Eastman and Reed forged an intense relationship that was alternately a bond between brothers and a decade-long contest between peers to see who could shine brightest on the stage of left-wing activism. Reed won his share of battles but lost the war, so to speak. In one of their final conversations, as Reed resigned from Eastman's *Liberator* magazine (the publication he started after government shut down *The Masses*), Max told Jack, "The trouble with you is you're getting too damned adult!" The barb dripped with irony, as Reed was calling the older Eastman a coward for soft-pedaling opposition to the European War. Eastman said that was the only way to stay in print while pushing for social revolution. Reed, for his part, acknowledged that "loss of gaiety was the price of revolution." A few years later, Reed died on Soviet soil, still clinging to the hope of a revolution to rid the world of capitalism and its economic violence. Eastman visited the Soviet Union in the early 1920s, met his second wife there, and transformed, over the next three decades, to become such an anti–Communist that he openly supported the fiery red-baiting rhetoric of U.S. senator Joseph McCarthy in the early years of the Cold War.[35]

Eastman was the son of two Congregationalist ministers, his mother the first woman to be ordained as a Congregational minister in New York state. He graduated from Williams College in 1905 and moved to New York City in 1907, gradually putting distance between himself and his parents' proselytizing, but heeding their lessons about social justice. He threw himself into an array of political, literary and social movements while settling in Greenwich Village a few years before it became known for counterculture experimentation.

The names of Eastman and Reed have been intertwined for a century, even though Eastman often acted more like an adult than Reed, lived for decades after Reed died, and eventually turned his back on socialism and communism. The core of their mutual legacy can be found in a passage written by American philosopher Sidney Hook. He was describing Max Eastman, but much of it could be applied to Jack Reed:

> Max Eastman was authentically American, sympathetic to the great rebels of the American past, intellectually independent, drawn to an undogmatic socialism on compassionate rather than economic grounds, an ardent supporter of women's rights at a time when it was dangerous even for a woman to be known as a feminist, defender of dissemination of information about birth control, an advocate of free love and open marriage, a pioneer for civil liberties, receptive of new ideas in almost every field. Max Eastman fought in more good causes than almost any man or woman of his generation, and yet he was by no means a purely literary radical—one of those who flaunt their radical ideas but never come within hailing distance of any political activity. Eastman put his very life and career on the line in pursuit of his radical ideas. More than once he had the courage to stand up to an enraged mob.[36]

They did not know each other in the fall of 1912, but Reed knew about *The Masses*, which had begun in 1911 as a monthly publication leaning toward socialism. The magazine struggled financially during first year. Serendipitously, its wealthy financial backers hired Eastman as editor. In the final weeks of 1912, Reed called Eastman after *American Magazine* refused to published his story "Where the Heart Is," an account of a young prostitute traveling back to the United States after taking what she called a well-deserved vacation in Europe and South America. Reed was more than a little pent-up after four months in Oregon; his return to New York produced head-shaking experiences for friends new and old who ran into him during his second go-round in the city.

To that point, Reed's preparation for a career in literary journalism and political activism consisted of distinct chapters. The first chapter: a boyhood of seclusion, illness, privilege and exposure to books, a boy born into an eccentric, well-traveled family. The second chapter: Harvard College, where he learned about the dark side of privilege while his family wealth disintegrated and his father's career lay in ruins. The third chapter: a post-college search for adventure for which his father handed him all of one hundred dollars. The fourth chapter: a year in New York, where he raced everywhere, 24/7, to find new people and new stories, laughing and loving and partying while taking careful note of the cruelty of wealth in America.

Eastman's impression of Reed, after he reluctantly agreed to hear a pitch for a story that nobody else would publish was "He had a knobby and too filled-out face that reminded me, both in form and color, of a potato. He was dressed in a smooth, brown suit with round pants' legs and a turned-over starched collar, and seemed rather small and rather distracted. He stood or moved about the room all through his visit and kept looking in every direction except that in which he was addressing his words." Eastman wanted Reed to leave him alone as soon as possible.[37]

"Where the Heart Is," written while Reed was in Portland, stunned Eastman with its "unlabored grace." *The Masses* published the story in January 1913. Eastman asked Reed to submit stories every month, and he put Reed's name on the masthead as a contributing editor. Then he invited Jack to perform some editing work in the office, which turned out to be a mistake. Their decade-long tempestuous relationship built on mutual love, respect and need was well under way.

"Jack had too many wayward ideas, too rich a flow of impulses," Eastman wrote. "He lacked judgment, and he had too much else to do. We agreed almost before he started that his help would be temporary, that what I needed was a paid associate who would sit up to a desk in the office—once in awhile, at least—and actually be there."[38]

Such was the devotion to his younger colleague and friend, however, that Eastman consistently defended Reed over the years with vigor and a precision of language intended to bury critics with reason instead of emotion. Eastman did this even after acknowledging his own misreading of the Bolsheviks' potential to have a positive impact on class struggle in Russia and the rest of the world. Few people wanted to hear this, but Eastman maintained that Reed ultimately developed his own doubts about whether a successful workers' revolution in Russia or anywhere else was more dream than reality. During that torturous time, 1918–1920, Reed remained true to himself, a man under construction since the late summer and fall of 1912.

"He did not want to sit aloft in a new priesthood, a new cult of intellectual complaisance, knowing what is good for the masses, because [Karl] Marx had explained it to him, and he had been superior enough to understand Marx, and therefore justified in hoodwinking and cheating the masses, and arousing them in any way he could to the action called for by an esoteric conception of history," Eastman wrote.[39]

When the federal government took *The Masses* and its editorial staff to court on charges of sedition in 1918, Eastman, Reed and others—a group advocating the restructuring of the United States' economic system—faced the very real possibility of 20 years in prison. Eastman knew Reed as well as anyone, yet he was still pleasantly surprised and emotionally stirred by Jack's eloquence on the witness stand. The experience helped him reflect on what made Jack Reed special.

> He was, with whatever gifts he had—and their extent will never be quite known—in the heart of one utterly American literary tradition, the tradition of imaginative laughter. We are not so far, I hope, from the great days of Davy Crockett and Attemus Ward and Mark Twain and Abraham Lincoln that we have to patronize and excuse and tolerate, and worst of all condescendingly understand as a "playboy" a man gifted with an irrepressible and absolutely divine gift of joking. All the oh-oh-ing about Jack Reed's joyful, and on the whole superlatively san exploits in imaginative laughter, as though they were something that had to be outgrown before he could become a man ... has always struck me as suffocating and sanctimonious. There is not one of John Reed's detractors as a "playboy" who wouldn't give his right hand for an occasional glimmer of the wit and gay magnetic lumorous fancies that bubbled out of him in speech and action more than half the time.[40]

Like a good older brother who took his role seriously, Eastman openly acknowledged Reed's maturation.

> Jack was a steadying influence on me—though he would be the most surprised to hear me say it. Not that he had stability, but he was more easefully daring than I, more instinctively belligerent. he did not have to fall back so often, in the class war we were waging, on naked resolution. He actually liked the battle; he liked dust and smoke—he liked the town! One day during that great year 1916 he called up and asked permission to dedicate a volume of poems to me. I stammered a yes that must have sounded more abashed than complimented.... His understanding was subtle—his dedication, when it appeared, proved to be a celebration of this very difference between us. He had turned that squeamish timorousness which made me admire him extravagantly into a cause for admiring me."[41]

The poem dedicated to Eastman, read, in part:

There was a man who, loving quiet beauty best,
Yet could not rest
For the harsh moaning of unhappy humankind,
Fettered and blind—
Too driven to know beauty and too hungry-tired
To be inspired.[42]

Chapter Three

Endless Storm: Harvard to Mexico

> I seem to discern in your verse a slap at this "generation of the thoroughly smug" ... at first it seemed funny, then it seemed unfair; and finally I made up my mind that it was simply stupid.
> No, Mr. Aggressively Contemporary Pound, here in America very few people indeed believe that these are "fair, peaceful, happy days."—Jack Reed, responding to a letter in *Poetry Magazine* that criticized his poem "Sanger"[1]

Jack Reed was a storm unto himself in a turbulent decade. In New York at the onset of the Bohemian Renaissance, and in Europe during the Great War, Reed's personality and behavior often diverted attention from his writing, which was controversial enough. As good as his published stories were, he did not sit behind a desk or in front of a typewriter long enough for the writing to overshadow his antics. He was a man of action, a writer who seemed more interested in seeing and doing than in writing.

He did not settle for writing from the sidelines. He jumped into the issues and events of a decade that shaped the rest of the 20th century—worker exploitation and labor strikes, immigration, women's rights, nationalism, war, imperialism, radicalism, civil liberties and the impact of corporate culture on all of the above. Reed's storm clouds were evident for anyone to see if they had encountered him at Harvard between 1906 and 1910. The anger was part of the package—a lonely freshman from the West mystified by Harvard's invisible social barriers, later an immature young man in New York's playground for young adults. But with the anger came conviction, an unshakable belief that he could use journalism as a platform to take on social injustice. Humor accompanied the anger, helping

Reed charm and disarm critics. In addition to understanding the nature of power at a young age (having witnessed his father's downfall), he also understood the value of whimsy as an art form (having witnessed bizarre and colorful behavior in his parents' home). He could not stop himself from poking fun at those who took themselves too seriously any more than he could conceal his righteousness toward those who determined the fate of individuals below their social status. He called his father a great fighter. Jack Reed was a loud, funny, angry, talented fighter.

At Harvard, he tried to join every club he could; many of them froze him out. As a journalist, he tried to be everywhere to see the world changing, including Paterson, New Jersey, for the silk workers' strike, and Ludlow, Colorado, where striking mine workers were killed. The Mexican Revolution. The European War. St. Petersburg and Moscow. He merged lessons from Charles Copeland—find adventure and heroism in the modern world and write about it—and Lincoln Steffens, who told his protégé that the best journalists do their best work when they write what they are passionate about, rather than what their publishers think their readers want.

* * *

Knocking Down Ivy League Doors

Harvard College awakened Reed to the realities of wealth and privilege. By virtue of enrollment, he could count himself among the elite students in the world. Nevertheless, he was a Harvard outsider; the invisible hand of privilege reminded him of that reality every day. He was deeply hurt by this.[2] Through persistence that was nothing less than annoying and energy that boggled the mind, Reed became a player in many social arenas on campus. By making new friends and having his voice heard, he gained some satisfaction—at a cost. Constantly having to prove himself to people born on third base while claiming they had hit a triple made him angry. Harvard taught Jack Reed about the power of the mind and spirit but Harvard also taught him about cruelty.

Harvard, he observed, was a place that could set a young man's brain and soul on fire. "Individualism was carried to the point where a man who came for a good time could get through and graduate without having learned anything," he wrote. On the other hand,

> anyone could find there anything he wanted from all the world's stores of learning. The undergraduates were practically free from control; they could live pretty much where they pleased and do as they pleased—so long as they attended lectures.

> Some men came with allowances of fifteen thousand dollars a year pocket money, with automobiles, and servants, living in gorgeous suites in palatial apartment houses; others in the same class stayed in attic bed-rooms.[3]

His first year year played out like that of countless freshmen in universities all over the world. Loneliness. Insecurity. Depression. Wondering whether he would ever have what it takes to make meaningful friendships or be recognized for his talents. Turns out he did. His uncle and grandmother had shown him how to create his own image as larger than life to the outside world. His mother had fed him an abundance of books about adventure and history. His father passed on grit and enough social skills to keep moving forward. John Reed, now known as Jack Reed at Harvard, made friends. And like his dad, he made enemies with his open disdain for pretentiousness. He turned his college life around in a hurry during his second year at Harvard. As a sophomore he hit the ground running and did not stop until graduation day. After failing to make the cut for the freshman crew team and then getting rejected for the job of assistant manager to the varsity crew team, Jack subsequently worked on two college newspapers, the *Harvard Lampoon* and the *Harvard Monthly*. He became president of the Cosmopolitan Club (with 43 nationalities among its members), manager of the Musical Club, and captain of the water polo team. He joined the campus cheerleading team, the swimming team, and the drama club. He was president of the Harvard Glee Club. He helped run the Hasty Pudding Theatricals, writing the music and lyrics for their Diana's Debut show. He was an Ivy orator and poet during his senior year. His last three years of non-stop activity foreshadowed his dual careers as a journalist and activist who dabbled in poetry, theater and hell-raising. He became acutely aware of social class tensions at Harvard. "The more I met," he said of his classmates, "the more their cold, cruel stupidity repelled me. I began to pity them for their lack of imagination and the narrowness of their glittering lives—clubs, athletics, society."[4]

He disrupted the sensibilities of serious-minded Harvard classmates whose strict rules of social conformity were an extension of their school's hallowed legacy. Most of them could not make sense of Jack Reed, who wanted to be a social climber but insisted upon poking fun at the people and clubs he tried to join. Had he toned down his act to show a perfunctory effort at decorum, the "aristocrats" (as he called them) may have been more accepting of this wild boy from the West. As it was, they opened a few doors, just a crack, here and there. He was brilliant at times, hilarious on occasion, and almost always a compelling presence. But his refusal to take himself or Harvard customs too seriously made his blueblood peers uncomfortable.[5] The social dynamics were not all that different from what his father had experienced in Oregon—an outsider will always be an outsider to those who lay claim to a high place in a social hierarchy. Even if he had committed himself to fitting in completely, his interactions with the Harvard elite could have ended badly—just because. Lineage, jealousy, who's in, who's out ... it was just more fun to bang on closed doors and burst into the party before getting kicked out than it was to wait for an invitation and promise to behave.

O'Connor and Walker's 1967 biography of Reed mentioned Reed's acceptance to the Hasty Pudding Club near the end of this Harvard career. The authors' interpretation: "In his first brush with the class struggle, rudimentary as it was on the campus of an Ivy League college in 1910, Reed betrayed it. But that would never happen again."[6] Reed himself, however, was not above betrayal himself. During his freshman year, he awkwardly ended a budding friendship with a Jewish undergraduate because he thought their association was hurting his social aspirations on campus. (Soon thereafter he acknowledged the insensitivity and selfishness of his actions and the friendship resumed.)[7]

It was difficult to tell whether Reed had social class warfare on his mind at Harvard or whether he was just another rebellious brat without money. Was he, as he suggested in "Almost Thirty," walking in the footsteps of his father, who desperately fought to send his boys to Harvard while fighting political corruption in Oregon? What did he want? He said he did not know. He wanted to be great at something, and he had no idea about how to go about doing that without creating havoc, running through campus, testing everything, leaving the debris of a storm in his wake.

"There was something Elizabethan in his huge vitality," wrote his classmate and close friend Edward E. Hunt, "and through everything he did there ran a strain of the grotesque which turned the most serious event into laughter. The college authorities were compelled by his pranks to revive the archaic punishment of rustication, a kind of academic jail sentence, the first of his innumerable incarcerations."[8]

The Harvard rustication/probation experience took place in Concord, Massachusetts, where Reed and other bad boys breaking rules were sentenced to a spartan school room that was part of a rural boarding house. Reed proved himself, as he would countless times over the next decade, irrepressible. From his Concord exile he wrote to his buddies in the Harvard Western Club about his clash with a moth miller that kept the Harvard outlaws awake at night.

"A large moth was severely injured about the neck and ears," Reed wrote. "Two old ladies who room below us and are Seventh Day Adventists thought that Christ had some again, and prayed violently all night. The hotel cat was so horrified by the tumult that the next morning she was found to have given birth to a litter of pups in the cash register."[9]

He knew his audience well. The Western Club had been organized by Reed to allow students from west of the Mississippi to speak, unfiltered, about the mysteries of Harvard social expectations. They were known as mischief-makers on campus; occasionally their club meetings would devolve into food fights.

Of all the classmates who enjoyed Reed's company and respected his intellect while cringing at his impertinence, perhaps none was more conflicted than Walter Lippmann, who in 1914 wrote an article for the *New Republic* titled—with nothing approaching flattery—"The Legendary John Reed."

"He came from Oregon, showed his feelings in public, and said what he thought to the club men who didn't like to hear it," Lippman wrote. "Even as an undergraduate he betrayed what many people believed to be the central passion of his life, an inordinate desire to be arrested." Reed, mindful of Lippmann's heft as a highly acclaimed thinker, and knowing that his friend was bound for greatness, invited Lippmann to a Western Club meeting. Lippmann accepted, but may have winced when Reed leaped from his chair and shouted, "Ladies and gentlemen, the future president of the United States!"[10]

His Harvard friends and acquaintances—future authors, editors and critics among them—were not shy about sharing their own Jack Reed stories. Journalist H.V. Kaltenborn was 28 years old as a Harvard undergraduate when he collaborated with Reed on Dramatic Club productions. "He was not a fiery left winger in those days," Kaltenborn wrote. "He was a nonconformist. He and I had planned to spend one brief vacation period together, walking through New England. This fell through when he was suspended or was rusticated.... He was extremely likable, good-humored, and attractive. He was possessed of great mental and physical vigor. Had he bothered to study he would have been a brilliant student. But he seemed rather bored by the intellectual discipline of college ... he hated authoritarianism of any kind."[11]

Was he calling attention to himself or searching for himself? Early on, most likely his sophomore year at Harvard, Reed began to feel comfortable with his rebel persona surrounded by stuffy conformists. "The change from West to East is a very great one," he wrote in a letter to his friend Robert Hallowell. "Out there the strength of body, here the fire of the mind.... You have no idea how it really thrills you to feel and think as we here feel and think together, how it makes you glad all over. That's something you can not get out West.... Don't you often feel that hunger for people to hear you open your heart and mind, and not be laughed at or misunderstood?"[12]

"Activity was obviously his realm, the drive for recognition his spur," Robert Rosenstone wrote in 1975. "Action might be central to his personality, but Reed thought of himself basically as writer. He was quite prolific, publishing more than twenty poems and nine stories in four years, along with numerous editorials, sketches, columns, jokes and pieces of light verse.... All this production did not mean his writing was mature. With so many commitments, he did most of his work in haste; there was never enough time to rewrite and edit."[13]

Wide Awake in the City That Does Not Sleep

Two letters that Reed wrote to Steffens, in July 1910 and February 1911, bore the stamp of a young man aware of his need for direction but not yet mature enough to create the structure needed in his life.

In the first letter he told Steffens about his planned trip to Europe on the cattle boat Bostonian with Waldo Peirce of Maine, a writer, cartoonist and Harvard graduate:

> From Manchester on foot to London, there to work at anything we can find until we get money enough to go to Germany, where we intend to cruise around for awhile, and then go down to the Black Forest path into France and up to Paris. Then Southern France and, Spain, to the Riviera, cruise around Italy in a fishing boat, Venice to Vienna, float down to the Danube through the Iron Gate, Constantinople, the south shore of the Black Sea, down the valley of the Anabasis, Persia, India and the East, to end the journey in San Francisco.
>
> My particular desire, is to make arrangements to write some magazine or syndicate of magazines for illustrate articles. We will have a very good camera, and will not only visit strange and wonderful places in a strange and unusual way, but will be in a position through letters, to meet and write of interesting people.

Whereupon he asked Steffens for ideas and contacts that can help him publish his travel stories in New York publications.

In a letter to Steffens dated February 23, 1911, written from Portland, the man-child is clearly evident, as Reed reports on his recently completed European travels:

> You will, without doubt, be surprised to hear from me at Portland, especially since I never wrote you from abroad and how much I gained from my acquaintance with Mr.

Fels, and how little I did to justify his kindness and yours. I became engaged to be married to a French girl at Nice, and came home on the run to arrange things for the family. I intend to start for New York Monday night or Tuesday morning and go to work at once. And my real purpose in writing you is to get your advice and if possible assistance in busting into journalism. What I really want I know but vaguely. But I am impatient to get to work, and ready for any amount of hard labor, short leisure, danger or drudgery, so long as I can do something worthwhile. Suppose that newspaper work is the stuff I need. But I want to talk to you first, if you can spare the time.[14]

As Europe teetered toward war, New York City seemed more exotic for a young Westerner lusting for urban life. Reed's writing this during time transitioned from college humor and critiques of campus life to word sketches of New York, a city that demanded the world's attention. As it was at Harvard, Reed's writing in New York did not receive the attention or polish of an author deeply committed to his craft. They were like extended postcards, with bursts of vignettes, reactions and spontaneous dialogue. In some respects his writing at that time may have been closer to the stream-of-conscious genre associated with Jack Kerouac a half-century later. Kerouac, despite the legend he created for writing without stopping, spent considerable hours at his typewriter trying to invent a new form of American prose. Jack Reed didn't have time for that. He was playing, seeing, talking, drinking, and hustling for work and kicks.

He would always be unfinished. Reed was a dreamer, romantic and poet. Later on, a political activist not interested in the art of political compromise. A revolutionary who underestimated the cost of personal sacrifice required to change a society. In New York he was a writer who commanded attention with his published works, but also a journalist who did not want to be told what to write or where to look for stories.

His New York home base was 42 Washington Square in Greenwich Village. From there he found the bars and apartments where he surrounded himself with people who worked, played, laughed and argued, sleeping and eating just enough to stay upright for the next day's endless possibilities. Their gatherings were intentionally informal, unscheduled and devoid of protocol, so it was not unusual for friends to come and go without explanation. Reed's arrivals and departures created a buzz, sometimes because he enjoyed drawing attention to himself. What really set him apart from his motley crew of new friends was his boyish and, to some extent, naïve fascination with not only the vibrant pulse of New York life, but also the dark underbelly that spoke of larger demons. Heeding the advice of Steffens and Copeland, he did not over-intellectualize what he saw. But he was determined to see everything.

"Within a block of my house was all the adventure in the world," he wrote. "Within a mile was every foreign country."[15] On foot, he traveled the world in New York: Chinatown, Little Italy, the Syrian quarter, German Village, the Jewish district of the Lower East Side. He walked through the Bowery and the Fulton Fish Market. He drank in saloons, some of them respectable, many of them the haunts of prostitutes, longshoremen, merchant mariners and old men waiting to die. "From them he learned strange lessons—how to buy cocaine or enter secret gambling dens, where to hire a man to kill an enemy," wrote Robert Rosenstone. "Sometimes he accepted unusual invitations—to a gangster's ball or a free Christmas dinner for derelicts given by a Tammany ward boss." On the other end of the spectrum, Reed somehow found the time and the means—oftentimes female friends with money, sometimes by borrowing cash from Lincoln Steffens—for days and nights at Fifth Avenue stores, uptown restaurants, Broadway plays, the Metropolitan Opera, the National Arts Club, Harvard football games at Princeton and Yale, the World Series, and some decadent goofing off at Coney Island.[16]

Reed wrote, with flashes of promise and groaning attempts to find his voice. He even tried investigative journalism. He produced an exposé of the New York City Fire Department, but he could not find a magazine or newspaper that would publish it, even after he reworked it as a profile of the fire chief. He wrote a scathing critique of fast-food lunch counters, 1911-style, but again there were no takers among editors and publishers willing to pay for the story in print. Among his first published magazine articles was a portrait of new immigrants arriving at Ellis Island and a half-hearted assessment of the flaws and virtues of big business in a free-market society. Like every good writer, Reed developed his voice through trial and error. Unlike most great writers, he did not appear to have the time or discipline to sit down at the typewriter for very long. He did not find the writing process as alluring as the images of real life that kept moving from a scene in front of his eyes to the writing voice inside his head and heart. He wanted to write, but living the stories was often more interesting than the grunt work of crafting sentences and paragraphs. "Ideas for stories were easier to conceive than to execute," wrote Robert Rosenstone.[17]

One breakthrough moment when John Reed, serious writer, muscled his way ahead of Jack Reed, mischief-maker, came with the publishing of "Where the Heart Is," a sweet and frank account of a prostitute who decides to take care of herself with a well-earned vacation.

Reed reported on a long conversation he had with the young woman over beers while they sat in a club called The Haymarket, which he described as "the most respectable place in town." Martha was one of the house girls. She remembered him from a few years back.

"I was in Paris two weeks, an' one day my friend beat it.... I would'a been on the street in another day if I hadn't run into the Englishman.... He was about sixty years old an' had a stomach.... His face looked like a walrus.... But he certainly treated me white. We travelled up through Belgium and Holland; Brussels, the Hague, Ostend, then took a trip through Germany.... I never missed a trick. Up at Waterloo I spent a whole day reading a history book. It seemed to me as if I was itching until I'd seen everything in the Baydicker—that's the guide-book. But after a while when we got around to Strassburg he began to get sore. 'Look here,' he says to me, 'chop the Cook's Towrist stuff, can't you?' So I simply cleared out one night and left him. I wasn't going to be anybody's dog, you bet. Just had enough money to get to Paris.... But I knew nothing could happen to me, with my luck. The very first night I went up on Monmarter an ran into an American girl who let me sleep in her bed.... All us American girls stick by each other, you know.... Monmarter is just like New York, except that it isn't so honest, if you know what I mean...."

She danced with a man who called himself a count, and who offered to take her to Rio. She was skeptical, asked around, and was reassured by another girl that taking the chance was a good idea.

"Suppose he'd take me somewhere where I didn't know the language and nobody talked American, and leave me? But I trusted to Gawd and went.... It took us two weeks on the boat,—then Rio. I guess Rio's the most beautiful place in the world. I had a great time there. Every Friday night we'd go to the High Life Club for dinner, an' Saturday night after supper the whole town would put on costumes—fancy dress you know,—an' ride up an' down in hacks.... I stayed there four months."

"No, I wasn't very happy.... You see, you get tired of wondering at things.... Everything in foreign countries is so much finer than you ever thought it would be.... Then you get excited when you see something that you've always heard about. It kind of gets on your nerves, and takes it out of you. I was going to stick around Rio for a year ... but I didn't."

"I can remember just as plain.... One night we came in rather tight after a big party at the club. Manuel dropped off to sleep, but I couldn't seem to close my eyes. It was in April, and the window was open, an' I could see straight up about a million miles in the sky. The stars are bearcats down there. I don't know what got me to thinkin about Broadway, but right off the bar I seemed to see it, wrigglin' and squirmin' with electric signs. with all the low brows coming out of the moving pitcher shows, an the shirt fronts comin' out of the theater—the hurdie-gurdies playing that 'Irish Rag'— at that moment i was sick as hound for old, honest, low-brow New York. You see, in foreign countries everybody is high brow. Then I saw the Old Market, with all the girls sitting around, an' the beer-stains on the table, an' the Sweet Caporal cigarette smoke.... I began to feel real tender for Big Bill there. So I gave Manual a poke ... 'I've got a cablegram from New York,' says I. 'It's very important. Coney Island will be open on the first. When's the next boat?' I says. 'I'm going to breeze.'"

"I will say the Count was O.K. He bought me a first cabin on the steamer, an told me to come again next year. That trip up the coast was the best time I ever had in my life. I lived strictly alone, an didn't allow a man on board to get fresh. Just read books; didn't talk to anyone; did a lot of thinking. I never was so happy. One morning I woke up with seven shillings, an' that day a young American spoke to me when I was killing time in Hyde Park.... I was getting sort of doped with London.... So that night I kissed the old lady good night, went up to my room an' packed.... We lit out at two in the morning.... I've often wondered what she thought in the morning."

"Well, from the first minute we began to see the old town loom up the bay I was so excited I couldn't talk. It hurt. I didn't wait for anything. When we landed I checked my stuff in the Erie Station and took a ferry. Then I took the El to Twenty-eight Street and blew in here. The old gink outside says, 'Here, you can't walk in here without a ticket'—An' then he looked closer. 'Well, what the—! Say, where have you been?' I couldn't answer him. I stood there like a deaf and dumb and blind bonehead—was was absolutely off my nut. An' then he held the door open and I sort of *fell* inside. There was Bill, and behind him all the crowd was dancing, and the little tables.... Home! That's what it was! Home! I heard the Big Fellow rumbling 'Martha! by God! The Female White Hope has come back!' O Gawd! You couldn't understand.... I just fell off a table and bawled.... Come on, let's dance."[18]

It was a turning point, although the story did not propel Reed into prominence as a journalist or writer. The home it found, *The Masses*, was a socialist publication that breathed fire and drew the ire of the federal government. Although it had a small slice of the mainstream magazine readership market, it was always hemorrhaging money and relied on wealthy backers who dabbled in radical politics. What made "Where the Heart Is" a watershed moment in Reed's life was its serendipity. Many editors, while acknowledging its high quality, passed on publication because it put a street girl in a sympathetic light. The editors were frank: our readers want information or entertainment, not moral ambiguity that compels them to question themselves or the world around them. Reed delivered the story to Max Eastman, editor of *The Masses*, a short time before he abruptly left New York in July 1912 for C.J.'s funeral. The story appeared in print in January 1913, less than three months after he returned to New York. Between the handoff of "Where the Heart Is" and its presentation to *The Masses* subscribers, Reed was more or less idle, 3,000 miles away from New York, in his hometown. Just as his father had suggested to Lincoln Steffens, after sacrificing his own pleasure for career, family and community, John Reed was was going to play as hard as he worked when he returned to New York.

He would write with his eyes—the eyes that Walter Lippmann later called "perfect." Eventually, what he saw more vividly than anything else was the unfairness of an American economic and political system that purported to be fair and democratic. The concept of America was alive and the possibilities seductive, but America itself was broken. The people were good, as Reed's stories illustrated, but the people were not in charge of their own fate in a country that was beautiful and unforgiving. People living on the streets and working in the mills had the goodness of his father and were crushed by the same forces—keepers of the economic and political status quo. In New York, Reed began fighting for the tramps. Armed with some talent, a lot of verve and Ivy League connections, he would take on the barons of industry, the political insiders and the abusers of power—through journalism. A Harvard man with no money who decided that his father essentially killed himself to send his sons to college, Jack Reed decided that his main reason for getting up in the morning would be war—not on America per se, but on the institutions Americans built that crushed the hopes and spirit of fellow Americans. That's "where his heart was."

And so when Julian Street and a friend admonished Reed in 1913 for betraying his social class by going to jail and organizing an extravagant pageant on behalf of striking silk workers in Paterson, New Jersey, Reed told Street and his peers that he would rather hang around murderers than self-satisfied Harvard men because the murderers were more interesting.[19]

War in Paterson

Reed reset his life again when he took on the Paterson labor conflict, first as a journalist and then as a producer of a political entertainment event at Madison Square Garden in the spring of 1913. He had been hanging out at one of Mabel Dodge's salon parties when Bill Haywood, the radical labor union organizer for the socialist Industrial Workers of the World, dominated the conversation with a rant about the abuse of workers—including violence executed by factory management and police. Haywood was fed up with the lack of press coverage of this story. Reed listened and then sprang into action, reporting on the strike, getting arrested (with lots of newspaper coverage for that), and then throwing himself into the elaborate pageant that featured the strikers themselves at Madison Square Garden.

The Harvard education (on campus, but outside the classroom) had done its job in terms of presenting competing (and often blasphemous) ideas of social structures for Reed and other students to dissect. Reed, however, was no more interested in discussing political ideology than he had been as an undergraduate. "Ideas do not mean much to me," he wrote many years later, when he was more somber and mature.[20] People meant a lot to him, particularly people who had little opportunity to live the life that America promised in exchange for hard work and following the rules.

The spoken words of people meant a lot to him because they tapped into the storyteller and the artist, sometimes the contrarian. When Bill Haywood spoke about the abuse of silk workers in Mabel Dodge's apartment, and Mabel floated the idea that a concert on their behalf—with the workers' participation—could actually work, Reed was ready to listen. He had already romanticized the working poor. The Paterson strike became his life for several months in 1913. He became reporter, activist and advocate for the silk factory workers as well as a producer, playwright, songwriter and publicist for the Paterson pageant. Seven years after joining dozens of clubs in college, two years after racing through western Europe long enough to get engaged and break it off, a year after he began soaking up New York like a sponge, Reed was running a marathon by sprinting. As if he had not already separated himself from Dodge's manufactured community of free-thinkers (where guests felt "vaguely guilty about their fortunate position," according to O'Connor), Jack Reed, the Storm Boy nobody could ignore, found the time to report on a landmark moment in American labor history that resonates a century later.

By 1874, half of the silk in the United States was produced in Paterson, one of the original textile towns in America. The nationwide abuse of foreign workers brought in for the purpose of production and exploitation—unlivable wages, unsafe conditions, complete control of their lives by the factory owners—had precedents in Paterson. In 1794, protesting calico-printers were locked out by their employers. A 16-hour shift was not unusual; women and children reported to their spinning machines at 4:30 a.m. and were whipped by foremen if they weakened late in the day. In 1828 and 1835 there were violent strikes for better working conditions.[21] The mill owners prevailed, as always. Thus, in 1913—during the so-called Progressive Era—after a couple of decades of muckraking journalism, including *The Jungle* by Upton Sinclair and *The Shame of the Cities* by Lincoln Steffens, the only "progress" made by silk workers in Paterson was that they were supposedly working 12 hours per day instead of 16.

Ideas do not mean that much to me. But raw images seen with his own eyes, unfiltered by the accounts of others, lightly edited by editors, unvarnished by the expectations of advertisers, meant everything to Jack Reed. (The socialist *Masses* was a free publication, did not pay its writers, and did not generate a lot of advertising revenue.)

"There's a war in Paterson," he wrote in a *Masses* story published in June of 1913.

> But it's a curious kind of war. All the violence is the work of one side—the Mill Owners. Their servants, the Police, club unresisting men and women and ride down

law abiding crowds on horse-back. Their paid mercenaries, the armed Detectives, shoot and kill innocent people. Their newspapers, the Paterson Press and the Paterson Call, publish incendiary and crime-inciting appeals to mob violence against the strike leaders. Their tool, Recorder Carroll, deals out heavy sentences to peaceful pickets that the police-net gathers up. They control absolutely the Police, the Press, the Courts.

Opposing them are about twenty-five thousand striking silk workers, of whom perhaps ten thousand are active, and their weapon is the picket-line. Let me tell you what I saw in Paterson and then you will say which side of this struggle is "anarchistic" and "contrary to American ideals."

Ushered into a patrol wagon (after his arrest for not moving when told to move), I was driven with much clanging of gongs along with picket-line. Our passage was greeted with "Boos" and ironical cheers, and enthusiastic waving. At Headquarters I was interrogated and lodged in the lockup. My cell was about four feet wide by seven feet long, at least a foot higher than a standing mean's head, and it contained an iron bunk hung from the side-wall with chains, and an open toilet of disgusting dirtiness in the corner. A crowd of pickets had been jammed into the same lockup only three days before, *eight or nine in a cell*, and kept there without food or or water for *twenty-two hours*! Among them a young girl of seventeen, who had led a procession right up to the Police Sergeant's nose and defied him to arrest them. In spite of the horrible discomfort, fatigue and thirst, these prisoners *had never let up cheering and singing for a day and a night*![22]

Reed was sentenced to 20 days in the county jail. He spent time in another holding cell with 80 prisoners, half of them strikers. Among the non-strikers was Bill Haywood of the IWW, who had organized the strike.

Surrounded by a dense crowd of short, dark-faced men, Big Bill Haywood towered in the center of the room.... His massive, rugged face, seamed and scarred like a mountain, and as calm, radiated strength. These slight, foreign faced strikers, one of many desperate little armies in the vanguard of the battle-line of Labor, quickened and strengthened by Bill Haywood's face and voice, looked up at him lovingly, eloquently. Faces deadened and dulled with grinding routine in the sunless mills glowed with hope and understanding. Faces scarred and bruised from policemen's clubs grinned eagerly at the thought of going back on the picket-line. And there were other faces, too—lined and sunken with the slow starvation of a nine weeks' poverty—shadowed with the sight of so much suffering, or the hopeless brutality of the police—and there were those who had seen Modestino Valentino shot to death by a private detective. But not one showed discouragement; not one a sign of faltering or of fear. As one little Italian said to me, with blazing eyes: "We all one bigga da Union. I.W.W.—dat word is pierced da heart of de people...."

Most of them were still weak and exhausted from their terrible night before in the lockup. Some had been lined up against a wall, as they marched to and fro in front of the mills, and herded to jail on the charge of "unlawful assemblage!" Others had been clubbed into the patrol-wagon on the charge of "rioting," as they stood at the track, on their way home from picketing, waiting for a train to pass! They were being held for the Grand Jury that indicted Haywood and Gurley Flynn. Four of these jurymen were silk manufacturers, another the head of the local Edison company—which Haywood tried to organize for a strike—and not one a workingman![23]

"War in Paterson" was the first manifestation of Reed's evolution into a serious journalist with an agenda far more controversial than the ones held by many respected reporters, writers, and editors in his field. The story was also a signal that Reed was following a path almost guaranteed to kill any hopes for commercial success in any profession. In this regard, he was too much like his father to play along with the power elite, the people who demanded loyalty and silence while they set the rules of markets, business, politics and interpretation of the law, keeping the unwashed masses an arm's length away. One difference between John Reed and his father, Charles Jerome Reed: C.J. bruised egos with wit and sarcasm while taking action to correct social injustice. He worked his way into influential positions in business and politics without the benefit of a college education, although he did marry into money. The doors of opportunity opened for him, but when he showed his true colors, the doors slammed shut. He was devastated, but he did open doors for his sons, John and Harry. By 1913, having seen beauty and cruelty on other continents and in New York, having lived for four years under Harvard's mysterious caste social structure, John Reed was ready to use the best weapons he had—storytelling and endless energy—to fight his father's fight against the abuse of power and privilege.

As he became a celebrity in New York, a common refrain about Reed was that his commitment to self promotion was greater than commitment to his work—and that his commitment to injustice was rather unseemly. Reed, however, was filling a void. It was the post-muckraking era of American journalism. Men and women who had exposed the flaws in America's institutions with shock and awe on the pages of large circulation newspapers and magazines were resuming their careers in a conservative publishing field while government at the local, state and federal levels engineered the slow machinations of democratic change.

Max Eastman gave Reed another opportunity to develop with a daily routine at his magazine, handing him the managing editor's role at *The Masses*. It was more of a grown-up's job than reporting. Reed did not last long behind the desk, although he produced quality stories and was a charming and effective fundraiser (he had a way with wealthy socialites). Faced with the never-ending grunt work of putting out a magazine, Reed behaved like something between a caged animal and a restless teenager. He pulled pranks to amuse himself, including the relocation of the company's safe from the newsroom to the sidewalk. Eastman could hardly wait to find a replacement editor and put Reed back where he belonged, on the streets, talking to people and telling their stories.[24]

He was still untamed by any definition of the word, but he did not let the opinion of others interfere with his new focus. His mother, forever concerned about appearances and social norms, began a decades-long diatribe against her son's association with socialism shortly after he resumed his New York life in late 1912 (she later objected in the 1930s to the emergence of John Reed Clubs, which were suspected Soviet fronts posing as character-building groups for boys). "I'm not a Socialist, any more than I am an Episcopalian," he told his mother in a letter. "My business is to interpret and live life."[25]

Nor did he listen much to Mabel Dodge, who had exposed him to a parade of talent, ideas, imagination and ego at her parties while taking him in as her lover. Dodge was not subtle or private about using sex as a weapon to keep young Jack Reed confined to her physical and psychic orbit. "I took my breakfast in bed, and he ate his at a little table by my bedside because I wanted him to," Dodge wrote in her memoir, *Movers and Shakers*. "But he might well have been gone from there for all he was with *me*. He drank his coffee with the morning paper propped up before him, his honey-colored round eyes just popping over *'the news!'* Any kind of news as long as it had possibilities for thrill, for action, for excitement."

His complicated relationship with Walter Lippmann had always produced more than a few slings and arrows. Reed respected Lippman for a willingness to use his intellectual heft to explore radical ideas about social structures. Lippman didn't always respond in kind, making sure that any public praise he offered Reed served as a caveat to a measured but stinging assessment of his immaturity.

"He assumed that all capitalists were fat, bald, and unctuous, that reformers were cowardly or scheming, that all newspapers are corrupt, that Victor Berger and the Socialist Party and Samuel Gompers and the trade unions are a fraud on labor," Lippman wrote in the *New Republic* in December 1914. "He made an effort to believe that the working class is not composed of miners, plumbers and working men generally, but is a fine statuesque giant who stands on a high hill facing the sun. He wrote stories about the night court and plays about ladies in kimonos. He talked with intelligent tolerance about dynamite, and thought he saw an intimate connection between the cubists and the I.W.W. He even read a few pages of Bergson."[26]

Reed distanced himself from other writers by grabbing attention with his actions as well as his words. He was doing things that good boys from Harvard didn't do, like getting arrested on the streets of labor rallies. Or following up his writing of the Paterson story with a mad, audacious

John Reed, in-house promotional advertisement in *Metropolitan Magazine*, publicizing his reporting on the Mexican Revolution, 1914 (courtesy Houghton Library, Harvard University, Cambridge, MA, hou00070co2111).

endeavor intended to bring social commentary off the pages of magazines and into Madison Square Garden—the Paterson pageant, where audiences met with the faces, flesh, blood and bones of laborers who had previously existed to them only as a concept. Jack Reed was funny and sometimes a bit much to take, but he was serious. The transformation to manhood, after Paterson, took the form of a journey to Mexico, where Reed took his brand of journalism to levels that were universally applauded.

The stories for which Reed is most widely known—the Paterson strike, the Ludlow Massacre, the Mexican Revolution, World War I and the Russian Revolution—had histories predating Reed, beginnings with no swashbuckling journalist on the scene. His Mexico stories, along with the Paterson and Russia coverage, were not the first articles alerting Americans to what was going on in those dramas. Reed's enduring contribution was to make these stories matter to an American readership that had grown to value escapism as much as quality journalism. The *Metropolitan*, which gave Reed his first big platform as he reported from Mexico, reached one million readers in 1913.[27] Large metropolitan newspapers, although capable of quality journalism, were easily manipulated by political pressure or the threat of advertising boycotts. Many of them supported a U.S. military invasion of Mexico. Reed supported Pancho Villa and his gangly army of armed peasants.

Pancho Villa and John Reed: Mutual Admiration

Two years before Reed arrived in Mexico, the world-famous adventurer/journalist/novelist Jack London traveled to Mexico to write about a citizen revolt for democracy against a "ruling oligarchy."

"All the names that you are being called, we have been called," London wrote as if speaking to the rebel peasants. "And when graft and greed get up and begin to call names, honest men, brave men, patriotic men and martyrs can expect nothing else than to be called chicken thieves and outlaws. I subscribe myself a chicken thief and revolutionist."[28]

The Mexican war became a cry for redistribution of land and wealth (although, ironically, instead of becoming a revolutionist, London turned hard to the political right after his Mexico experience). The cover of John Reed's internationally acclaimed book *Insurgent Mexico* calls the conflict the world's first socialist revolution. Many American journalists covered the story when Pancho Villa's guerrilla army gained traction through unexpected victories against the government's military forces.

General Pancho Villa (left), 1914 (courtesy Houghton Library, Harvard University, Cambridge, MA, 518429_04).

Nobody gained the kind of access to Villa that Reed secured. "One of Reed's most effective qualities as a reporter was his ability to disarm his subject by empathizing with him," wrote journalist Barbara Gelb in *So Short a Time*. "Reed was able to get astonishingly candid answers from the revolutionary leader, who was regarded as an enigmatic and almost mythical figure by Americans on both sides of the border."[29]

Three. Endless Storm: Harvard to Mexico

Reed got Pancho Villa talking as easily as he got Martha the house girl talking in "Where the Heart Is."

"One hears a great many stories of Villa's violating women," Reed wrote. "I asked him if that were true. He pulled his mustache and stared at me for a minute and an inscrutable expression. 'I never take the trouble to deny such stories,' he said. 'They say I am a bandit too. Well, you know my history. But tell me, have you ever met a husband, father or brother of any women that I have violated? Or even a witness?'

"It is fascinating to watch [Villa] discover new ideas," Reed continued. "Remember that he is absolutely ignorant of the trouble and confusions and readjustments of modern civilization. 'Socialism,' he once said, when I wanted to know what he thought of it, 'Socialism—is it a thing? I only see it in books, and I do not read much.'"[30]

The reporter had attended earnest Socialist Club meetings among Harvard undergraduates. He learned about socialist ideology in dry Harvard classrooms. He had witnessed fire-and-brimstone speeches by socialist I.W.W. leaders as they brought overworked and uneducated American laborers into its ranks. At this point in his life, however, Reed had something in common with Pancho Villa: a disregard for intellectualizing socialism. (His disdain for pedantic policy-making proved part of his undoing among the Russian political elite who courted him years later.) Both Villa and Reed considered their relationship with socialism simple, although not simplistic: leaders and their followers need to see the world through the eyes of the impoverished. Convince people that the lives of the poor and uneducated do not have to be predetermined.

Insurgent Mexico reports on this exchange between Reed and a soldier in Pancho Villa's guerrilla army:

> "What are you fighting for," I asked.
> Juan Sanchez, the color bearer, looked at me curiously. "Why, it is good, fighting," he said. "You don't have to work in the mines!"
> "We are fighting," said Isidro Amazo, "for Libertad."
> "What do you mean by Libertad?"
> "Libertad is when I can do what I want!"
> "But suppose it hurts someone else."
> He shot back at me Benito Juarez's great sentence:
> "Peace is the respect for the rights of others!"
> I wasn't prepared for that. It startled me, this barefooted Meztizo's conception of Liberty. I submit it is the only correct definition of Liberty—to do what I want to! Americans quote it to me, triumphantly, as an instance of Mexican irresponsibility. But I think it is a better definition than ours—Liberty is the right to do what the Courts want....
> But, just to be square, I'll have to report Juan Sanchez' remark.

"Is there war in the United States now?" he asked.

"No," I said, untruthfully.

"No war at all?" He meditated for a moment. "How do you pass the time, then?"[31]

The stories from Mexico drew international attention. His fame was in the same realm as that of his namesake, Jack London, who had also reached stardom through talent, thrill-seeking and self-promotion. There is no historical evidence that Reed and London ever met each other, which was probably a good thing for both men. Both Jacks became disillusioned with Pancho Villa and his murderous ways. That awakening helped turn London into a hard-right conservative. On the other hand, the realization that Villa did not deserve hero status failed to make Jack Reed waver, or even flinch, in his commitment to expose exploitation of the working class. If anything, the Mexico experience hardened him. The bouncing, entertaining Storm Boy of Greenwich Village developed a steely resolve to follow his public war wherever it took him. The fall of a violent Mexican bandit previously held up as hope for the oppressed likely made one lasting impact on Jack Reed. He had to know, after Mexico, that he was going to lose his war. Pancho Villa lost. Charles Jerome Reed had lost. So would John Reed.

Chapter Four

Two Women: Mabel Dodge and Louise Bryant

"You see, my dearest lover, I was once a free person. I didn't depend on anything. I was as humanly independent as it is possible to be. Then along came women, and they set out deliberately, as they always instinctively do, to break that armor down, to make the artist a human being and dependent on human beings. Well, they did it, and so now without a mate I am half a man, and sterile."—John Reed in a letter to Louise Bryant, July 5, 1917[1]

In addition to carrying the labels of rebel and revolutionary, Jack Reed earned a reputation as a romantic. The word "romantic" applied to his vision of working class laborers as noble men and women capable of controlling their own destiny. It also applied to his habit of falling in love with foreign cultures. And it applied to his relationships with women.

He was engaged twice, got married without an engagement, and offered engagement (unsuccessfully) to a woman who tortured him with sex and control. In between there were trysts, some of which he tried to rationalize to the women with whom he had long-term relationships at the time. He took full advantage of the sexual revolution that occured in a quasi-underground manner in urban America in the early 20th century. Jack Reed had an eye for women, but he always kept the other eye on a different prize. Sometimes it was the discovery of new places or people that could change his world outlook. Other times it was literary recognition. Often it was a celebration of laughter and kicks in a life laced with risk.

He had several friendships with women based on interests in literature, art, politics and philosophy rather than romance or sex. He did not, however, show much interest in compromising his ambitions for any woman. He was a romantic in politics and love. Just as the daily grind of public policy or journalism interested him less than political victories or bylines, Reed did not often have the time or desire for the unglamourous work of a long-term relationship. Two women, Mabel Dodge and Louise Bryant, invested much of their time and emotional capital trying to make Reed understand what a man's commitment to a woman really means. Both women were intriguing and erratic—and very different from each other in terms of pedigree and style.

Mabel Dodge

Mabel Dodge, eight years older than Reed, was the daughter of a wealthy banker from Buffalo. Her first marriage came at age 21, but within two years she was a widow. Later she married Edwin Dodge, a wealthy Boston architect. Between 1903 and 1912 the couple lived in luxury in Florence, Italy. She had an abundance of friends who were rich, creative or famous. Among them was Gertrude Stein, who managed to write a profile entitled "A Portrait of Mabel Dodge at the Villa" without ever mentioning Dodge or the villa in the text.[2] When the Dodges returned to the United States in 1912, their marriage was rocky. That summer Mabel became familiar with the Greenwich Village counterculture. Her need for attention and the acknowledgment of her importance compelled her to organize weekly gatherings at her Fifth Avenue apartment, where debates and alcohol flowed freely—with Mabel as host and facilitator. The gatherings became known as Mabel's salon.

The salon, a concept she had learned about in Europe, had already established its reputation as an island for unruly free expression when John Reed joined the party. He was in attendance when I.W.W. leader Bill Haywood—armed with less education than just about anyone in the room—challenged the talkers to walk the walk by doing something about the Paterson silk workers' strike. Reed heeded the call to action, quitting his first post-college full-time job at *American Magazine* to work with Dodge on an audacious project—a pageant at Madison Square Garden to dramatize the plight of the mill workers, using the striking laborers themselves onstage to reenact the courage, misery and violence that made the conflict a watershed moment in American labor history.

Reed and Dodge worked closely together for weeks on the pageant. Reed, consistent with his approach to any endeavor he cared about at the moment, went all-in, working around the clock. Dodge, also true to her nature, took great pleasure in her role as coordinator, financial backbone and de facto producer, all the while setting her sights on Reed for her next sexual conquest. Friends noticed their stolen glances and attempts to restrain their flirtations.

"When I saw that look on her face, I knew it was all over for Mabel for the time being and also probably all over for Reed," said Hutchins Hapgood, a good friend of Mabel's.[3]

The pageant achieved critical acclaim but fell far short of its revenue goals and its mission, which was to help the workers with a strike fund. Reed was physically and emotionally drained following the event; he recuperated in Europe, accompanying Mabel, her son and his nurse on a trip through several countries. According to Robert Rosenstone, Mabel withheld sex from Reed until she made arrangements for her son's care so that she would be alone with Reed in Italy. Dodge wrote about their lovemaking in her autobiography, openly praising Reed for his skills. But she chafed at his divided attention. When traveling friends from the States found him in Italy, he did not hesitate to leave Mabel behind to frolic with them on short road trips or drinking sessions.

By November 1913 Reed and Dodge were living together in her Fifth Avenue apartment, his growing reputation as a literary journalist further spiced by his romantic relationship with a woman known as "man-eating Mabel." Her attempts to monopolize Reed's time continuously clashed with his relentless pursuit of stories and adventure for its own sake. When he secured the assignment in Mexico that would take his journalistic reputation to an international level, Mabel chased after him. His departure, he claimed, was the end of their relationship. But she caught up with him in Chicago, and they made wild love all the way to El Paso while he set his sights on chasing down Pancho Villa.[4]

By February 1914, his reports from Mexico, published in *Metropolitan* magazine, put him "in the first ranks of American literary journalists."[5] He and Mabel reconnected in New York, and for most of 1914 they considered themselves a couple. Their dueling interests—Mabel insisting upon his complete surrender to the relationship, and his unflinching commitment to writing, kicks, and fame—defined their tempestuous relationship. She tried to make him jealous by dropping hints of an affair she had had while he was in Mexico. Reed did not take the bait. One of his written responses, upon reading of her time with another man, was "I will write all our names across the sky in flames."[6] He broke up with her in Europe via transatlantic cable while covering the Great War; he had fallen in love with a married woman. That affair was short-lived, and when he returned to the States, he bought two gold rings and showed them to Mabel—not as a formal proposal, but as a sign of commitment to each other. She rejected him, and he went into a drinking tailspin. It wasn't until 1916 that Reed accepted the end of their relationship.

Louise Bryant

Louise Bryant's first husband was a dentist with a successful practice and an upper-middle class lifestyle in Portland. He was also a frustrated artist who acquiesced to the new-fangled notion of open marriage. Louise had love affairs in her studio. She was vain; in her late 20s she began a lifelong habit of lying about her age. In November 1915, longing to get out of Portland and flee to New York, she met John Reed (who was on a brief visit to spend time with his mother) through friends after reading his articles in the *Metropolitan* and *The Masses*. She orchestrated a "chance encounter" with the intent of starting a relationship that would jump-start her career as a writer. Reed, as he had done before and would do again, fell in love immediately. She enjoyed his company because he was funny. She told friends about his youthful vigor, adventurous spirit, ruggedness and fame.[7]

She was born in Nevada in rustic surroundings. Her father was a self-made, self-educated man who became a teacher and abandoned his family. She achieved average grades in high school, attended college (which was unusual for young women of her background) and continued to earn average grades. Louise worked as a teacher in Puget Sound and at a cannery (although her accounts of her early life are subject to debate, due to contradictions) before settling in as a society reporter for a local newspaper while living in a rented house boat, making friends with people of much broader financial means, including her future husband Paul. After their wedding, he encouraged her to rent a studio to write. She did so and began to carve out her own identity. She developed a reputation for flightiness and pretension. In college she had shown disdain for sorority girls and the narrow confines of middle class life, but as a young wife she resembled a sorority girl who wanted to bust out.[8]

In the middle of the decade, the on-again, off-again romance between Louise Bryant and Jack Reed featured a famous interloper, poet and playwright Eugene O'Neill. Reed befriended O'Neill, drawing him into his eccentric social circle of writers. O'Neill went out of his way to present

Louise Bryant portraits, undated (courtesy Houghton Library, Harvard University, 518309_1).

himself in the least flattering light imaginable, looking and acting like a street bum, hating people in general, hating himself, drinking more than the well-lubricated Bohemians, while at the same time trying to establish himself as a distinguished poet. For period of time, wrote biographer Barbara Gelb, it seemed like the only person who recognized O'Neill's talent was Jack Reed. As O'Neill ventured into the outer periphery of Reed's circle, Jack introduced him to Louise, just as he had introduced all of his New York friends to Louise while trying to help her career and confidence. Reed and Bryant spent the summer of 1916 in Provincetown, which was evolving into a hideaway for artists and writers working and living in Greenwich Village. At Reed's urging, O'Neill eventually joined the group in Provincetown.

Bryant was drawn to O'Neill's sullen nature, and they got to know each other through the Provincetown Players, a chaotic collection of writers and amateur actors who strove to produce unpolished, alternative theater that Broadway would not touch, for the sake of art that challenged the boundaries of social acceptance. Reed was in and out of this playground

John Reed (right) and friend in Provincetown, undated though likely 1916 (courtesy Houghton Library, Harvard University, 518317_03).

atmosphere, leaving for magazine assignments and political events. During one of Reed's business trips, Bryant seduced O'Neill. Mabel Dodge found out because Mabel Dodge knew everybody and everything about this New York crowd. Dodge, Reed's ex-lover, told Reed about the fling between Louise and Eugene, but Reed refused to believe her.

The Provincetown Players returned to New York in the fall of 1916, but Reed, Bryant and O'Neill stayed behind. As they worked on their individual writing projects, Reed and Bryant lived together in one house and O'Neill lived by himself in a nearby apartment. Bryant continued to sleep

Four. Two Women: Mabel Dodge and Louise Bryant

John Reed (right) with friends in Provincetown, undated though likely 1916 (courtesy Houghton Library, Harvard University, 518317_01).

with O'Neill when Reed left for assignments, then returned to Reed's bed when he came back to Provincetown. She did not mention this to Reed, who did not ask. Louise told O'Neill that Reed's kidney infection prevented him from making love to her. For his part, Reed told Bryant he was abstaining from sex because he didn't know if he could infect her. Bryant, according to Gelb, convinced herself that she was living within the conscripts of Bohemian free love.[9]

In September of 1916, Reed and Bryant returned to New York City. On November 9, 1916, without fanfare, they got married. The sleeping arrangements, which included O'Neill but were not discussed, continued as they were in Provincetown. According to Gelb, Louise was feeling triumphant with her power over two men. Reed was earning good money as a magazine writer in high demand. He and Louise pooled their resources and bought a house on Croton-on-Hudson, a village in the town of Cortlandt in Westchester County, New York. They threw in a few pieces of furniture for functionality while maintaining a minimalist approach to housekeeping consistent with their counterculture ethos. This was their weekend retreat from the city. During this time, O'Neill was establishing himself as an accomplished poet, and the Provincetown Players were establishing their theater as a cool avant garde operation, a risk-taking, freewheeling alternative to Broadway.

Reed's health, precarious since childhood, was worsening. He traveled to Baltimore for tests that eventually led to a kidney removal operation. Occasionally he acknowledged fears that his life could be in danger. He and Louise wrote each other an endless series of romantic, schmaltzy letters while he was hospitalized. The language they used in correspondence may not have been unusual for the times, when letters served as a vehicle for the expression of deep emotions. A century later, the letters read like teenagers falling in love for the first time. During Reed's hospitalization, O'Neill moved into the New York apartment Louise was sharing with Reed. Bryant became very sick, with symptoms that were vague enough for friends to speculate that she had had an illegal and botched abortion. Reed became upset when he read one of her letters suggesting that she had kept some information from him.[10]

Upon his return to New York in December, Reed's health improved. He prepared for a trip to China for an assignment that the *Metropolitan* was promoting heavily. The trip and the assignment disappeared, however, as the publication succumbed to nationalistic fervor.

On February 3, 1917, the United States cut off diplomatic ties with Germany. Magazines that had been publishing Reed's stories asked him to keep his political views to himself and out of print. The *Metropolitan* was forced to shut down when advertisers became skittish about their association with a socialist publication. Most prominent journalists, at this point in history, tried to adapt to the changing political landscape by either shifting or softening their social commentary or by staying away from politics altogether. Many of them had already started doing this a few years earlier when public interest in muckraking journalism faded. Reed, for his part, amped up his own war on capitalism, writing in socialist publications that paid little or not at all, and taking an aggressive tone at anti-war rallies, where he insisted on making the connection between the European War and capitalist exploitation of the working class, calling it "a trader's war." Friends and peers were cautious, not wishing to be found guilty by association while everyone's patriotism came under scrutiny. To cover his lost income, Reed did land a full-time newspaper position at the New York *Mail*, a conventional reporting job that did not allow him to write about politics, period.

Bryant had difficulty establishing herself as a professional journalist, although not for political reasons. She had some success promoting O'Neill's work before he emerged as a first-rate writer. The literary magazine *Seven*

Arts, on her recommendation, bought O'Neill's story "Tomorrow" after the *Metropolitan* rejected it. At the same time, *Seven Arts* editor Waldo Frank rejected a poem written by Bryant.

"Our magazine was very serious, almost religious—we considered ourselves the organ of cultural nationalism," Frank said. "We were disciples of Walt Whitman and were creating the voice Whitman wanted." Frank did not take Louise Bryant seriously. "She was just around," he said. "She was a 'flaming youth' girl, an Irish beauty, thin, with pale skin, very romantic. She was intellectually alive and responsive, although not profound."[11]

Bryant did manage to land a job as a war correspondent in France. She was motivated by rage after Reed confessed to her that he had had an affair. While still avoiding the topic of whether or not she was sharing her love with two men, Reed agreed to help her secure accreditation as a war reporter through the Bell Syndicate. He championed her skills to his contacts in Washington and abroad. But while Bryant did obtain a passport and credentials, her comportment made an impression on a State Department official not unlike the one expressed by Waldo Frank: "I suppose I will have to issue a passport to this wild woman. She is full of socialistic and ultra-modern ideas, which accounts for her wild hair and open mouth. She is the wife of John Reed, a well-known correspondent."[12]

The couple continued to write letters to each other while Louise was in France, although some of their letters were delayed by wartime complications. She told Reed that she detected an attitude shift among expatriots from anti-war to anti–German. She spent considerable energy trying to obtain military clearance to report from the front lines of battle, and seemed baffled by the rejections, despite her lack of overall reporting experience. She also told Reed that he was an immensely popular writer among the French. "Artists you do not know at all love you over here," she wrote. "They think you are the greatest man in America." Meanwhile, Reed seemed to recognize that his fight against capitalism and his refusal to back the war against the Central Powers had a palpable effect on his friendships. He suggested to Louise that he was beginning to "bore" his beloved mentor, Lincoln Steffens. The couple tried to apologize to each other for their personal actions that led to this odd separation, without getting into specifics. "Oh, dearest, I could talk to you now," she wrote. "I could air every part of my heart and brain. I understand you and I understand myself better than you think. We would be happy—more deeply happy than we have every been—this just had to happen—not this particular little mess, but something to make us find each other."[13]

For his part, Reed tried to reassure Louise that he was working on his inner demons, making veiled references to lust. He added that while he longed for her, only he could address his obsession with women. He referred to a woman he had recently met in Washington. "I burst out and talked of you and what you meant to me for about an hour—why, I don't know ... I was decent and nice to a girl and I pitied her—she wanted to make love. I didn't and couldn't. I've been true all right. But I think perhaps there's something terribly wrong about me—that I may be crazy, for I had a desire once, just the other day." Again he reassured her that he did not act on his desire, that he was "frozen." And while this was a torturous process for him, he warned her that it would be worse if she tried to manage his actions if and when they reunited. "It would be intolerable for both of us if you felt you had to direct and censor my thoughts, my actions—as you have in the past—as you did even in your letter telling me not to drink."[14]

In near-panic about his health, love life, career and the memories of mass suffering and mutilation he had witnessed in Europe, Reed believed, as he approached 30 years of age, that his youth was gone. He wrote "Almost Thirty" at this time, the waning months of 1916; it is alternatively revealing, poignant, wistful and somber. He foreshadowed the Lost Generation in this never-published essay: "Sometimes it seems to me the end of the world's youth, too. Certainly the Great War has done something to us all.... I've watched civilizations change and broaden and sweeten in my lifetime, and I've watched it wither and crumble in the red blast of war. And war I have seen, too, in the trenches, with armies.... A good many of my beliefs have got twisted by the Great War.... The War has been a terrible shatterer of faith in economic and political idealism.... I am waiting, waiting for [the war] to end, for life to resume so I can find my work."[15] Meanwhile, Reed showed up every day for the grind of daily newspaper work, collecting a paycheck, writing profiles about celebrities and boxers and other topics he found meaningless, but which were in demand by the *Mail's* readers.

Following a trend throughout the zigzags in Reed's life, the gloom and doom of his mood evaporated by July 1917 when he again reunited with Louise in New York. He burned with intensity and joy over developments in Russia, when the revolution also smoldered with passion, danger and hope. The tsar had abdicated his throne in March. The provisional government did nothing to give hope to peasants, farmers and laborers, and thus the Russian bourgeoisie became targets of ire and impatience. Reed made no secret of his belief that this was his calling, the ultimate class war, the social revolution that would tower above all revolutions.

Four. Two Women: Mabel Dodge and Louise Bryant

In Russia, Reed and Bryant reached the zenith of of their passion for each other, their politics, and their journalism careers. They saw validation of their outsider status as idealistic youths insisting that there was a better way to attain economic justice and individual liberty than the American model. The Bolshevik Revolution gave Bryant a level of journalistic credibility that she had not come close to attaining before. Years of hard work had not improved her reputation for style over substance, but, in collaboration with Reed, she learned how to integrate documents, interviews and observations with her narratives. The result was a book, *Six Red Months in Russia*, that received some acclaim and a long list of speaking engagements when she returned to the States.[16] She left Reed behind in Russia to return to New York to write her book. When she arrived, she learned for the first time that Reed (a) had been named Russian consul to the United States and (b) he had been removed from the post almost immediately after Washington officials objected.

Upon returning to New York, Louise wrote to Eugene O'Neill and insisted that they meet. O'Neill was engaged, and his fiance was not happy about Louise's message. Friends of Bryant and O'Neill were mystified by her attempt to reunite with her old lover.[17]

She pestered a Senate committee investigating Bolshevism, insisting that the panel needed to hear her testimony. The committee was reluctant in the aftermath of her arrest following a speaking engagement at which she burned President Wilson's photo in effigy. In jail she went on a hunger strike while Reed reached near panic over her actions. Eventually the Senate allowed her to testify on her insights about Bolshevism, but—whether due to sexism, her personality or the quality of her remarks—the senators gave little indication that they took her seriously.[18]

Louise Bryant outlived Reed by a decade and a half, but any trace of her alluring nature and vibrant intellect disintegrated when he died in October 1920. She remarried but drank heavily and went through a series of well-documented humiliations due to her behavior in public.[19] Her legacy remains as the woman who alternately stood by and ran with Reed on her own terms during his chaotic career as radical journalist, political agitator and revolutionary.

Art Young, one of Reed's best friends when they worked together on *The Masses*, wrote, "Poor Louise committed slow suicide—went the sad road of narcotic escape." Young received a letter from Louise shortly before she died in 1936 at the age of 41: "Know always I send my love to you across the stars. If you get there before I do—or later—tell Jack Reed I love him."[20]

"In thinking it over, I find little in my thirty years that I can hold to," Reed wrote in 1916. "I haven't any God and don't want one; faith is only another word for finding oneself. In my life as in most lives, I guess, love plays a tremendous part. I've had love affairs, passionate happiness, wretched maladjustments; hurt deeply and been deeply hurt. But at last I have found my friend and lover, thrilling and satisfying, closer to me than anyone has ever been. And now I don't care what comes."[21]

CHAPTER FIVE

Crossing Borders and Boundaries

"I have become an I.W.W. and am now in favor of dynamiting."—Jack Reed in a letter to friend Bob Andrews in 1912[1]

Long before online surveillance, the Patriot Act, domestic Cold War spying, or the first incarnation of the Red Scare, a bad joke about supporting violence to make a political point was a good way to make friends nervous or catch the attention of federal authorities, especially if the comment was made in writing. But Jack Reed was far from alone when suggesting, in jest or not, that the extremes of injustice in America demanded extreme responses. The ranks of socialists, communists, anarchists and anti-capitalists of different stripes became impossible to ignore in the early years of the 20th century. It took a world war and a U.S. federal government assault on free speech to put out the fires of of violent dissent. Reed got the memo, so to speak, and he ignored it. Amendments and interpretation of the Alien and Sedition laws, along with the Espionage Act, made criticism of the U.S. government illegal. The *New York Times*, along with other prominent and smaller publications, risked the loss of mailing privilege for their war commentary. Knowing all this, and having been arrested and assaulted himself while covering labor conflicts and anti-war rallies, Reed stood his ground, effectively taunting the U.S. government. He was not as far left on the political spectrum as the violent, bomb-throwing anarchists of his day, but he may have been considered more dangerous.

For a few years, his words and actions were in step with the politics of the times; nearly a million Americans, 6 percent of the vote, cast ballots for Socialist Party candidate Eugene Debs in the 1912 presidential election. Debs received the same level of support in the 1920 election while he was in prison. By the end of the 1910–1919 decade, however, friends, family, mentors and peers began treating Jack Reed like the last guest at a party who didn't realize the night was over.

Those who had cheered for Reed hoped he would adjust to the realities of post–Progressive politics; they hoped he would adapt to rising nationalism, distance himself from the violent ways of the International Workers of the World and the anarchists, and find a way to play safe enough to continue publishing without attracting the ire of the federal government—as most of the muckrakers from the 1890s and early 1900s had done by 1915. Walter Lippmann expressed his concern over Reed's judgment. So did Steffens, Julian Street, Max Eastman and others.

His critics saw what they wanted to see, even decades after his death. In 1958, Bernard W. Gwertzman, writing for the *Harvard Crimson*, sprinkled broad misconceptions of Reed with a dash of accuracy in an article titled "John Reed: The Eternal Cheerleader."

> As poet, war correspondent, Communist and Harvardman, John Reed saw life as one Big Game. You could lose the game, but it wasn't worth dying for. Life was too exciting....
>
> Reed was impetuous—a romantic who saw beauty in fighting for something even if everyone else was against him. But at the same time he craved popularity.
>
> His friends had expected his impulsiveness to vanish, but he always cherished the memory of those moments when, in front of the Harvard stands, cheerleader Jack Reed could summon help to "dash old Elie's hopes."

Gwertzman quotes Reed saying, "As songleader of the cheering section, I had the supreme blissful sensation of swaying 2,000 voices in great crashing choruses during the big football games." He went on to compare Reed's Harvard cheerleading to a Communist rally in the Soviet Union, when Reed hoisted Vladimir Lenin on his shoulders. Still a man-child in the eyes of a Harvard classmate in 1958.[2]

Between 1913 and 1916, Reed's lust for adventure and his search for purpose took him south of the U.S. border and across the Atlantic Ocean, where he found beautiful cultures on the verge of destruction as they wrestled with the same economic and political issues plaguing his homeland.

Mexico, Continued

In March of 1913, five months after leaving his mother in Portland and returning to New York, Reed was on assignment in Mexico. His reporting

Five. Crossing Borders and Boundaries

General Pancho Villa, third from the right, along with his officers who fought in the Mexican Revolution, 1914 (courtesy Houghton Library, Harvard University, Cambridge, MA, 581429_03).

vaulted him into celebrity and stamped him as a journalist worth taking seriously. The *Metropolitan's* in-house advertisements for Reed's articles gave readers the image of a cowboy journalist wearing a sombrero, a revolver and a gun belt.[3]

Insurgent Mexico was based on a collection of articles Reed had written for the mainstream *Metropolitan*, whose editor, Carl Hovey, told him, "Nothing finer could have been written." Old friend and frequent critic Walter Lippmann had this to say in a letter to Reed: "Your ... articles are undoubtedly the finest reporting that's ever been done. It's kind of embarrassing to tell a fellow you know that he's a genius.... You have perfect eyes, and your power of telling leaves nothing to be desired. I want to hug you, Jack. If all history had been reported as you are doing this, Lord—I say that with Jack Reed reporting begins. Incidentally ... the stories are literature."[4]

Reed had more on his mind than fame with the public or acceptance by New York literary types. His Mexico adventure was more than a thrill ride with the charismatic Pancho Villa. He was serious about land reform for the Mexican peasants as a model for the United States.

Newspapers and magazines, taking their cue from the U.S. government, were openly discussing the possibility of stabilizing Mexico by invading it. The public sentiment for ending chaos in Mexico had all the earmarks of U.S. foreign intervention over the next century, including the European War in 1916, Vietnam in the 1960s, and Iraq/Afghanistan at the turn of the next century, with political leaders arguing that we could set up democratic models for nations that could not govern themselves.

His stature enhanced by the Mexico reporting, Reed made his case against U.S. invasion in an op-ed column in the *New York Times* that was reprinted by the *Metropolitan* and the American Association for International Conciliation. Referring to the Mexican revolts, counter-insurgencies and warring factions that Americans had difficulty keeping track of, Reed wrote, "It is common to speak of the Orozco revolution, the Zapata revolution and the Carranza revolution. As a matter of fact, there is and has been only one revolution in Mexico. It is a fight primarily for land."

In the *New York Times* piece, he foreshadowed his commitment, five years later, to the Bolsheviks' two-steps-forward-two-steps-backwards route to revolution in Russia. The peasants and the peons in Mexico, led by Pancho Villa, were making progress, Reed insisted.

> We Americans, if we enter Mexico, are going to check all this. The first American soldier across the Rio Grande means the end of the Mexican revolution.... The Government of the United States has already expressed itself as opposed to the confiscation of private property; and the land question in Mexico cannot be settled in any other way....
>
> We Americans honestly believe that we will benefit the Mexicans by forcing our instruction on them. We do not realize that the Latin temperament is different from our own—and that their idea of liberty is broader than ours. We want to debauch the Mexican people and turn them into little brown copies of American businessmen and laborers, as we are doing to the Cubans and the Filipinos....
>
> The American soldiers will have nothing serious to anticipate in the opposition of the Mexican army. It is the peons and their women, fighting in the streets and at the doors of their houses, that they will have to murder. It is the patient, generous, ignorant race that has struggled for liberty and self-consciousness for four hundred years—unorganized and inadequately armed—that they will have to shoot down.

In two years, Reed would restate the same essential message, with different settings, different armies, different cultures and different words, as he reported from the Balkans and Russia during the First World War.

In the offices of the *Metropolitan* magazine, after Reed had returned from Mexico, former president Theodore Roosevelt, himself a highly-paid, high-profile correspondent for the publication, hollered at him for glorifying Pancho Villa.

"Villa is a murderer and a bigamist," Roosevelt said. Reed shot back,

Five. Crossing Borders and Boundaries 79

Execution of a revolutionary at Jojutla, Mexico, 1914 (courtesy Houghton Library, Harvard University, 518429_02).

"Well, I believe in bigamy," leading Roosevelt to shake Reed's hand vigorously, TDR-style, and reply, "I am glad, John Reed, to find that you believe in something." Any hope by witnesses that this uncomfortable exchange was really good-natured bantering dissolved later when Reed heard the former president brag that he had ordered a soldier shot in Cuba. "I always knew you were a murderer," Reed said. A *Metropolitan* editor had to separate the two men away to avoid an office fistfight.[5]

Roosevelt had deployed a popular strategy of Reed's critics, who held that his romanticism and idealism clouded his judgment and made him a less-than-stalwart journalist.When Reed returned to New York after his first round of reporting on the the European War, Lippman dismissed Reed as more of a romantic than a reporter: "Reed has no detachment, and is proud of it."[6]

Insurgent Mexico contained this portrait of Pancho Villa:

> Villa was an outlaw for twenty-two years. When he was only a boy of sixteen, delivering milk in the streets of Chihuahua, he killed a government official and had to take to the mountains. The story is that the official had violated his sister, but it seems probably that Villa killed him on account of his insufferable insolence. That in itself would not have outlawed him long in Mexico, where human life is cheap; but once a refugee he committed the unpardonable crime of stealing cattle from the rich haciendados. And from that time to the outbreak of the Madero revolution the Mexican government had a price on his head.

Pancho Villa's rebels on the march (courtesy Houghton Library, Harvard University, Cambridge, MA, 518429_01).

> Villa was the son of ignorant peons. He had never been to school. He hadn't the slightest conception of the complexity of civilization, and when he finally came back to it, a mature man of extraordinary native shrewdness, he encountered the twentieth century with the naive simplicity of a savage.[7]

Peers frequently referred to Reed's eyes and ears, as well as his heart, more than his analytical skills. The early articles about Manhattan, SoHo, Harlem and Greenwich Village burst with urgency and discovery; the Paterson labor conflict reporting screamed righteousness and disbelief; the Mexico stories possessed colorful, piercing descriptions of what Americans considered a lawless land underneath theirs. Reed's description of Villa as a military leader, however, had the markings of a writer who could analyze as well as describe.

> In the field, too, Villa had to invent an entirely original method of warfare, because he never had a chance to learn anything of accepted military strategy. In that he is without the possibility of doubt that greatest leader Mexico has ever had. His method of fighting is astonishingly like Napoleon's. Secrecy, quickness of movement, the adaptation of his plans to the character of the country and of his soldiers, the value of intimate relations with the rank and file, and of building up a tradition among the enemy that his army is invincible, and that he himself bears a charmed life—these are his characteristics. He knew nothing of accepted European standards of strategy or of discipline.... But he does know that guerrilla fighters cannot be driven blindly in platoons around the field in perfect step, that men fighting individually and of their own

Five. Crossing Borders and Boundaries

The United Mine Workers of America's "military headquarters" in Trinidad, Colorado, while supporting striking coal mine workers employed by the Colorado Fuel and Iron Company in nearby Ludlow in 1914 (photograph by Lewis R. Dold, courtesy Houghton Library, Harvard University, 518259_02).

free will are braver than long volleying rows in the trenches, lashed to it by officers with the flat of their swords. And where the fighting is fiercest—when a ragged mob of fierce brown men with hand bombs and rifles rush the bullet-swept streets of an ambushed town—Villa is among them, like any common soldier.[8]

The Ludlow Massacre

One month after Reed left Mexico, the *Metropolitan* sent him to Ludlow, Colorado, the scene of another bloody class war. Arriving in late April, ten days after armed security forces set fire to tents in a colony established by striking coal mine workers, Reed was surveying the aftermath of a horror known as "the Ludlow Massacre." The reality may have been worse than the label. It was common laborers against the National Guard and armed security forces employed by John D. Rockefeller, Jr.[9]

On April 20, 1914, the Colorado branch of the National Guard as well as armed guards in the employ of the Colorado Fuel and Iron Company and

Coal mine workers on strike at their tent colony in Ludlow, Colorado, 1914 (courtesy Houghton Library, Harvard University, 518250_03).

various soldiers of fortune opened fire on a tent village inhabiting miners and their families. Two dozen people were killed, including four women and 11 children asphyxiated and burned to death under one tent. The striking workers, who had been armed for months, fired back. The violence was a resumption of sporadic combat that had recently abated upon the arrival of the Colorado National Guard. The eruption on this day had been building; people in the tents had been evicted from their company-owned homes when the CF & I refused to meet their contract demands. During months of negotiations, the company garnered public support for its cause by accusing the United Mine Workers of America of inciting violence against replacement workers.

The company's claims were not without some merit. When striking miners clashed with replacement workers, several deaths had been reported. Newspapers were quick to point out that unions organized by socialists, including the IWW, were not shy about suggesting violence as a means to an end. The bombing of the *Los Angeles Times* editorial offices in 1910 had been just one of several acts of terrorism that scarred the labor movement and its connections to the Socialist Party; it was relatively easy for leaders in government and business to portray all socialists and their sympathizers as radical, deadly and ungodly. Meanwhile, the writings and speeches of

Five. Crossing Borders and Boundaries 83

respected Socialist intellectuals (Eastman, Steffens, Debs, Emma Goldman and many others) throughout the decade lent some theoretical legitimacy to the concept—if not the application—of social and economic revolution.

On the other side of the labor revolt was a level of worker exploitation that had been on full display in Colorado for anyone paying attention. Between 1884 and 1912, 1,700 Colorado residents died in mining accidents. Many miners worked in company towns, where all land and real estate was company-owned. Company housing included curfews for employees. The conditions reflected a national landscape where radicalized labor unions squared off against corporate abuse. Immigration and industrialization changed the face of the nation while courts, businesses, and governments at the local, state and federal levels signed off on restrictive and unconstitutional laws to deny basic human rights.

The Colorado Fuel and Iron Company employed more than 7,000 individuals and controlled nearly 72,000 acres of coal land in the early 1900s. John D. Rockefeller bought CF & I in 1902 and nine years later transferred controlling interest to his son, John D. Rockefeller, Jr., who ran the company from New York. The work had long been known as dangerous and deadly, but there was nothing the workers could do about it once they had signed on. The colliers, as coal miners were known, were entirely dependent upon company-owned stores where employees bought living necessities. Unionizing efforts began in the 1880s. Strikebreaking efforts included the hiring of replacement miners from Mexico and Europe.

The United Mine Workers of America called their strike in September of 1913 after the CF&I refused to meet the following demands: recognition of the union as a bargaining agent; compensation for digging coal at a ton-rate based on 2,000 pounds instead of 2,200 pounds; enforcement of an eight-hour work day; payment for laying track, timbering and handling impurities; weight-check men elected by workers to balance the calculations of company weight-check men; the right to use any stores, boarding houses or doctors not chosen or approved by the company; strict enforcement of Colorado's laws on mine safety rules; abolition of scrip or promissory notes in lieu of wages; and elimination of the company guard system.

The company's refusal to address the demands led to the eviction of 1,200 coal miners and their families from company housing, leading to the erection of a massive tent colony.

Reed merged what he saw in Ludlow with old-fashioned journalistic grunt research to write an acclaimed article for *Metropolitan* magazine that is still referenced by historians. In *More Powerful Than Dynamite: Radicals, Plutocrats, Progressives, and New York's Year of Anarchy*, author

Striking coal mine workers on the march in Ludlow, Colorado, 1914 (courtesy Houghton Library, Harvard University, 518259_01).

Thai Jones referenced Reed's account of what happened after militia reinforcements and a second machine gun and 7,000 rounds of ammunition arrived to help the National Guard and company security.

> "Go in and clean out the colony," their commander told them. "Drive everyone out and burn the colony." When these soldiers attacked, the defense cracked; "both machine guns," wrote John Reed, "pounded stab-stab-stab full on the tents." Inside, the bullets shattered mirrors and splintered furniture. By sunset resistance had been subdued, and the soldiers roamed unhindered, ransacking the settlement. The "men had passed out of their officer's control," investigators would later conclude, "had ceased to be an army, and had become a mob." They looted "whatever appealed to their fancy of the moment ... clothes, bedding, articles of jewelry, bicycles, tools and utensils," and then began to systematically burn the tents, dousing the canvas with oil before tossing on the matches.[10]

Reed's *Metropolitan* story in the summer of 1914 was important for several reasons. The magazine was widely read by New York City's intellectual elite, most of whom at least professed to care about social injustice. The *Metropolitan* had been home to several well-known writers who were either overtly radical or identified themselves as Socialists, but in 1914 the magazine was trying to appeal to readers and advertisers aligned with liberals and progressives. Reed was still a welcome and marketable presence for the *Metropolitan*, but he didn't notice or didn't care that many top journalists were tempering their words. The principal owner of the Colorado Fuel and Iron Company, Rockefeller, ran his feudal business from an office on Broadway in Manhattan—thus, the highest echelons of American political and economic power had easy access to Reed's reporting for a sophisticated New York readership.

Reed's story, using government documents and first hand accounts, included these excerpts:

> On the morning of the 17th of October (1913), a body of armed horsemen galloped down the Ludlow road and dismounted in a railroad cut near the colony. At the same time Felts' armored automobile appeared from the direction of Trinidad, swung around and trained its machine gun, immediately on the tents. Astonished and terrified, the strikers swarmed out, dragging their guns with them, but a guard named Kennedy, afterward an officer in the military, approached with a white flag, shouting:
>
> "It's all right, boys; we're union men." And as the strikers lowered their guns, he said:
>
> "What I wanted to say was that we are going to teach you red-necks a lesson!" and, lowering the white flag, he dropped on the ground. At the same time the dismounted horsemen fired a volley into the group, killing one man instantly. In a panic, the strikers poured back to the tents, across the field to a gulch where they had agreed to go in case of attack, and as they ran the machine gun opened up on them. It riddled the legs of a little boy who was running between the tents, and he fell there. The strikers immediately began to fire back, and the battle kept up from two o'clock in the afternoon until dark. Every time the wounded boy tried to drag himself in the direction of the tents, the machine gun was turned on him. He was shot not less than nine times. The tents were riddled, the furniture in them shot to pieces....
>
> Nine out of ten business and professional men in the coal district towns are violent strike sympathizers. After Ludlow, doctors, ministers, hack-drivers, drug-store clerks and farmers joined the fighting strikers with guns in their hands. Their women organized the Federal Labor Alliance, which is to spread all over the country, even among women whose husbands are not union men, to provide food and clothing and medical attendance for workers on strike. They are the kind of people who usually form law and order leagues in times like these; who consider themselves better than laborers, and think that their interest lie with the employers. Many Trinidad shopkeepers had been ruined by the strike....
>
> Lucia Bartellotti rocked slowly backward and forward, the tears running down her cheeks; they said she had been crying steadily for a week and could not sleep. She burst out monotonously, as one recites a piece:
>
> "I can't remember nothing. I am so terrible and the shooting all the time, and me try to get down in our cellar under the tent. And then Mis'Fyler comes and says: For God's sake, go down the well; they are going to kill all the women and children! When I come up again in the night, the tents burning and women and children burning alive, screaming, and I don't know what else. My husband is shot in the back when he is running away because he does not know the customs of this country; and why they should shoot as us, God knows."

Fifty more people were killed in the ten days following retaliatory attacks by miners against the coal mines. President Woodrow Wilson sent in national troops, which quelled the chaos; they disarmed both sides and arrested both strikers and militia. Rockefeller hired experts to help him craft meaningful reform for treatment of coal miners. A federal government task force investigation produced a report recommending many of the changes sought by the striking workers.

Reed had this to say about Rockefeller's response to the tragedy:

> I want to add one significant fact for the benefit of those who think that Mr. Rockefeller and the coal operators are innocent, though misguided. At the triumphant conclusion of the legislative session, it is said the Mrs. Welborn, wife of the president of the Colorado Fuel & Iron Company, told her friends of the "lovely telegram" her husband had received from John D. Rockefeller, Jr. It read, according to Mrs. Welborn: "Hearty congratulation on the winning of the strike. I sincerely approve of all your actions, and commend the splendid work of the legislature."[11]

The War of Traders

There was palpable anti-war sentiment in America for more than half of the decade between 1910 and 1920. It was crushed by the press and leaders of all three branches of the federal government. Americans watched events unfold in Europe and expected war to break out; a major war had not been fought on European soil for 30 years while secret alliances, an arms race, bitter rivalries and resentments simmering for decades created unbearable tension. Most Americans did not want their country involved, and their president won re-election while promising to keep America out of European conflicts, but the hindsight of history has made those sentiments and promises seem naive and hollow. Europeans had also displayed anti-war sentiments; their political leaders had the final say.

Carl Hovey, editor of the *Metropolitan*, sent Reed to Europe, despite his reporter's public denouncements of the adversaries' motives. It was a war of profits, Reed declared. It was a war of economic lust, not economic need. He was not the only one making these declarations, but those who did were increasingly cast by federal authorities and the press as, at the very least, unpatriotic, and, at worst, dangerous to America's notion of liberty. Still, Reed—at this point acknowledged as one of the best reporters in the country—secured another high-profile assignment on the world stage. It did not turn out well for anyone.

A disconnect between Reed's idealism and the brutal reality of human history crashed upon him. His righteousness bubbled over the surface again

Five. Crossing Borders and Boundaries

as the attitudes of Europeans—indifference, fatalism, bigotry—stabbed him continuously, reminding him of what he could not change, and what, possibly, nobody could change. At this point in his life, he had not envisioned an end game for his own country or for any society in the grips of class conflict. What unfolded in front of Reed in Europe was, as he saw it, the eventual destruction of civilizations that possess the best of the human spirit.[12]

War broke out in August of 1914. The *Metropolitan* wasted no time assigning Reed to cover the conflict. Even though the magazine had been trying to distance itself from the far left, Reed was too marketable to keep home. "When there is war, Jack Reed is the man to write about it," the magazine had declared upon sending him to Ludlow a few months earlier. He reported from England, France, Switzerland, Italy, Germany and Belgium, witnessing combat while accompanying three armies. Reed was in Europe for five months before the French government kicked him out of their country. He returned a month later and spent seven months covering the war on the Eastern Front, which led to his book *The War in Eastern Europe*.

At this point in his career, Reed's aggressiveness and convictions often made him as much of a story as the events and people he wrote about. He became something beyond star journalist. To some, he was out of control. To others, he was self-serving. Reed's take was that acquiescence to wartime hysteria—along with the desensitization to killing through high-tech weaponry and propaganda—destroyed beautiful cultures, leaving him no choice other than to smash journalistic protocol whenever he could. He was not going to write what people told him to write or wait for the story that authorities promised would arrive. He was following the trail blazed by his father, C.J. Reed, "the great fighter ... with a fine scorn for stupidity." And he was following an old lesson from Steffens, who had told him that the best stories come from the hearts of capable reporters, not from the minds of editors—but who was now telling him to bide his time until the political climate had changed.[13]

He crossed the French-German border on the Western Front for several reasons, none of which earned him the respect of authorities or many of his peers and friends back home. He wanted to get away from Mabel Dodge, who had followed him to Paris as part of their volatile and almost schizophrenic love affair. This, of course, was not long after she had followed him from New York to Chicago to El Paso before he covered the Mexican war. He also need to escape a furious husband (not Mabel's) whose wife had slept with Reed in France; the husband armed himself and announced to anyone who would listen that he was going to kill Reed. Mabel found out about the affair when she heard of the threat. Her response was to take an overdose of morphine, as she had done in New York when Reed tried to break up with her. Reed appeared amused by all of this and told his friends as much, although he was careful to add that when his German-American mistress became ill, he nursed her back to health—and he made sure Mabel didn't kill herself. "He is the only fellow I know who gets himself pursued by men with revolvers, who is always once more just about to ruin himself," wrote Walter Lippmann.[14] As he worked his way to the German side of the front, he told a friend that German authorities gave more access to foreign correspondents than other governments did, as long as the reporters didn't blame Germany when they got shot.[15]

Reed did not get shot by bullets, but his reputation took a serious hit. He told fellow traveler and New York journalist Robert Dunn that he feared commitment to a relationship more than anything else.[16] His actions gave credence to his words. He had put himself in physical danger in Paterson and in Mexico, and he had put himself in political danger by aligning himself with radicals in New York. Now he was covering a war as an American journalist while the world knew he did not support the Allied side. He didn't support the Central Powers, either, but that mattered little to the propagandists and nationalists rapidly gaining control of the American press.[17]

One of innumerable absurdities that sprinkle the landscape of Reed's life occurred after he and Dunn made their way across the German border, frustrated with military and political restrictions imposed on their efforts at independent reporting in wartime. They talked their way into the trenches with German soldiers and officers. On their way to the Western Front separating France from Germany, they purchased two bottles of champagne to calm their nerves. With mortar shells flying over their heads, giving them the action that they claimed to have craved, Dunn and Reed settled their nerves with generous gulps from the bottles. A German officer noticed and suggested that Reed and Dunn grab a rifle and fire a shot in the general direction of the Allied side. And so they did, although Dunn claimed the bullets traveled more toward the sky than toward the German adversaries, the Allied soldiers.[18]

Although discretion was not a word often associated with Jack Reed, he did not turn the trench episode into another fantastic story for the entertainment of friends and peers. Nor did he use the story to perpetuate his own legend, as he had done with the murder charge involving Waldo Peirce back in 1910 (he had tried to sell that story, failed, and eventually received some monetary compensation after selling the story rights to Julian Street).[19] The man who could not wait to tell the tale was Dunn, who cabled his editors in New York, whereupon the episode went about as viral as a story could in 1915. As the news spread, the reaction fast and furious. The French government, Princeton University president John Hibben, esteemed journalist Richard Harding Davis, pro–Allied newspapers ... all condemned Reed and Dunn for committing a potentially lethal pro–German prank. As usual, "Big Stick" Teddy Roosevelt—former president, now contributing editor for thr *Metropolitan*—delivered the loudest smack, telling Dunn he would have Reed "shot on sight" for hanging out in German trenches in the first place.[20]

Nonetheless, in one of those paradoxes that color nearly every aspect of Reed's life, Roosevelt eventually wrote a letter to the French embassy in Washington in support of Reed's efforts to gain re-entry into France after he was called back home by his editors. *Metropolitan* editors were angry and embarrassed, but they wanted Reed back where they felt he belonged—writing about war, because it was generally believed in the publishing field that Reed had few peers as a war correspondent. Nearly a century later, historian Daniel W. Leham wrote, "By the age of twenty-six, Reed was filing battlefield reports from the 1913 Mexican Revolution for New York's Metropolitan Magazine and was the brightest star in that magazine's constellation of writers, a fiery group that included Joseph Conrad, Susan Glaspell, D.H. Lawrence, Rudyard Kipling, and George Bernard Shaw."[21]

When the *Metropolitan* asked Roosevelt to grease the wheels for Reed's return to France, the former president obliged out of loyalty to the late C.J. Reed, the man who paid such a steep personal price for doing TDR's dirty work investigating the Oregon land scandal. "The letter of introduction, dictated by Roosevelt in Reed's presence, was a curious document," wrote Julian Street in "Soviet Saint," an article published in the *Saturday Evening Post* a decade after Reed's death. "It stated that Jack was sorry he had fired toward the French, that he wished to go to France, and that if permitted to do so, his writings would doubtless benefit the French cause. But that was not all. At the end came a sentence somewhat as follows: 'Nevertheless, I am bound to say that if I were Marshal Joffre and Reed fell into my hands I should have him court-martialed and shot.'" Reed brought to the letter to Washington and discussed the matter with the French ambassador, who told him thanks but no thanks, it's probably a bad idea for you to step foot on French soil.[22]

Incredibly, the *Metropolitan* sent Reed back to war, this time in the

Balkans. Although *The War in Eastern Europe* did not generate the kind of awe from peers that *Insurgent Mexico* or *Ten Days That Shook the World* did, it was and remains highly respected war reporting. Ironically, Reed's own words about America's role in the war, "This is not our war," applied, with a twist, to himself and his journalistic style. This was not Jack Reed's war. It took a stretch of his imagination and a leap of faith to identify the good guys or beloved underdogs. But his writing and reporting still sparkled at times.

The Reed legend had kept growing, for better and for worse, during the "time out" his editors imposed upon him in New York, sandwiched between his European assignments. Lippmann, a premature curmudgeon whose temperament may have been the polar opposite of Reed's aggressiveness and buoyancy, took a huge swing, in print, at his old Harvard Socialist Club peer in an apparent attempt to set the world straight about this gifted writer and dashing young adventurer possessed with a flair for self promotion and irrepressible impishness. The article in the *New Republic* was titled "The Legendary Jack Reed."

> By temperament he is not a professional writer or reporter. He is a person who enjoys himself. Revolution, literature, poetry, they are only things which hold him at times, incidents merely of his living. Now and then he finds adventure by imagining it, oftener he transforms his own experience. He is one of those people who treat as serious possibilities such stock fantasies as shipping before the mast, rescuing women, hunting lions, or trying to fly around the world in an aeroplane. Reed is one of those intractables to whom the organized monotone and virtue of our civilization is unbearable. You would have to destroy him to make him fit. At times when he seemed to be rushing himself and others into trouble, when his ideas were especially befuddled, I have tried to argue with him. But all laborious elucidation he greets with pained boredom.... I don't know what to do about him. In common with a whole regiment of his friends, I have been brooding over his soul for years, and often I feel like saying to him what one of them said when Reed was explaining Utopia. "If I were establishing it, I'd hang you first, my dear Jack." But it would be a lonely Utopia.[23]

The wild winds of Storm Boy showed no signs of calming when Boardman Robinson decided to accompany Reed to the Balkans. Robinson, an illustrator for the *New York Tribune*, was a robust, loud, hard-drinking Englishman. A match made in heaven or hell, depending on how seriously one took John Reed. The question of whether Reed could effectively report the war, given the public thrashings he took for his embarrassing moment on the Western Front or his open disdain for the Allies' economic motives, competed with another question regarding his return to Europe. Why would anyone in their right mind willingly venture into a region ravaged by typhus and cholera?

The Balkans had been decimated by three wars in three years. Serbia was occupied by Austrian troops. Typhus was everywhere. Armies and nations crumbled while tens of thousands of men died from bullets, bombs, gas and the trauma of what they saw and heard. In the Shabats region Reed and Robinson were shown a photograph of a hundred women and children who were chained together and decapitated.[24]

When they made their way from Italy to Salonika to Serbia, they were well aware that typhus had wiped out one-sixth of the Serbian population while cholera was knocking on the door. The astonishing beauty of the mountains at Vardar stabbed at the heart while the images and words of a slaughtered culture resonated. "We Serbians have no longer any uniforms," a Serbian trooper told Reed. "We have fought four wars in three years—the First and Second Balkan Wars, the Albanian revolt, and now this one. For three years our soldiers have not changed their clothes."[25]

The crossing of geographical and military borders—as well as boundaries of common sense and self preservation—continued as the two journalists pressed forward to the Russian front. It was May 1915, and Russian Allied forces had just finished another retreat, this one 200 miles, after the Central Powers inflicted more carnage than any nation should be able to survive. "It is like that," a Russian officer told Reed. "Advance, retreat. Advance, retreat." How long can this war last? Reed asked. How long can Russia withstand this beating? "What do we care," the officer said, with a disturbing smile, "so long as England gives money and the earth gives men?"[26]

Reed had a lifelong habit of falling in love with cultures he had not fully examined (the same could be said for his romantic flings), and this could have been the moment a passion for all things Russian entered his bloodstream. On his way to the front he noticed the Moldavian hills, brown and gold, and the landscape of Bucovina, "white winding roads, dazzling villas set in green, and occasional shining town—order and prosperity," whereupon his senses again felt the stab of poverty and the cruel contrasts of different worlds side by side with an invisible but impenetrable barrier. Across the landscape he saw "the wet tin roofs of a clump of wooden shacks, thatched huts the color of dirt, a wandering muddy track that served as a road."

With the help of second- and third-rank military officers and local police, Robinson and Reed continued their journalistic journey through a world that most Americans and Europeans were blissfully unaware of: Tarnopol, Lemberg, across Poland, long train rides, desolation, despair, beauty and hope. "One had the impression of vast forces hurled carelessly here and there, of indifference on a grand scale, of gigantic waste." Images of the cold, efficient German army returned as he looked at the ravages of war on the other side. The Allies were sending money, but money was not going to help Russia. Russians knew it. Reed knew it. The Allies knew it.[27]

The impressions of people and cultures and the invincibility of the human spirit during war is what the author of *The War in Eastern Europe* promised his readers in the book's introduction—not battles or strategy or troop advancements and retreats. Reed made good on his promise, although it would be easy to misunderstand passages if taken out of the early 20th-century context.

On the Jewish race: "For a thousand years the Russians and their church have done their best to exterminate the Jews and their religion. With what success? Here in Rovnov, were thousands of Jews shut in an impregnable world of their own, scrupulously observing a religion incessantly purified, practising their own customs, speaking their own language, with two codes of morals—one for each other and the other for the Gentile. Persecution has only engendered a poison and a running sore in the body of the Russian people. It was true that Miroshnikov said, as we drank kvass in a little Jewish bar—that all Jews were traitors to Russia. Of course they are."[28]

He did not blame the Russian people for their tragic history or current plight. "Russians are not patriotic.... The Tsar to them is not the head of government; he is a [deity]. The government itself ... the bureaucracy—commands no loyalty from the masses.... As a rule, they do not know what their flag looks like, and if they do it is not the symbol of Russia."

Reed quoted a middle-aged civilian saying, "We Russians do not know how great we are. We cannot grasp the idea of so many millions of people to communicate with. We do not realize how much land, how much riches we have.... And no Russian realizes how many races are embraced in this nation; I myself know of only thirty-nine."

He continued,

> Yet this vast chaotic agglomeration of barbarian races, brutalized and tyrannized over for centuries, with only the barest means of intercommunication, without consciousness of any one ideal, has developed a profound national unity of feeling and thought and an original civilization that spreads by its own people....
>
> Russian ideas are the most exhilarating. Russian thought the freest, Russian art the most exuberant.... Russians are, perhaps, the most interesting human beings that exist.... In America, we are the possessors of a great empire—but we live as if this were a crowded island like England.... Our streets are narrow and our cities congested.... Russia is also a great empire; but these people live as if they knew it was one.[29]

* * *

World War I affected Reed deeply. In Rome, on September 18, 1914, as he began the reporting for *The War in Eastern Europe*, he brooded at his typewriter, sorting out his impressions, trying to overcome his repulsion as the continent lurched toward war on a scale never seen before. He mused over soldiers marching through the streets, the quietness racked by mounting war preparation. The Italian government had imposed strict price controls, and everybody was out of work. Italy's working class, which had voiced its objection to proposals that the country come to the aid of its allies, found itself with no better option for earning a living than the Tripoli Volunteer Force, which offered wages and benefits otherwise unattainable in the Italian economy. Rumors had serious currency. "Priests and monks had visions of the end of the World, and of the Beast of the Apocalypse ... in the form of the German Emperor to lay waste the earth," he wrote. "The German Secret Service was credited with miraculous omniscience—spies were everywhere,"

> but perhaps as marvelous a thing as any, was the thought of the millions of men involved,—the hurling of mighty populations upon the frontiers of nations, the subjugation of the strong life of the world,—the intellect, the dreams, the love of the entire earth, almost, in the desire to kill, and disposed of by the commands of two or three specialists whose vocation was killing. All art, literature, production, amusement, family life, politics of western civilization checked and forgotten. It was tremendous.... In Russia, the remnants of those who who had been murdered by the Cossacks in 1905, the martyred living dead in Siberia, the sons and brothers of massacred Jews in the Pale, were all caught up in a mighty enthusiasm for the cause of the White Czar who persecuted them.[30]

He visited Geneva, which he called "the gayest place on earth, apparently." He described crowds in the streets, women in extravagant costumes, cafés filled with Berliners, Parisians, Londoners, talking about women, clothes and wines, boulevard strollers with flowers in their coat buttons, holding canes casually over their shoulders, dowagers with pearls and lorgenettes, leaning back inside fashionable automobiles ... it was all for show, according to Reed. The European cosmopolitans showing no outward signs of nationalism were running scared, as far as he was concerned.

> And then everybody would scrape his pockets for a few coppers to pay the bill,—for no one had any money. At the hotels, one lived upon credit. The chauffeurs of the splendid automobiles had gone to war,—so small boys drove them, also upon credit. At night, many automobiles stood in the street, because the owners couldn't afford garage-charges. It was rather pathetic, the bluff of it all. The elegant ladies in extravagant gowns had holes in their stockings; the dowagers could not afford manicures; the boulevardiers wore dirty collars and went unshaven; and the bizarre dogs had not been recently clipped. Everything was just the least bit off-color. And this, too, seemed like the end of a phase of our civilization.[31]

The *Metropolitan* refused to publish the story he produced from these notes, his first impressions of the Great War as an eyewitness. The draft sits in his personal collection of papers at Harvard University. Eventually he would have better luck getting his words and views on war into print, but he had stamped himself, emphatically, as a man out of step with the times, crossing a serious boundary by criticizing the Allies not only for their politics but also for abandonment of national character while swept up in war fever.

* * *

Back on the home front, Reed damaged relationships with Charles Copeland, Lincoln Steffens and his mother with his anti-war crusade. He burned bridges by reporting what he saw, what he heard, and what he knew about economics and history: that Europe and the United States were selling war under false pretense. Western leaders were rationalizing, not justifying, the sacrifice of blood, limbs and lives belonging to young men for the sake of corporate profits, according to Reed and American socialists labeled as radicals. Nobody in a position of economic or political power, and nobody who wanted to maintain whatever social status they had achieved in life, wanted to be linked publicly with such ideas, which were deemed illegal under the Alien and Sedition Act.

At this point, Max Eastman and the socialist *Masses* magazine still had room for Reed's writing. For it Reed wrote:

> Consider the French army, rent with politics, badly clothed, badly provisioned, and with an inadequate ambulance service; opposed always to militarism, and long since [subjected to] fighting. The French army has not been fighting well. But it has been fighting, and the slaughter is appalling. There remains no effective reserve in France; and the available youth of the nation down to seventeen years of age is under arms. For my part, all other considerations aside, I should not care to live half-frozen in a trench, up to my middle in water, for three or four months, because someone in authority said I ought to shoot Germans. But if I were a Frenchman, I should do it, because I would have been accustomed to the idea by my compulsory military service.
>
> The Russian army, inexhaustible hordes of simple peasants torn from their farms, blessed by a priest, and knouted into battle for a cause they never heard of, appeals to me even less....
>
> And crossing over to the Austrian side, I call to mind that hideous persistent story about the first days of the war, when Austria sent her unequipped regiments against the Russians. Only the first ranks had rifles and ammunitions; the ranks behind were instructed to pick up the guns when the first ranks were killed, and so on....
>
> But I could fill pages with the super–Mexican horrors that civilized Europe is inflicting upon itself. I could describe to you the quiet, dark, saddened streets of Paris, where every ten feet you are confronted with some miserable wreck of a human being,

or a madman who lost his reason in the trenches, being led around by his wife. I could tell you of the big hospital in Berlin full of German soldiers who went crazy from merely hearing the cries of the thirty thousand Russians drowning in the swamps of East Prussia after the battle of Tannenburg....

But that is not the purposed in this brief article. I want to try and indicate the effect of military obedience and discipline upon human beings. Disease, death, wounds on the battlefield, Philosophical anarchism, and International Socialism, seem to be futile as incentives to Peace. Why? As for the bloody side of war, that shocks people less than they think; we're so accustomed to half a million a year maimed and killed in mines and factories. As for Socialism, Anarchism, and democratic or individualist faith—I don't speak of Christianity, which is completely bankrupt—the Socialist, Anarchists, et al, *were all trained soldiers!*[32]

* * *

Reed had made up his mind very quickly that he would not be able to report the European War with the flair, color and details of *Insurgent Mexico*; he even offered an explanation in the opening pages of *The War in Eastern Europe*, telling his readers that circumstances demanded he write more about what the war does to the social and cultural fabrics of civilizations. The book, generally considered in third place among Reed's biggest journalistic efforts (behind *Ten Days That Shook the World* and *Insurgent Mexico*),[33] nonetheless demanded admiration from writers and editors around the globe. His entire World War I experience captured a wide range of Jack Reed's persona, from intrepid reporter to zealous critic, from playful globetrotter lacking in judgment to a young man burning with naked conviction.

* * *

He had returned to Europe in February 1915 after three months on the *Metropolitan's* bench. During those three months in New York, Reed wrote a conventional profile of evangelist Billy Sunday, focusing his critical eye on the reverend's moneyed backers trying to establish a codified system of morals in the United States. Sunday himself received respectful treatment in Reed's article. The journalistic approach had similarities to Reed's profile of Henry Ford, in which the socialist writer focused on the threat that the uber-capitalist posed for other American capitalists who considered his innovations radical. Ford was empowering his workers with a livable wage, benefits and a reasonable workday, Reed argued. This was not the formula that built the United States into an industrial superpower. Ford, therefore, was a dangerous man. The article was headlined "Why They Hate Ford."

Upon returning to war reporting, Reed cranked up his aggressiveness, in vain, for finding the explosive story while his comportment in front of disapproving authorities—even those who could end his life—became more outlandish. He seemed to have made up his mind about something, in a manner not unlike the resolve he established in the summer and fall of 1912. This was less than three years after his father's death, but both Reed and his country had crossed many thresholds in that short period. Conflicts that turned into tragic crises over immigration; the widening gap between urban wealth and poverty; organized violence to keep organized labor in check; the evaporation of muckraking journalism; domestic terrorism targeting corporate power, and anti-war sentiment that turned on a dime in to fervent nationalism—all of it put Reed on a collision course with the United States government.

* * *

He crossed the lines between the reporter and his subject; between advocacy journalism and crusade; between criticizing government and declaring it unworthy of American ideals; between scolding capitalists and declaring them undemocratic; between talking socialism and promoting it with the voice of a poet and the rage of a man who knew how to get people's attention. In the spirit of humorist Finley Peter Dunne's definition of good American journalism, Reed tried to comfort the afflicted and afflict the comfortable. He also declared, aloud and in print, that the afflicted had more value to this country, and more "American" character, than the comfortable. The targets of his scorn were the the leaders of institutions who considered themselves the embodiment of Americanism. By doing this, he implicated his own people, the writers and editors and artists who needed big-money capitalists to back their magazines and publishing houses. Reed wasn't the only journalist who did this in the first half of the decade between 1910 and 1920, but as his country marched to war while identifying enemies at home, Reed became more professionally isolated. It is difficult to say what made him more dangerous to authorities and himself—his political views, his understanding of power, the personalization of social conflict, his talent, his charisma or the fact that he acted like he had nothing to lose.

Was the socialist (and, eventually, communist) crusade actually calculated martyrdom? Perhaps he did not want to live in a world that crushed the poor and the working class. Perhaps he became unhinged from holding onto a grudge against the Portland elite's treatment of his father. Perhaps he saw the pursuit of wealth creating a fog that diminished the beauty of life or the inheritance of wealth (as in his family) as a cruel illusion.

Reed, according to some historians (Zinn, O'Connor and others), had made rebellion look cool. He looked like he was having fun. Friends and foes and followers did not know what to make of him. His laughter was memorable, but by 1917, he sounded different. Julian Street, according to Richard O'Connor, "believed that Jack had become much less the laughing cavalier of the revolution-to-be and was beginning to assume some of the humorless and dogmatic qualities of the doctrinaire Marxist."[34]

CHAPTER SIX

The Retreat of American Journalism

John Reed created distance between himself and his editors with his criticism of the Great War. He created distance between himself and other journalists with his open contempt for monied backers of the publications they needed to remain relevant in print. The disconnect had been developing for years. Reed was a young, aggressive reporter at a time when aggressive reporting was falling out of favor with the public. He was still getting paid well in the years just prior to U.S. engagement in the world war, and his star was still rising, but he had been warned about taking his politics too far. The muckrakers who dominated journalism for 20 years prior to Reed's first New York byline began to pull their punches and retreat to neutral corners.

"Although Reed and his magazine [the *Metropolitan*] were first able to suppress their internal contradictions and differences, the outbreak of World War I tore the lid off that alliance," wrote Daniel Lehman. "Reed broke both with his nation and with mainstream U.S. socialists, refusing to support either military preparedness or U.S. involvement in World War I." The magazine, in a blunt display of acquiescence to emerging nationalism, ran cartoons of a sleeping America while German soldiers dug trenches in the sand traps of Long Island golf courses.[1]

U.S. president Theodore Roosevelt, in a speech to the U.S. House of Representatives in 1906, said: "In [John] Bunyan's Pilgrim's Progress you may recall the description of the Man with the Muck-rake, the man who could look no way but downward with the muck-rake in his hands; who would neither look up nor regard the crown he was offered, but continued to rake to himself the filth on the floor. I hail as a benefactor every writer or speaker, every man who, on the platform, or in a book, magazine or newspaper, with merciless severity makes such an attack, provided always that he in turn remembers that the attack is of use only if it absolutely truthful."[2]

Roosevelt chose his words in response to a series of *Cosmopolitan* magazine articles that criticized his political allies under the headline "Treason in Senate." By lashing out against his former allies in the press, Roosevelt blurred some lines for historians. The rise of investigative journalism overlapped Progressivism, when popular demand for changes in American life emerged in response to the power of corporations and the unforeseen negative impact of industrialization. Roosevelt befriended journalists, knowing that he owed much of his political capital and legacy to their work that was followed by government reform, including the Pure Food and Drugs Act and the Federal Meat Inspection Act of 1906. Roosevelt pushed for these laws after publication of *The Jungle*, Upton Sinclair's exposé of the meat-packing industry, published in 1904.

Although many prominent journalists decried Roosevelt's pushback, he actually qualified his criticism by suggesting he salutes the muckraker, "provided always that he in turn remembers that the attack is of use only if it is absolutely truthful." (The irony is that *The Jungle*, although filled with undeniable truth, is a work of fiction.) Lincoln Steffens told Roosevelt, "Well, you have put an end to all these journalistic investigations that have made you." In 1932, David Graham Phillips, also known as a muckraker of that era, said, "The greatest single definitive force against muckraking was President Roosevelt, who called these writers muckrakers. A tag like that running through the paper was an easy phrase of repeated attack upon what was in general a good journalistic movement. Looking back, it seems to me clear that the muckraking magazine was the greatest single power that ever appeared in this country. The mere mention in one of these magazines of something that was wrong was usually sufficient to bring about at least an ostensible reformation."[3]

Investigative journalism, as understood today, is rooted in late 19th-century calls for reform in government and big business. C.J. Reed and his eldest son hitched their wagons to Steffens, one of the most famous investigative reporters in the history of American journalism. C.J. Reed was a friend of Steffens as they worked together to expose the Oregon land scandal. Jack Reed saw Steffens as a journalistic giant and a father figure in the aftermath of C.J. Reed's death. Throughout his tumultuous career in journalism and political activism, Jack sought Steffens' advice, even when they clashed over how to survive in a censored, nationalistic environment. When Reed called Steffens a muckraker in his biographical essay "Almost Thirty," he did so with admiration. Steffens may not have been fond of the label, but he would not have a chance to discuss it with Reed, as the document did not become available to the public until a decade after Reed's death.

The muckraking era lit one of many fires that burned inside of John Reed the writer and Jack Reed the man. The demise of investigative journalism in the mainstream press set him up as a target of scorn when the public's journalistic appetite shifted toward lifestyle features and jingoistic political news. Although Reed is not remembered as a muckraker, his marketability and star power as a respected, well-compensated, and reform-seeking journalist was on the rise 1913–1915—the immediate aftermath of muckraking's death. Those years represent a demarcation point for the history of investigative journalism, which came to a halt for a variety of reasons (among them emerging nationalism, the European War, fear of political extremists, government crackdowns on dissent, and the limits of public demand for changes to American institutions).

In the 1880s, the decade of John Reed's birth, Henry Demarest Lloyd of the *Chicago Tribune* investigated corruption in business and politics with articles in the *Atlantic Monthly* and *North American Review*. Among his articles were "The Story of a Great Monopoly" in 1881, "The Political Economy of Seventy-Three Million Dollars" in 1882, "Making Bread Dear" in 1883 and "The Lords of Industry" in 1884.

During the same decade, Ida B. Wells, an African-American journalist and activist, wrote about racism, lynchings and women's rights. When she wrote a series of articles on civil rights and criticized the Memphis board of education for under-funding Memphis schools, she lost her job as a school teacher. She started her own Memphis newspaper, *Free Speech*, but a white mob destroyed her printing press after she published articles condemning the lynchings of three African-American businessmen. Knowing that she had been targeted for hanging as well, Wells moved to New York and wrote about lynchings and Jim Crow laws for *New York Age*.

The combined circulation of ten magazines that concentrated on investigative journalism was three million readers in 1906, according to historian John Simkin. Harold Evans, author of *The American Century: People, Power and Politics*, wrote, "Crooks in City Hall. Opium in children's cough syrup. Rats in the meatpacking industry. Cruelty to child workers.... Scandal after scandal in the early 1900s as a new breed of writers investigated the evils of laissez-faire America.... The muckrakers were the heart of Progressivism, that shifting coalition of sentiment striving to make the American dream come true in the machine age. Their articles, with facts borne out by subsequent commissions, were read passionately in new national mass-circulation magazines by millions of the fast-growing aspiring white-collar middle class."[4]

Evidence of reform-minded journalism gained momentum in the last two decades of the 19th century before turning into a tidal wave in the early years of the 20th century. In January of 1903 *McClure's Magazine* had three powerful works of investigative reporting in a single issue; they were written by Lincoln Steffens, Ray Stannard Bake and Ida M. Tarbell. Charles Edward Russell put the spotlight on the need for monopolies in "The Greatest Trust in the World" (1905) before setting his sights on the spread of democracy worldwide in "The Uprising of the Many" in 1907. Perhaps Steffens' most famous book, *The Shame of the Cities* (1907), exposed corruption in city and state politics nationwide. Brand Whitlock made capital punishment a journalistic target in "The Turn of the Balance." Thomas W. Larson, a Boston finance executive, tried his hand at journalism with success; his article published in *Everybody's* magazine, headlined "Frenzied Finance," exposed stock market abuses and insurance fraud. Tarbell's book *The History of Standard Oil Company* details the reckless and abusive process of eliminating market competition by building a monopoly in a free-market capitalist society.

In *The Era of the Muckrakers*, published in 1933, author C.C. Regier listed reforms between 1900 and 1915 that were made possible by the investigative journalists who became known as muckrakers: prison reform, sanitation and health standards in food manufacturing, child labor laws, federal employers' liability legislation, land preservation and conservation, eight-hour work days for women, race-track gambling regulations, women's pension laws, worker compensation laws, an income tax amendment to the U.S. Constitution, the break-up of Standard Oil and Tobacco companies, Niagara Falls and the state of Alaska protected from industrial development, and insurance laws.[5]

The journalistic party was winding down at about the time John Reed's career gained traction. Some, such as Steffens and David Graham Phillips, blamed Roosevelt for using his "bully pulpit" to turn public opinion against the press. Ray Stannard Baker said, "Latterly I believe Roosevelt did a disservice to the country in seizing upon a movement that ought to have been built up slowly and solidly from the bottom with much solid thought and experimentation, and hitching it to the cart of his own political ambitions. He thus short-circuited a fine and vigorous current of public opinion into a futile partisan movement." A century later, however, graduate students in Professor Rick Musser's journalism history class at the University of Kansas had a different take: "During the 1910s, Americans' interest in muckraking journalism waned and publishers shifted focus as their audience's tastes changed," they wrote. "Magazines like *Vanity Fair*, *The Smart Set* and *Vogue* focused on the lifestyles of the rich, while the squalid lives of the underclass became the staple of tabloid newspapers and confessional magazines."[6]

Roosevelt followed his House speech with another premeditated attack on muckrakers at the Gridiron Club, a roundtable forum comprised of journalists, government officials and business owners gathered to talk public policy. Known for his political dexterity, Roosevelt carefully sprinkled his speech with praise for quality journalism. Yet again he was criticized for doing considerable damage to the efforts of respected reporters, editors and publishers who were attempting to curb the abuses of public trust in American institutions. Roosevelt, however, had the public on his side for two reasons: the proliferation of copycat investigative journalism that was not high quality, and thus came closer to the lowest interpretation of Bunyan's muckraker, and public fatigue with years of news coverage that put our forms of self-government and successful free enterprise in a negative light.

"His exasperation with the proliferation of increasingly sensational and shoddily investigated exposure journalism had been slowly building," wrote Doris Kearns Goodwin in *The Bully Pulpit: Theodore Roosevelt, William Howard Taft and the Golden Age of Journalism*. "The carefully documented quest for truth had been supplanted by slapdash, often slanderous accusations."[7]

"I get sick of people who are always insisting upon nothing but the dark side of life," Roosevelt told humorist Peter Dunne.[8] An accompanying and more eloquent sentiment came from literary critic Edwin E. Sosson: "The public cannot stand at attention with its eyes fixed on one spot indefinitely," he wrote. "It is bound to get restive, and seek diversion in other interests."[9]

C.C. Reiger, author of *The Era of Muckrakers*, quoted a letter he received from John S. Phillips that stated, in part, "This phase of journalism died down because of the unwarranted and exaggerated imitations done without study and containing much that was untrue. The result of these things was a revulsion and a loss of public interest."[10]

The backlash against the crusading journalists was abrupt, and in

Six. The Retreat of American Journalism

some respects just as scathing as the muckrakers' words condemning public corruption. One of the first targets of scorn was *McClure's Magazine*, which had set an almost impossibly high bar for quality investigative journalism. *Life* magazine published a searing satire on *McClure's* most prominent writers—Tarbell (depicted as Ida Tarbarrell), Ray Stannard Baker (Ray Standard Fakir), and Lincoln Steffens (Sinkem Beffens). Steffens was practically set on fire, journalistically speaking, with this quotation fabricated for the sake of satire: "I'm not really great. I'm only eminent, unparalleled, superlatively remarkable." The article laid out Sinkem Beffens' reporting process: "With only his suit-case and his gold rake stuffed with diamonds, he can take the morning train for an unknown city, rake off in a few hours the thick slime of municipal corruption and have a shame-shrieking article ready for *McClure's* by night."[11]

Also contributing to the demise of *McClure's* as a standard-bearer for exposure journalism was chaos within the company as it reached the peak of its power. Owner Sam McClure tried to expand his company into a media giant with multiple magazines while also seeking investors into other business enterprises. He lost the trust of his star reporters with his grandiose schemes and obsession with his own success. He openly compared his "facilities for getting to know public opinion and the opinion of able thinkers" to Abraham Lincoln's.[12] Investigative reporter Ellery Sedgwick, the future editor of *Atlantic Monthly*, said, "A week in the McClure office was the precise reversal of the six busy days described in the first chapter of Genesis. It seemed to end in a world without form and void. From Order came forth Chaos."[13] At the peak of the magazine's power, Sam McClure lost his writers' respect by engaging in a scandalous international love affair while holding up *McClure's* as a beacon of public morality in its fight against corruption. There was no shortage of federal, state and local government leaders and employees who were more than happy to see the power of *McClure's* dissipate. The same could be said for the untold number of American citizens who suffered from scandal fatigue. They were ready to give the benefit of doubt when the motives of big business were questioned.

Although historians have alluded to the impressive list of reforms that muckrakers can take credit for without argument, C.C Reiger added a caveat to his 1933 study of muckrakers: "On the other hand, in 1911, when muckraking ceased, many important reforms, some of which were adopted in the first Wilson administration, were still unrealized, and furthermore, it was already apparent that many of the old evils were appearing in new guises. Monopolies had been abolished in theory, but it still existed in fact. Despite the amendment providing for direct election, senators were frequently chosen by the same old bosses. The direct primary, for which so much had been hoped, was proving a disappointment in many states. Business might be less open in its defiance of law, but there were many subtle ways of evading legislation that clamored for exposure."[14]

Into the void stepped John Reed. He was not an investigative reporter in the muckraking sense, but he did make a lot of noise while occupying space between the public and government with his words and actions. With the exceptions of his reporting from Ludlow, Colorado, during the coal miner strike as well as *Ten Days That Shook the World*, Reed did not demonstrate a large appetite for the document-hunting or painstaking devotion to corroboration and fact-checking that was and remains the hallmark of respected investigative journalism. He was a storyteller, his eyes and ears his primary tools, a man who could get people talking so that he cold retell their stories. He thought of himself as an artist, a writer who could create a portrait of truth from his observations. He called himself a poet, although he knew himself well enough to acknowledge that his attraction to politics probably meant that he wasn't meant to be a poet.[15]

The bridge between the muckraking era and John Reed has three sections: (1) Roosevelt's warning that a continuation of journalistic attacks on successful capitalists and our government institutions would invite socialists and radicals into our serious public discourse (Reed, in fact, went there); (2) Reed's first high-profile platform as a salaried reporter at *American Magazine*, a publication founded by the acclaimed muckrakers who had made *McClure's* magazine a journalistic legend; and (3) the swagger that Lincoln Steffens passed on to Reed. Steffens presented himself as man revealing character through his exposés. He possessed an ego that was on full display during his unpleasant departure from *American Magazine*. Following a series of Lincoln's complaints about editing and the placement of his stories, publisher Phillips told Steffens, "It seems to me you have had more out of this magazine than anybody else in proportion of what you have put in." The magazine, in fact, had been covering Steffens' travel expenses, which included bills for his wife and mother-in-law. "My husband has become famous, but at a high price," said Steffens' wife, Josephine. Steffens himself said, six months before the partners bought out his share of the company, "Either I am to write as I please without being edited; or I quit."[16]

John Reed, a disciple of Steffens, demonstrated a fair amount of bombast and arrogance himself as his journalistic reputation soared. The backlash against his reporting, politics and ego didn't stop him. Nor did it help him.

Chapter Seven

The Classic and the End Game

A year and a half before he wrote *Ten Days That Shook the World,* John Reed himself was shaken by doubt and a developing sense of his own limitations. In the spring of 1917 he wrote an essay that few people have read during the past century and which almost nobody read before he died. "Almost Thirty" sits in a manilla folder at Harvard University's Houghton Library, used by every Reed biographer to cobble together a coherent narrative and to assemble an analysis of his thinking and decision-making in a quixotic life. He told his story on his terms, without trying to impress a professor, an editor or even the readers of books and magazines. He was trying to connect dots. The 8,000-word essay is raw and tender, with the qualities of a dream tinged with acceptance of what he cannot change. "Almost Thirty" hints at the end of Reed's life. The writing voice is not that of a man who wants to die, but possibly a man who suspects the end is near. He wanted to create something larger than his life, something that would help his life make sense. He was running out of time.

Returning to the United States from the European War in late 1916, in the midst of pro-war hysteria, a clampdown on civil rights as a means for tighter national security, and press censorship for journalists and publications deemed unpatriotic, Reed became sick, reflective and depressed. He sat down to write about his childhood, his father, his restlessness and the arc of his life. He wanted to begin something new, but he sensed the end of something important.

A great deal of my boyhood was illness and physical weakness, and I was never really well until my sixteenth year. The beginning of my remembered life was a turmoil of imaginings—formless perceptions of beauty, which broke forth in voluminous verses, sensations of pain. Then came a period of intense emotion ... a furious energy drove me to all kinds of bodily and mental exercise, without any particular vision—except that I felt sure I was going to be a great poet and novelist. After that I was increasingly active and restless, more ambitious of place and power, less exalted, scattering myself in a hundred different directions; life became a moving picture, thought about only in brilliant flashes, conceived as emotion and sensation. And now, almost thirty, some of that vitality is gone, with it all the sufficient joy of mere living. A good many of my beliefs have got twisted by the Great War. I am weakened by a serious operation. Some things I think I have settled, but in either way I am back where I started—a turmoil of beginnings....

I must find myself again. Some men seem to get their direction early, to grow naturally and with little change in the thing they are to be. I have no idea what I shall be or do one month from now. Whenever I have tried to become some one thing, I have failed. It is only by drifting with the wind that I have found myself, and plunged joyously into a new role. I have discovered that I am only happy when I am working hard at something I like. I never stuck long at anything I didn't like, and now I couldn't if I wanted to; on the other hand, there are very few things I don't get some fun out of, if only the novelty of the experience. I love people, except the well-fed smug, and am interested in all new things and all the beautiful old things they do. I love beauty and chance and change, but less now in the external world and more in my mind. I supposed I'll always be a Romanticist.[1]

He had found part of himself, slowly, at Harvard, transforming from an introverted Westerner to Eastern campus big shot, before finding another part of himself, at a furious pace and in spectacular fashion, in New York. He found himself a third piece of the puzzle in Russia, doing, as Max Eastman said, what he was born to do. Round three of self-discovery for Jack Reed came with a price. He lost his country and many friends. "Almost Thirty" offers reasons to believe he understood this before he sat down to write his epic, *Ten Days That Shook the World*. Perhaps he understood that even before he returned to Russia in late 1917. He lost his life three years after writing "Almost Thirty," two years after writing *Ten Days That Shook the World*. The end came at 33, an age where there could have been decades of artistry ahead of him.

From the time he reached Petrograd in August 1917 to the time he returned to the States six months later, Reed abused his body by not sleeping, eating wretched food or not eating at all, and plunging, as he wrote to himself, into something something new and beautiful, something with chance and change. Convinced more than ever that economic and political revolution for the working class was a matter of life and death for every global citizen who believed in the premise and promise of self-government, Reed had trouble envisioning satisfaction in the next phase of his life. He had bypassed multiple opportunities to tone down his rhetoric or to rein in his aggressive style to practice a safer form of journalism. So many of his friends and peers had done so. When he sat down to write "Almost Thirty," he saw the formless images of his life take shape.

The world at large swung violently between abject misery and denial. European nations had celebrated wildly at the onset of the war, but from 1914 to 1919 the continent's social structures teetered on the brink of extinction, its human spirit undeniably shattered. Famine turned once-wealthy regions into ghostly-looking charred ruins. Austria-Hungary and Turkey were states of chaos, with ethnic, racial and nationalistic hostilities worse than ever before. Revolution gripped Germany, Bavaria and Budapest. In Russia, where the mother of all revolutions had turned a nation upside down, counter-revolutionaries gained steam with help from foreign governments, including the United States. In America, hope for the end of war and a new beginning gave way to domestic terrorism and state-sponsored attacks on citizens. Real, perceived and fabricated threats to America took the form of Bolsheviks, Germans, Communists, Socialists, anarchists and the *New York Times*, which briefly lost its mailing privileges for its critical coverage of U.S. war policies.

In Russia, the tsar abdicated his throne in March 1917 and was replaced by a provisional government promising land reform for the benefit of peasants and laborers. American authorities, needing political stability in Russia to neutralize the German military, desperately wanted the new Russian power structure to succeed. Reed knew better. Looking beyond the surface, drawing upon his experience in Eastern Europe as a war correspondent, he saw what the U.S government did not want Americans to see—the potential or, possibly (as if scripted by Karl Marx), the inevitable rise of the Soviet of Workers and Soldiers Deputies. As a journalist and activist, he drew a linear connection from the silk workers in Paterson to laborers in Ludlow, Lawrence, Mexico, a dozen or so countries in Europe, and in Russia. They were "human capital" creating wealth for the capitalists. The underclass was fighting back. Its target—"the well fed smug"— included, as far as Reed was concerned, everyone who used the poor to enrich themselves, including the middle class and the wealthy. The bad guys ranged from the Portland business leaders who had ostracised C.J. Reed, to the Rockefellers who bankrolled the Ludlow Massacre, to congressmen and senators who declared war, to the Russian provisional government. Re-energized with a purpose, Reed made plans to return to Russia. His objective was nothing less than to change the world.

Louise Bryant, a trailblazer for women's political, social and sexual freedom (and Reed's wife since November 1916), became a tremendous journalistic ally at this juncture in Reed's life. She had covered the European War in France after one of their break-ups. She returned to the States and set Reed's passions on fire, telling him of simmering revolts primed to boil over throughout Europe. She wanted to go to Russia with him. At this point in Bryant's career, securing credentials from a press syndicate was not a problem. But for Reed, it was a problem. His trail of anti-capitalist rhetoric, his journalistic assaults on government, his unyielding anti-war stance, his sophomoric (and well-publicized) episode in the trenches of the Western Front, and a *Masses* headline he wrote, "Knit a Straight Jacket for Your Soldier Boy" ... all of it created a wall denying him publication in American newspapers and magazines with mainstream audiences. Max Eastman and *The Masses* would publish Reed, but they could not afford to send him to Russia. Or pay him at all, for that matter. Ditto for *The Call*, another left-wing publication. Finally, Eastman—a man who knew far more than Reed about how to talk socialism while courting the capitalists he needed—persuaded Eugene Boissevain and other wealthy backers of *The Masses* to finance Reed's Russian assignment.[2]

Reed faced other obstacles in his efforts to secure a passport. One concerned compulsory military service; he was, officially, in good health, despite the loss of a kidney. The other complication was a federal order denying travel for Americans planning to attend a global Socialist conference in Sweden. Reed worked through the first problem with help from connections in high places, appealing to General Crowder, who ruled that nephrectomy disqualified Reed from serving in the military. The second obstacle came down, mysteriously, when Reed appealed to influential friends who persuaded the State Department to accept his promise that he would not take an oath to represent the Socialist Party at a conference in Sweden—or anywhere in Russia. As his past and subsequent actions suggested, this agreement could not have passed the straight-face test on either side. Reed was going to do what Reed was going to do, and American authorities would be watching every move.[3]

On board the Danish steamer *United States*, Reed and other passengers waited for a week at Halifax while British inspectors searched for contraband; Reed told friends that the English felt they could do anything to anyone on the high seas without explanation. Marine officers knocked on Reed's cabin door and announced their intentions to inspect the inside. Reed hid his letters to the Stockholm Socialists before offering the soldiers whiskey and conversation. They happily accepted, and the search ended before it began. Reed was on his way to make history.[4]

Seven. The Classic and the End Game

He found himself again, as he had implored himself to do. Arriving in Petrograd in September 1917, he and Bryant took a small apartment together. Reed knew a little Russian from his time covering the war in Eastern Europe. Neither he nor Bryant were interested in making contacts with non–Russian diplomats or businessmen. They made contacts with like-minded socialists, writers and Americans, many of whom gathered in their apartment to discuss the greatest revolution the world could not see. The living conditions were spartan, without nearly enough heat or food. Reed would start a fire on the tiled bathroom floor to warm a can of soup for his guests. A frequent topic of conversation: whether American aid for the revolutionaries was a fantasy or whether someone could convince U.S. authorities that self-government in Russia would be in the best interests of the United States and the rest of the world. Back home, the United States was reeling from one crisis after another, including politically-motivated domestic terrorism, the jailing of anti-war demonstrators and a growing number of left-wing and anarchist organizations promising to disrupt the capitalist system by any means necessary.[5]

John Reed in Russia, undated (courtesy Houghton Library, Harvard University, hou00070co2105).

Naturally, Reed took it upon himself to step out of his role as a journalist for the sake of direct activism. He drafted a report, outlining the case for U.S. support for Soviet rebels, and delivered it to Colonel Raymond Robins of the Red Cross who had invited Reed, Bryant and other Socialists to a dinner party attended by diplomats and American businessmen. At the party, Reed sat next to a Tammany Hall politician, a proud war profiteer who had a searing opposition to the revolution and a steadfast refusal to cloud his judgment with facts or new information. Reed's hope for a genuine Socialist movement in America began to fade, although his conviction about the inevitability of Russian revolution remained intact.[6]

Outside their apartment in Petrograd, Reed and Bryant entered a world of surrealism in a nation that was just beginning to take steps from the Middle Ages to the 20th century. Reed saw factory workers living multiple lives as production laborers, management trainees, political activists and armed revolutionaries. Conversations and arguments about the latest political developments never ceased. Crowds on the streets of Petrograd fought for newspapers. Crime spiked to levels never seen before, as law and order became collateral damage of the dismantling of the old regime. Reed witnessed several hundred people beat a soldier to death because he had been caught stealing. Mysterious men whispered to women shivering in bread lines in the rain, suggesting that Jews were orchestrating the chaos, while Soviet political leaders lived in luxury. Meanwhile, high stakes gambling clubs continued uninterrupted throughout the city. Prostitutes wearing expensive jewelry and furs worked the streets and cafés. German spies took notes—names, observations, questions, speculation and deductions.[7]

It was not difficult to find resistance to the Bolsheviks, just one of many pieces of the resistance to the provisional government. Most Russians with any sort of economic standing were more concerned about losing what they had than about what the Russian peasants (whom they were loath to call "fellow Russians") could gain. Reed spent many evenings with a Russian family who offered meals and place to crash during his journalistic journey. "[T]he subject of conversation at the dinner table was almost invariably the coming of the Germans, bringing law and order."[8] On October 15, 1917, the prominent Russian capitalist Stepan Georgevish Lianozov, known as the Russian Rockefeller, and who was loyal to the Cadet political faction, told Reed:

> Revolution is a sickness. Sooner or later the foreign powers must intervene here—as one would intervene to cure a sick child, and teach it how to walk. Of course, it would be more or less improper, but the nations must realize the danger of Bolshevism in their own countries—such contagious ideas as proletarian dictatorship, and world social revolution.... There is a chance that this intervention may not be necessary. Transportation is demoralized, the factories are closing down, and the Germans are advancing. Starvation and defeat may bring the Russian people to their senses.[9]

* * *

From the moment he began attending meetings connected, directly or indirectly, with the Bolsheviks' cause, Reed was watched continuously by secret agents reporting to U.S. diplomats.[10] Perhaps he should not have been surprised, seven months later (April 1918), that all of his Russian papers, notes and pamphlets were confiscated upon his return to New York to write his book about the Russian Revolution. After a tortured process of appeals, U.S. authorities returned all of Reed's papers five months later, in September 1918. This could not have happened without the help of Lincoln Steffens, who now had cozy relationships in the highest echelons of power, including President Wilson's closest advisor, Colonel House. Reed was nearly broken at this point, having endured two trials for sedition following his return from Russia (no convictions), having pushed his body and mind beyond exhaustion. American newspapers and magazines were refusing to publish his work. The Macmillan publishing house cancelled his book contract for the story of the workers' revolution in Russia. Every scrap of information he had collected to write *Ten Days That Shook the World* sat for months in the offices of federal security agents. Reed lost sleep and weight, and he began to lose the side of his personality that friends and a fair number of adversaries had found endearing for years. His social behavior (always an acquired taste, despite the charm) became uncomfortably bizarre. Eight years of adventure-hunting, story-hunting, storytelling, racing around the globe, searching for his calling, fighting, being the life of the party ... all of it was slipping away as he ached for his Russian papers. His personal war on unchecked authority, begun in earnest in 1912, was coming to a halt. Given his fragile health for much of his youth, and the abuse he inflicted upon his body, Reed may have known that his personal endgame was near—as he had hinted in "Almost Thirty."

Papers finally in hand, in November 1918 Reed rented the top floor of the Greenwich Village Inn and shut out the world. This was no small feat, as the Village had been his playground and launching pad for fame. But Reed was desperate, a man running out of time, the Russian Revolution narrative there for the taking by others who did not know what he knew, had not seen what he had seen, and could not write like he could write—and who had not lived for this moment, as he had. He wrote *Ten Days* in two months. The joy returned, possibly one of the few times in his life when joy emerged in solitude for this insatiably social creature. He was on fire, reliving the drama of the revolution. The physical world he inhabited while creating a 20th-century masterpiece contained piles of newspapers, pamphlets, placards, books, notes, a Russian dictionary, writing paper, a typewriter, desk and endless cigarettes. Nothing else mattered. One day, when he took a break and ventured into Sheridan Square for a cup of coffee, he ran into Max Eastman, who expressed astonishment over

Reed's appearance: "gaunt, unshaven, greasy-skinned, a stark sleepless half crazy look on his slightly, potatolike face." Reed began talking about the book and could not stop. He had an "unqualified, concentrated look of joy in his eyes," according to Eastman. Reed "was doing what he was made to do."[11]

In his ragtag, disheveled condition—bone-weary, malnourished, unbathed and over-caffeinated—Reed's body and soul took on the features of the Russian underclass. He brought mind-pictures back to life on the pages rolled in his typewriter. The peasants and the factory workers fought their battles under gray skies and shortened days of September and October 1917. The rain never stopped, and oftentimes it pounded. Although the best of Petrograd featured architectural splendor worthy of a large nation's capitol city, many of its streets (and the streets of surrounding villages) turned into steep, slippery mud that made a walk of any length hazardous. The mud made its way into every building by way of traveling boots. It happened every year, but in 1917 it was worse than ever because municipal governments had either stopped operating with any efficiency or manpower or employees had refused to work in response to political paralysis. The mother of all revolutions unfolded in the months preceding the fabled Russian winters, featuring cruel winds, lockdown fog and darkness from three in the afternoon to to ten o'clock the next morning. In Petrograd, Reed reported, a week went by with no bread for anyone, milk for about half of the babies in the city, and no basic food staples for most of the hotels and private houses. Lines for milk and bread consisted largely of women holding their babies for hours in bitterly cold rain (that, Reed noted, had been going on since 1915, under the tsar; months into the provisional government transition, nothing had changed). The nights were darker than dark, with few street lights and little electricity available for a few hours each evening. Residents of apartment houses took turns guarding their communities with loaded rifles. The provisional government showed no signs of noticing or caring.

At the same time, Russian cultural life thrived in Petrograd. Theaters were open every night. Major ballet dancers and opera singers continued to entertain the cultural elite. Art lovers had plenty of painting exhibitions to attend. Young women of bourgeois families continued their rituals of attending lectures on art, literature and philosophy. Young women from the provinces traveled to Petrograd to take French and singing lessons, while "ladies of the minor bureaucratic set" held afternoon teas and discussed, among other things, the difficulty of hiring good servants during the revolution. One afternoon, Reed was at the home of a Russian friend when the man's daughter came home in hysterics because a female streetcar conductor called her "comrade!"[12]

Although timing and detail made *Ten Days That Shook the World* historic journalism, it was Reed's ability to convey the beat and throbbing of a country's heart that made Russia's impossible political and social environment understandable to the outside world. Reed described the machinations and nuances of political conflict and paralysis at great length, then seasoned and spiced the narrative with bursts of passion reminiscent of his early Greenwich Village descriptions.

> In the new Russia every man and woman could vote; there were working class newspapers, saying new and startling things; there were Soviets; and there were Unions ... all Russia was learning to read and *reading*—politics, economics, history—because the people wanted to *know*.... In every city, in most towns, along the front, each political faction had its newspaper—sometimes several. Hundreds of thousands of pamphlets were distributed by thousands of organizations, and poured into the armies, the villages, the factories, the streets. The thirst for education, so long thwarted, burst with the Revolution into a frenzy of expression.... Russia absorbed reading matter like hot sand drinks water, insatiable. And it was not fables, falsified history, diluted religion and the cheap fiction that corrupts—but social and economic theories, philosophy, the works of Tolstoy, Gogal and Gorky.[13]

Ten Days That Shook the World is not an easy read for a 21st-century student of journalism, world history or political science. The story comes from an outsider on the inside showing readers what it took to end a 300-year system of oppression from the ground up—including the stench, the raw, emotional responses to micro-developments, and the use of military and insurgent documents in an arena of chaos where everyone had an agenda and everyone talked openly because they were Russians, with no political context for the modern world. Nobody knew what was happening next, or what had just happened, and everyone was scared.

Endless meetings involving warring factions, hostile takeovers and abrupt walk-outs contained drama that Reed was more than happy to draw with his unique skill set as a writer. His narrative overflowed with energy and historical perspective that had begun during childhood and developed (although not refined) with his Harvard schooling. He used his remarkable ear for conversation to turn ordinary conversations into poetry. He put the dialogue of economic and social revolution where it belonged, in scenes were worlds collided. The bourgeois tried to ignore the revolution, but when they tried to treat waiters and hotel servants as they always had, the service workers acted bold. They were organized, and they refused tips. The proletariat found the possibilities and promise of self-government intoxicating; they had Reed on the scene to let the world know what it felt like.

Reed described a day after the Bolshevik victory, the second world-changing upheaval in the same country in eight months. "On November 8, 1917, day broke on a city in the wildest excitement and confusion, a whole nation heaving up in long hissing swells of storm. On the surface, all was quiet; hundreds of thousands of people had retired at a prudent hour before getting up early and going to work: In Petrograd the streetcars were running, the stores and restaurants open, theaters going, an exhibition of paintings advertised. All the complex routines of common life—humdrum even in wartime—proceeded as usual. Nothing is so astounding as the vitality of the social organism—how it persists, feeding itself, clothing itself, amusing itself, in the face of the worst calamities."[14]

As a reporter, Reed took the time to explain why resistance to the Bolsheviks came from segments of the Russian political class that had orchestrated their own revolution against the tsar. The answer lay in the complexity of moving parts, shifting allegiances, newly-formed wings of already splintered parties—but it also lay in the simple reality that the middle class showed no signs of following through on the essential promise of the 1905 revolution or the March 1917 government takeover by moderate Socialists and the Menshevik party. That promise was threefold: an end to the war, land distribution to the peasants, and worker control of factories. Political moderates and tsar loyalists losing faith in the provisional government's ability to govern—and there were many—openly pined for a successful German invasion of their country for the sake of law and order.

Neither land distribution nor factory worker empowerment could be accomplished without Russia's withdrawal from the war with Germany. The third manifestation of the Russian Revolution, the October 1917 version, revealed that resolution of each issue was completely dependent on resolution of the other two. First the tsar and then the provisional government left the front-line soldiers exposed to die in hideous fashion at the hands of a German war machine by not providing them with enough food, clothing, provisions, ammunition or reinforcements. The provisional government needed an army at Petrograd and the White Palace to stave off insurrection. Soldiers at the capitol home base were well cared for, pointedly supplied with as much alcohol as food to keep them compliant. Eventually, however, the soldiers did not want to be part of a government that killed its own people. Nor did they want to fight Germans, knowing the fate that awaited them. These soldiers clung to the hope that the provisional government would prevail without insurrection and without sending them to the Eastern Front.

The provisional government did not go quietly after the Bolsheviks and their following claimed victory in early November 1917. The government had myriad components that included supposed tsar loyalists who were not all that loyal. The bourgeois, bureaucrats, provincial and municipal workers, splinter factions calling themselves Revolutionary Socialists in honor of the March 1917 political revolution—nobody could make a powerful case that the provisional government had a coherent plan beyond continuation of a losing war and the stonewalling of land grants to peasants that had been promised when the tsar finally stepped down in March 1917. In November, government services still worked for those who were already comfortable. For the tens of millions of Russians who were starving, as well as the tens of thousands of Russians fighting Germans on the Eastern Front who were also starving, the provisional government had no meaning beyond the status quo that had existed for 300 years. Such was the desperation of resistance to the Bolshevik takeover that one of the counter-revolutionary groups was offically named the Committee for Salvation. At an emergency meeting of the Duma in Petrograd, the Committee for Salvation managed to enlist the support of the Union of Railway Workers, the Post Employees and the Telegraph Employees, all groups announcing their refusal to work for the Bolshevik regime. Telephones were cut off at Smolny, an important government complex. The audience at the Committee for Salvation meeting was openly incredulous, defiant and contemptuous of the lower classes that now felt empowered by the Bolshevik takeover. Reed quoted a common cry in the crowd: "These Bolsheviki will try to dictate to the intelligentsia? We'll show them!"

"It was war," Reed reported. "War deliberately planned, Russian fashion; war by strike and sabotage." He tried to be at every gathering where an important political dialogue took place among people who not only cared but who were taking action. Thus Reed could offer contrasts. At the Congress of the Soviets: "There, great masses of shabby soldiers, grimy workmen, peasants—poor men, bent and scarred in the brute struggle for existence." At the Committee for Salvation conference: "here the Menshevik and Socialist Revolutionary leaders ... rubbed shoulders with Cadets like oily Shatsky, sleek Vinaver; with journalists, students, intellectuals of almost call camps. This Duma crowd was well fed, well dressed; I did not see more than three proletariats among them all."[15]

Reed had always been fascinated by social contrasts, which compelled him to write like a romantic poet before flipping a switch to journalistic urgency. In his childhood Oregon household, contrast took the form of exotic Chinese servants who helped his parents entertain conservative

Portland businessmen at high-profile parties. Within his family, rowdy, globe-trotting uncle Roy and John's flamboyant grandmother contrasted with his mother, Margaret Reed, who was obsessed with decorum to maintain social status. At Harvard, the elite clubs made sure the non-wealthy students knew their place while the secret clubs did the same to the elite. In New York, the dualism of haves and have-nots violated Reed's senses, pulling him into the seedy side that Harvard men were supposed to avoid (or at least not talk about). In Mexico, he championed the uneducated, uncivilized Pancho Villa while the outlaw rebel humiliated a national army with his wits, audacity and conviction. And in Europe, Reed squatted in the mud and blood of trenches filled with body parts of sacrificial lambs just a few months after sitting in the Oval Office with Woodrow Wilson, just a few years after going toe to toe in a newsroom argument with Teddy Roosevelt.

He drew the contrasts between the proletariat and their Bolshevik leaders ... a peasant with long hair, boots, sheepskin coat, bowing to all corners of the room ... a soldier, gaunt, ragged and eloquent ... another soldier, with a disordered beard and flaming eyes ... Leon Trotsky, the new head of foreign affairs, calm and venomous, conscious of power ... all listening to Vladimir Lenin, their chosen president whom Reed described in *Ten Days That Shook the World:*

> A short, stocky figure, with a big head set down on his shoulders, bald and bulging. Little eyes, a snubbish nose, wide generous mouth and heavy chin; clean shaven now but already beginning to bristle with the well known beard of his past and future. Dressed in shabby clothes, his trousers much too long for him. Unimpressive, to be the idol of a mob, loved and revered as perhaps few leaders in history have been. A strange popular leader—a leader purely by virtue of intellect: colourness, humourless, uncompromising and detached, without picturesque idiosyncrasies—with the power of explaining profound ideas in simple terms, of analyzing a concrete situation. And combined with shrewdness, the greatest intellectual audacity.[16]

The reporting sustained its authority and credibility in spite of (and perhaps because of) Reed's opening and closing caveat: that he sympathized with the peasants and factory workers, the ranks of whom comprised practically all of the front-line soldiers getting slaughtered in battles that the world knew Russia could not win. They had been promised land and bread forever. What they received were rearranged political structures in 1905 and in March of 1917; nothing had changed for them. With Bolshevik leadership, they were winning a civil war. No credible source could deny what Reed reported when he told of the lies spread by the Socialist Revolutionaries and the Mensheviks in their attempts to feed the fire of hatred that the bourgeoisie had towards the Bolsheviks. Newspapers loyal to the provisional government reported that the Red Guard, having shifted loyalties to the Bolsheviks, looted the Winter Palace, massacred yonkers guarding the building, killed government ministers in cold blood, and tortured and raped women before the victims committed suicide. Reed reported these claims as fiction, noting that Socialist Revolutionaries and Mensheviks had traditionally been loyal to facts to the point of missing truths. He suggested that an obvious sign of deception was their encouragement of mothers and fathers to read the names of alleged victims to the crowd gathered at the Duma, setting off a tidal wave of hysteria. He noted that newspapers published a story of Prince Tumanov's body found floating in the Moika Canal; the prince's family said no, our son is in jail, whereupon the press reidentified the floating dead as belonging to General Denissov. "The General having also come to life, we investigated, and could find no trace of any body having been found."[17]

Elements of the underdog's fight—drama, tension, desperation, sabotage—failed to cloud Reed's clarity of thought when he reported what the Bolsheviks were up against while trying to set up a sustainable governing infrastructure. When it was not fighting off counter-revolutionary forces, the new government had to put people in place to create an economy that worked, along with local governments run by local people—the same people who had been denied education, human rights and dignity for 300 years.

> Men literally out of themselves, living prodigies of sleeplessness and work—men unshaven, filthy, with burning eyes who drove upon their fixed purpose full speed on engines of exaltation. So much they had to do, so much! Take over the Government, organize the City, keep the garrison loyal, fight the Duma and the Committee for Salvation, keep out the Germans, prepare to do battle with Kerensky, inform the provinces what had happened, propagandize from Archangel to Vladivostock ... against them not only the organized bourgeoisie, but all the other Socialist parties except the Left Socialist Revolutionaries, a few Mensheviki Internationalists, and the Socialist Democrat Internationalists, and even the undecided whether to stand by or not. With them, it is true, the workers and the soldier masses the peasants an unknown quantity—but after all the Bolsheviks were a political faction not rich in trained and educated men.[18]

For all the confusion amidst stupefying chaos bordering on anarchy (without the help of the so-called Anarchist wing of the Bolsheviks), the Land Decree—the heart and soul of the Russian Revolution—stood as a model of simplicity with depth as Lenin read the document to the Congress of the Soviets. It had five provisions:

1. All private ownership of land abolished immediately without compensation.

2. All landowners and all lands belonging to the Crown, to monasteries, church lands with all their livestock and inventoried property ... transferred to township Land Committees and the district Soviets of Peasants' Deputies.

3. Any damage done to the confiscated property now belonging to the "whole People" is regarded as a serious crime, punishable by revolutionary tribunals.

4. Guidance during the realization of the great land reforms will be based on ... 242 local peasant recommendations drawn up by the editorial board of the Izvestia of the All-Russian Soviet of Peasants' Deputies in August of 1917.

5. The lands of peasants and of Cossacks serving in the Army shall not be confiscated.

The Land Decree was not, Lenin immediately noted after reading the document from the podium, a product of the moderate Socialists or the provisional government "erecting a framework" for change—words that had run hollow for eight months since the March 1917 transfer of power to moderates. Lenin reminded the newly empowered proletariat that the revolution was not accomplished through compromise and that it was not to be finished or successful without similar upheavals throughout Europe.[19]

* * *

In *Ten Days That Shook the World,* Reed reported what he saw. He offered no critical analysis of Lenin's vision beyond the immediacy of victory and reaction to a continuous state of crisis. Nor did he raise questions about the new government's suppression of press freedom or the subsequent uproar from Bolsheviks who wanted the restrictions lifted before the civil war faded into history.

Trotsky read an Official Bolshevik Resolution at one of many important assemblies as the revolutionaries tried to prepare the rest of Russian history. He spoke of confiscating privately-run printing plants, including the equipment and all supplies of paper used for newsprint.

The buildings, printing presses, paper and ink in capitol cities and in provinces would become property of the Soviet states, "so that political parties and groups can make use of the facilities of printing."

"The reestablishment of the so-called 'freedom of the press,'" he continued, "the simple return of printing presses and paper to the capitalists—poisoners of the mind of the people—this would be an inadmissible surrender to the will of capital, a giving up of one of the most important conquests of the Revolution; in other words, it would be a measure of unquestionably counter-revolutionary character ... [the Bolshevik Party] categorically rejects all propositions aiming at the reestablishment of the old regime in the domain of the press.[20]

From the floor of the assembly, a Bolshevik protester named Karelin shouted at Trotsky, reminding him that three weeks prior, Bolshevik leaders vigorously defended freedom of the press: "The arguments in this resolution suggest singularly the point of view of the old Black Hundreds and the censors of the Tsarist regime—for they have also talked of poisoners of the mind of the people."

Without editorializing, Reed simply quoted Trotsky defending the anti-free press resolution: "The monopoly of the press by the bourgeoisie must be abolished. Otherwise it isn't worthwhile for us to take power. Each group of citizens should have access to print shops and paper.... The passing of power into the hands of the Soviets will bring about a radical transformation of the essential conditions of existence, and this transformation will necessarily be evident in the press.... If we are going to nationalize the banks, can we then tolerate the financial journals. The old regime must die; that must be understood once and for all."[21]

Reed had blinders on at this point. The Russian Revolution, an all-consuming immersion, became his revolution. Lenin's ability to frame an argument against press freedom with his steel-trap mind met no resistance from Reed, one of the most famous and talented journalists of his era, a reporter who had thrived on the adversarial role of a free press. Later, when Lenin overruled Reed's astonishing appointment as a Russian consul to the United States, Reed did not protest or even complain. Eager to spread the word of the Bolshevik revolution by strengthening the Communist Party base in the United States, Reed—relishing the role of agitator against his homeland—had been thrilled that American officials found his appointment unacceptable. He did not want to agitate Lenin, however. Lenin cancelled Reed's appointment after hearing a rumor that Reed had considered editing an American propaganda newspaper in Russia. Reed was disappointed, but he told George Sisson (former *Cosmopolitan* editor and now working for the U.S. Committee of Public Information in Russia) that he would serve the Bolshevik cause in any manner deemed appropriate by their leaders. He had never came close to offering that kind of loyalty to his own government.[22]

Reed was not alone in overlooking the heavy-handedness of the Bolshevik regime. Max Eastman, on one hand Reed's journalistic soulmate and on the other hand his non-biological older brother, saw Reed's appointment as a sign of hope for a new Russia. Eastman went over the moon for Reed in a column for *The Evening Call:*

> John Reed's appointment as consul general in his own country by the Bolsheviki is the most beautiful and astute expression they have yet given to the international character of the class struggle and the social revolution. In his own country, John Reed has been proscribed by the respectables and indicted by the courts as a traitor. He will present his credentials from the sovereign proletariat of Russia to a bourgeois government that has already put him jail.... John Reed was born to fill a high place in revolutionary times. He is one of the few universal men—the men who combine that arrant imagination and headstrong will of adventure which are the attributes of poetic genius, with a diligent and real power to achieve and understand. There is nothing that needs to be done, either in the technical routine of a consul general's office or in the extraordinary and delicate duties of a revolutionary emissary, that John Reed is not abundantly equipped to do.... Starting off with brilliant emotions, perceptions and world combinations in mind, I have watched him add to these native gifts the habit of verification and clear analytic understanding. And I know that his history—the intimate history—of those great days at Petrograd will be a light in the world's literature.[23]

Eastman had accurately predicted the enduring power of *Ten Days That Shook the World*, which was praised by U.S. diplomat and Russian expert George Kennan several decades later. Eastman had always been fascinated by Reed, even when he was simultaneously exasperated, times when he had to shake Reed and tell him to get real. His passionate tribute to Reed, however, could have been written for Reed's benefit as much as it served the purpose of public enlightenment. Eastman had believed in the ideology of Karl Marx, as many Americans had during the decade of World War I. But in the 1920s, after Reed's death, Eastmen visited Russia and came away horrified by the abuses of Soviet Communism. He may have seen the dark side of Bolsheviki socialism earlier, as the dust settled from their victory in 1917. Knowing Reed as well as he did, Eastman may have understood what was happening when Reed became obsessed with writing a poem about America while trying to return home for *The Masses* sedition trial. Reed wrote the poem while being detained in Sweden. It was his longest poem, and his last:

America, 1918

Across the sea my country, my America
Grit with steel hard-glittering with power
As a champion, with great voice trumpeting
High words, "For Liberty.... Democracy..."

❧ ❧ ❧

Deep within me stirs, answers—
(My country, my America!)

Seven. The Classic and the End Game

As if alone in the high and empty night
She called me—my lost one, my first lover
I love no more, love no more, love no more...

❧   ❧   ❧

By my free boyhood in the wide West
The powerful river, fish wheels, log rafts
Ships from behind the sunset, Lascar-manned
Chinatown, throbbing with mysterious gongs,
The blue thunderous Pacific, blaring sunsets,
Black smoking forests on surf beaten headlands,
Lost beaches, camp fires, wall of hunting cougars...
By the rolling range, and the flat sunsmitten desert.
Night with coyotes yapping, domed with burst of stars,
The gray herd moving eastward, towering dust
Ropes whistling in slow coils, hats flapping, yells...
By miles of yellow wheat rippling in the Chinook
Green-golden orange-groves and snow-peaks, looming over...
But raw audacious cities sprung up from nothing
Brawling and bragging in their careless youth...
I know thee, America!

❧   ❧   ❧

Fishermen putting out from Astoriea in the foggy dawn their double bowed boats,
Lean cow-punchers jogging south from Burns, with faces burned leathery and silent
Stringy old prospectors trudging behind reluctant pack-horses across the Nevada alkali...

❧   ❧   ❧

By my bright youth in golden eastern towns...
Harvard ... pain of growing, ecstasy of unfolding,
Thrill of books, thrill of friendship, hero-worship,
Intoxication of dancing, tempest of great music,
Squandering delight, first consciousness of power...

❧   ❧   ❧

Manhattan, zoned with ships, the cruel,
Youngest of all the world's great town,
The bodice bright with many a jewel,
Imperially crowned with crowns...

❧   ❧   ❧

Who that hath known thee but shall burn
In exile till he come again
To do they bitter will, O stern
Moon of the tides of men!

❧   ❧   ❧

In dim Roumanian wine-cellars I am not welcome,
Pulsing with hot rhythm of scornful gypsy fiddlers...
In Grand Street coffee rooms, haunt of Yiddish philosophers,
Novelists reading aloud a new chapter, collecting a dime from each auditor,
Playwrights dramatizing the newspaper headlines, poets dumb to deaf America...

❧   ❧   ❧

Dear and familiar and unforgettable is the city
As the face of my mother...

        ❧ ❧ ❧

Have I omitted you, truck quaking West Street, dingy Death Avenue,
Gracious old Church of the Sea and Land, Inwood, tip of Manhattan,
The rag shops of Minetta Lane, and the yelping swirl of the Broad Street Curb,
Macdougal Alley, gilded squalor of fashionable artists,
Coenties Slip, old sea-remembering noth at the back of downtown?
Nay, across the world, three thousand miles away, without map of guide-book,

        ❧ ❧ ❧

Ask me and I will describe them and their people,
In all weathers, drunk or sober, by sun and moon...
I have watched the summer day come up from the top of a pier of the Williamsburg Bridge,
I have slept in a basket of squid at the Fulton Street Market,
Talked about God with the old cockney woman who sells hot dogs under the Elevated at South Ferry.
Listened to the tales of dago dips in the family parlor of the Hell-hole,
And from the top gallery of the Metropolitan heard Didur sing "Boris Godounov."

        ❧ ❧ ❧

Dear and familiar and ever-new to me is the city
As the body of my lover...

        ❧ ❧ ❧

All professions, races, temperaments, philosophies,
All history, all possibilities, all romance,
America ... the world...![24]

CHAPTER EIGHT

Radicals, Revolutionaries and Reed: Berkman, Goldman, Haywood, Debs

Convulsions in the global economy between 1910 and 1920 gave radicals reason to believe that the masses would support their hostility toward capitalism. Serious people took radical politics seriously. Workers of the world were paying attention to labor union leaders. Jack Reed was simultaneously a journalist, an activist and a revolutionary during this time. As he spoke for disenfranchised laborers, he became forever linked to radicals who now live in the margins of history.

In 1914, a year removed from robust economic gains throughout every major industry, a business philosophy of "industrial leanness" exacted a human that was hard to ignore. In Kalamazoo, Michigan, closing factories produced one thousand unemployed workers unable to find jobs. In Pottsville, Pennsylvania, the Lehigh and Navigational Company laid off 10,000 workers. The completion of the Panama Canal meant that 30,000 workers had to search for new jobs. General Electric Co. in Schenectady, New York, laid off 3,000 workers.[1]

The desperation was palpable. In Pendleton, Oregon, farmers donated 1,200 rabbits in one day—for hundreds of men and women in surrounding cities trying to feed their families but could not find work. And in Los Angeles, a widow, Mary E. Erickson, unable to find work and fearing starvation, threw a brick through a plate glass window in order to wind up in jail and get fed.[2]

"For revolutionaries, such incidents presented an opportune crisis," wrote Thai Jones in *More Powerful Than Dynamite: Radicals, Plutocrats, Progressives and New York's Year of Anarchy*. "Nothing radicalized the working classes like a business panic.... Pointing out that Congress' new billion dollar budget had failed to allocate a single penny to 'aid the out of works,' the Socialist Party offered a platform of jobs bureaus and government relief through public projects."

"Anarchists scoffed at such reformism, urging direct action," Jones wrote. He quoted anarchist Alexander Berkman: "The problem of unemployment cannot be solved within the capitalist regime. If the unemployed would realize this, they would refuse to starve; they would help themselves to the things they need. But as long as they weakly wait for the government miracle, they will be doomed to hunger and misery."[3]

Progressives put their faith in the American political system to help advance people left behind in a competitive, capitalist economy. Anarchists wanted to blow up the system—figuratively for the most part, literally in some cases. Socialists wanted to keep the system intact while resetting American economic and social values through the ballot box. Communists wanted an economic, social and political revolution on a global scale, with America following Russia's example.

Each group worked furiously in the years leading up to World War I, during the war and in the immediate aftermath of the armistice, striving to shape the United States into nation with a re-engineered system for dealing with unforeseen problems emerging from industrialization, urbanization and the political power of big business.

By 1919, labor unrest had morphed into social chaos. "There were dressmakers strikers, railway strikes, cigar makers' strikes, miners' strikes," wrote Bruce Watson, author of *Sacco and Vanzetti*. "Even police went on strike, leaving Boston to rampaging drunks and looters. That summer, savage race riots set off by white mobs broke out in Chicago, Washington, D.C., and two dozen other cities."[4]

As a talented, connected and popular journalist, John Reed could have remained on the sidelines—exactly where most accomplished journalist say they belong. But he never pretended to be a reporter without jumping into the fray. As his peers pointed out numerous times, he enjoyed the conflicts from the inside—not from the sidelines, and not the from the front row. But he would move on. He would not commit himself to any particular group's cause for very long, whether it be his dozen or so clubs at Harvard, fundraising for the Paterson silk workers, riding with revolutionaries in Mexico, or even the Provincetown Players. Commitment to a strictly defined mission or a special interest meant submission to a collaborative process, a set of agreed-upon values, in-house politicking, and a slice of dogma. It meant playing by someone else's rules. Reed moved from cause to cause, inspired by Progressives, aligning himself with socialists (for a while), befriending radicals, sounding like an anarchist on occasion. In the end, he committed himself to communism, then died before he could undertake his next (inevitable?) transformation. Left behind, however, were hints that, had he lived longer, his politics would evolve past Bolshevik ideology. He may have had no choice. Bolsheviks may have had more than enough of their new friend, the man once known as Storm Boy.

America had many high-profile radicals with diverse backgrounds in the years leading up to and following the Great War. Some were homegrown. Others came from someplace else. Some were self-taught, taking their books as seriously as they took their own lives, while others used university education to shape their worldviews. Reed was among the latter, but he did not align himself with any individual or cause for long. As he cried for revolution, he did so as a moving target, compelling and armed with humor, refusing to take himself too seriously. He worked hard at being funny and often succeeded, but his words and actions frightened and angered political allies and adversaries.

Emma Goldman, Alexander Berkman, Eugene Debs and Bill Haywood—four radicals who tried to remake America during the Great War's decade of social chaos—crossed paths with Reed directly and indirectly. Their paths in the century's second decade offer context for Reed's high-speed transformation from wide-eyed New York newcomer to spectacular reporter to audacious activist to dangerous revolutionary. Given the extreme nature of political activism, which included violence and killings, and the equally extreme measures taken by government and business to eliminate dissent in the years 1910–1920 (violence and killings were part of this package as well), Jack Reed may not have appeared as dangerous as others who fought for revolution. Or maybe he did.

Alexander Berkman

In the late 1800s and early 1900s, America had many "halfway anarchists" who confined their radicalism to conversation in cafés, writes Thai Jones. The author of *More Powerful Than Dynamite* referred to Peter Kropotkin, a Russian aristocrat committed to revolution by violence, and, if necessary, killings. "In the midst of discontent, talk, theoretical discussions, an individual or collective act of revolt supervenes," Kropotkin wrote.

"One such act may, in a few days, make more propaganda than thousands of pamphlets." Whereas "propaganda of the deed" made many halfway anarchists squeamish, Alexander Berkman declared, "the killing of a tyrant is in no way to be considered the taking of a life."[5]

On July 23, 1892, Berkman took a train to Pittsburgh and bought a new suit before walking into the Chronicle-Telegraph Building and shooting steel magnate Henry Clay Frick of the Carnegie Corporation—an attempted assassination of a man fully committed to breaking labor unions by any means necessary. Berkman, a Russian emigre who edited *Mother Earth*, an anarchist magazine published by Emma Goldman, had made a conscious, deliberate choice to become one anarchist whose actions carry more weight for the cause than mere words.

"It is disgusting to witness the brazen hypocrisy of newspapers and magazines," he wrote. "The United States, according to statistical figures, employs more children in stores, factories and mines than any other 'civilized' nation." Berkman saw, as Reed and other radicals did, a clear connection between capitalism and the easy destruction of human life. Commenting on the development of a newer, more efficient machine gun that could fire 500 rounds in one minute, Berkman wrote, "Think of what that means! A single company of soldiers will, by means of the new Lewis gun, have a destructive power equal to a whole regiment at present. Wonderful human achievement."[6]

As far as Berkman was concerned, elections were meaningless to the common laborer. "He may vote blue, white or red, but however he casts his ballot, he always votes to continue his own slavery," he wrote.[7]

In Berkman's world, the leaders of the political status quo served the interests of abusive capitalists who used human life like it was part of the machinery or chemicals in their industrial plans. He called them parasitic speculators, property patriots, hired plug-uglies, pathological degenerates, government squealers, slimy creatures, Judases, Hessians, harpies, troglodytes. He referred to the Socialist Party of America, founded at the turn of the century, as "friends with somewhat similar aims." But he abhorred the socialists' faith in elected democracy, American style, even though the party's candidate for president, Eugene Debs, earned nearly a million votes in his 1912 White House bid. Berkman and other anarchists believed that participation in elections and acquiescence to the policies of the U.S. government made real change for the working class impossible.[8]

Friends referred to Berkman's "graveyard humor," although he had nothing approaching the mirth and playfulness of John Reed. Like Reed, he had friends who witnessed a decline in his ability to laugh at himself as the weight of his crusade for justice became a burden without relief.[9]

As it was with Reed, Berkman's passion for radical politics seemed intertwined with his lust for women who were bold enough to carve their own activist causes and join others. Among his lovers were Emma Goldman and other Russian émigrés named Anna, Masha, Nadya, Kolya and Luba. As it was with the formally-educated Bohemian writers, poets and artists experimenting with open sexual relationships, foreign-born migrants such as Berkman—a cigar maker and shirt packer who took pride in his poverty—considered the constraints of social conventions such as marriage and monogamy closely aligned with the numbness of working for industrial masters.[10]

Compared to radicals such as Berkman and Frank Tannenbaum, Reed could have been cast as a poseur, a bourgeoise bad boy who dabbled in radical politics but was really in it for the money. Berkman had no appetite for those who called themselves radical and revolutionaries while performing work for the institutions that anarchists wanted to bring down. Nevertheless, Reed's fight for social, economic and political upheaval in America outlasted Berkman's—although his life did not. On June 17, 1917, Berkman and Emma Goldman were arrested for sedition. They served two years in prison before being deported to Russia. On December 21, 1919, they joined nearly 250 other deportees on a transport ship, *Buford*, nicknamed *The Soviet Ark* because its passengers were Russians with histories of revolutionary politics, or at least the reputation of associating with such undesirables.[11] During the two and a half years between Berkman's arrest in New York and his deportation, Reed took his rebellion to Russia, back to America and then Russia again, where the crusade ended with his death.

Berkman shared Reed's belief that the Russian Bolshevik Party represented the best hope for the world's working class. "The Boylsheviki alone have the faith and strength of actually putting the program of the Social Revolution into operation," he wrote.[12]

Reed and Berkman traveled in the same circles—at anti-war rallies, pro-labor rallies, meetings where activists plotted disruption of American institutions, and at Mabel Dodge's Manhattan salon. When Berkman and Emma Goldman were arrested for the final time before their deportation, it was Reed who jumped onto a stage where they were speaking, creating a commotion that allowed the pair to escape police for about 12 hours before they were apprehended the next morning. Berkman and Goldman attended Reed's funeral in Russia in 1920. They carried his wife, Louise Bryant, to a car after she collapsed during the eulogies.[13]

Emma Goldman

Emma Goldman began working for a living at home in St. Petersburg in 1882, at the age of 13, knitting shawls for women who wanted to look fashionable. She spent most of the next two years working in a glove factory. In 1885, she emigrated to Rochester, New York, where she found employment in a clothing factory. In her autobiography, she compared a teenager's impressions of Russian working conditions with American working conditions.

The St. Petersburg glove factory, she said, "was far from our place. One had to get up at five in the morning to be at work at seven. The rooms were stuffy, unventilated, and dark. Oil lamps gave the light; the sun never penetrated the work room. There were six hundred of us, of all ages, working on costly and beautiful gloves day in, day out, for very small pay. But we were allowed sufficient time for our noon meal and twice a day for tea. We could talk and sing while at work; we were not driven or harassed."[14]

In Rochester she was told her factory was state of the art. "Certainly, Garson's clothingworks were a vast improvement on the glove factory on the the Vassilevsky Ostrov. The rooms were large, bright and airy. One had elbow space. There were none of those ill smelling odours that used to nauseate me in our cousin's shop. Yet the work here was harder, and the day, with only half an hour for lunch, seemed endless. The iron discipline forbade free movement (one could not even go to the toilet without permission) and the constant surveillance of the foreman weighed like stone on my heart. The end of each day found me sapped, with just enough energy to drag myself to my sister's home and crawl into bed. This continued with deadly monotony week after week."[15]

She was living with her sister, who let her know that $1.50 of her weekly earnings (60 percent of her pay) would go to household expenses. Emma, a 15-year-old Russian immigrant oblivious to protocol, decided that she needed a raise. She asked for and was granted a meeting with the factory owner, bypassing the foreman because she felt that would be a waste of time. She told Mr. Garson that her pay, $2.50 per week, did not cover her board and that she would like to be able to afford an occasional book or a theater ticket for 25 cents. "Mr. Garson replied that for a factory girl I had rather expensive tastes, and that his 'hands' were well satisfied, that they seemed to be getting along all right—that I, too, would have to manage or find work elsewhere." And so she did, securing a job at another factory for $4 per week.[16]

Less than four years after asserting herself as a factory worker asking

Eight. Radicals, Revolutionaries and Reed

for better treatment from her employer, Goldman moved to New York City, where she met Alexander Berkman. Berkman was imprisoned in 1892 for his attempted assassination of Henry Clay Frick. A year later, at the age of 24, Goldman was arrested for inciting a riot among unemployed workers.

Long before she attended John Reed's funeral in Russia in 1920, Goldman was a presence at the early stages of his political and social awakening. A year after Reed graduated, 1911, he attended a Harvard Socialist Club meeting featuring Goldman as a speaker. Reed was there to defend the free speech rights of Harvard radicals. Goldman couldn't actually relate to Harvard undergraduates experimenting with political philosophies that threatened the status quo on their revered campus, and Reed in fact had moved on, fast and far away from Harvard. Goldman, who had lived in a society ruled by the tsar, was already marching towards anarchism as a belief system. Reed, who had once thought that class differences between Harvard students was a big deal, was discovering the brutal reality of America's social class system on the streets of New York: "I couldn't help but observe the ugliness of poverty and all its trains of evil, the cruel inequality between rich people who had too many motor cars and poor people who didn't have enough to eat. It didn't come to me from books that the workers produced all the wealth of the world, which went to those who did not earn it."[17]

Goldman was a regular at Mabel Dodge's salon, where she, Berkman, Reed and a fiery crew of intellectuals, artists and radicals flattered each other by showing up with their reputations before challenging each other with rhetoric and one-upmanship. She attended I.W.W. meetings where the line between socialist principles of overhauling the existing social structures blurred with the anarchist vision of literally blowing them up.

Reed and Goldman crossed paths throughout the decade, occasionally working on plans to recruit and rally laborers to take their fate into their own hands through strikes, marches and disruption of business and government. By 1915, they knew each other so well and they had such name recognition that Reed could set aside his considerable ego for comrade Emma. At a protest rally condemning Goldman's arrest for advocating birth control, Reed and Goldman were scheduled as the final two speakers. A dozen speakers who went before them had a lot to say. Reed, whose sense of comic timing rivaled his gift of gab, addressed the crowd with 11 words: "I am too tired. I too want to hear Emma Goldman." Then he sat down.[18]

Reed did not identify himself as an anarchist, as Goldman did, and he did not engage in violence, but some of his words did foreshadow acceptance of the Bolshevik belief that a true revolution almost guaranteed bloodshed. In 1915 he told the Intercollegiate Socialist Society that workers of the world, if they wanted to get the attention of their abusive employers, should know how to use deadly weapons. Arming citizens with the Second Amendment is dangerous when the workers answer to the capitalists, he told the audience. On the other hand, if the workers themselves were in charge of all industries, including the munitions plants, the social equation would be changed. It would be interesting, Reed said, to see whether working conditions for factory laborers would improve when the laborers are armed and trained.[19]

Reed and Goldman had each other's backs. At a June 1917 anti-conscription rally at Hunt's Point Palace in the Bronx, organized by Goldman and Berkman, Reed showed up ostensibly as a reporter but really to protect the speakers in any way that he could. Local police officers, emboldened by the nation's embrace of militarism and the federal government's assault on free speech, watched passively while soldiers in the audience threw electric light globes at the stage before moving in on the speakers. Reed jumped onto the stage, grabbed a speaker, and whisked him off to safety, while Goldman and Berkman left the building. The next morning Goldman and Berkman were arrested for interfering with the military draft.[20] Reed wrote an article for *The Masses* that described the episode and the convictions of Goldman and Berkman. "In America," he wrote in the story that appeared in the September 1917 issue, "the month just passed has been the blackest month for freedom our generation has known. With a sort of hideous apathy the country has acquiesced in a regime of judicial tyranny, bureaucratic suppression, and industrial barbarism, which followed inevitably the first fine careless rapture of militarism ... the law is merely the instrument of the most powerful interests and there are no constitutional safeguards worthy the powder to blow them to hell.... Meanwhile, organized labor takes it."[21]

As he kept his sights on nothing less than turning the world upside down by mobilizing common laborers against forces that were bigger in numbers, better financed and more comfortable with more to lose, Reed's frustration slid toward a sense of futility, and he found himself sniping at allies such as Lincoln Steffens and Emma Goldman who had lost faith in the Bolsheviks. Author Granville Hicks reported that in 1920, when Goldman arrived in Russia on the *Buford* with other deportees, Reed greeted her warmly but he became irritated with her doubts about the Bolsheviks' ability to govern, feed the people and give them meaningful work.[22]

Big Bill Haywood

Reed met Bill Haywood (who is consistently referred to as Big Bill Haywood in historical accounts of the time) at a Mabel Dodge salon gathering in 1913. Haywood introduced Reed to the Paterson, New Jersey, silk workers strike and its significance in the big picture of social class struggle—workers with no education or financial resources fighting for their lives against the corporate barons with endless resources, politically and monetarily. Haywood struck Reed as informal, raw but measured and, most of all, authentic. He was completely unfazed by talking to educated society women of the Bohemian set. Watching Haywood hold court led Reed to believe they had more than politics in common—he seemed like he could hold a conversation with anyone. Reed wanted to see Haywood in his element, fighting the good fight, taking on the big bad guys while defending the little guys who built things. Reed wanted to see the Paterson strike.[23]

They reconnected in a Paterson jail, after each man had been arrested—along with scores of striking workers—without any charges filed. Haywood introduced Reed to strikers who could help them tell the story of the America laborer fighting for an eight-hour work day.

Reed and Haywood served each other's purposes in Paterson. Reed was kept behind bars for only four days, but his incarceration and flair for self-promotion gave Haywood's labor organization efforts a tremendous boost. The officer who arrested Reed asked for his occupation. "Poet," Reed replied. The New York newspapers loved Reed's cheekiness. They "made more fuss about one reporter," police captain McBride said bitterly, than they had about scores of strikers he had jailed.

Although Reed admired Haywood, the Paterson strike helped him realize that social and economic justice is less about leaders and more about root causes of a society's dissatisfaction. "When it came time for me to go out, I said good-bye to all those gentle, alert, brave men, ennobled by something greater than themselves. They were the strike—not Bill Haywood, not Gurley Flynn, not any other individuals."[24]

So many unfolding events and loose ends left by history converged to build the radical John Reed. Reed had been on the streets of New York for two years, and it helped form his self identity and redefine the world around him, but it was Haywood who took him by the proverbial hand to show him what the world really looked like for people sacrificing their bodies for industry profits.

They had striking differences and similarities. Reed came from a family of affluence and attended Harvard. Haywood was an uneducated mine laborer working in the metal mines of Colorado. Reed spent most of his life repelled by violence until his final years, when he suggested a revolution could not be pulled off without bloodshed. Haywood was known as a violent man who grew to embrace passive resistance. Both men were compelling public speakers, with attractive physical features and personalities—Reed the urbane, charming playboy with a wink and a wild side, Haywood "tall, broad shouldered and strong, with one dead eye and a black Stetson cowboy hat perched upon his scarred and scowling face."[25]

In Roughneck: The Life and Times of Big Bill Haywood, author Peter Carlson drew a multi-layered profile of a complex man feared by capitalists and politicians and adored by the press—for a few years—until the political winds shifted violently. "For awhile, in the heady, giddy days before World War I, when Americans seemed eager for reform, Haywood was tolerated, deemed almost respectable. He was courted by writers and intellectuals, invited to fashionable Fifth Avenue soirees, and summoned to Washington to explain his political philosophy and entertain a federal commission with his remarkable life story. But the guns of World War I blasted away the atmosphere of tolerance." In early September 1917 the *New York Times* described Haywood as "the most hated and feared figure in America."[26] Reed's life had a similar arc as his politics moved further to the left and stayed there; he went from being one of the highest paid journalists in the country to an outlaw under three federal indictments for alleged anti–American activities.

Haywood was mysterious and unpredictable, reveling in the myths the press had created for him. "Frequently described as a 'giant' who stood 'well over six feet' or 'almost seven feet,' Haywood was, when measured in the cold light of prison, just a shade over five feet, eleven inches. It was his presence that was huge."[27] He did not use profanity. He would call himself "a two-gun man from the West" before pulling out his red I.W.W card and his scarlet Socialist Party card in front of a cheering crowd. When federal agents destroyed his Chicago office in search of evidence to put him in prison, they found a plaster cast of a human face. Without losing his cool, Haywood told the officers that it was the death mask of a friend, Frank Little, a half-breed I.W.W. officer who had been dragged out of his bed and hung from a railroad trestle by vigilantes deputized by the federal authorities.[28]

In 1916, when *Metropolitan Magazine*—home for Reed and other radicals—began to soften its left-wing edges to comply with emerging nationalism, its editors used Haywood as an example of how not to run a reformist party. "Two and a half years ago the Socialist Party was still dominated in part by men of the Haywood type.... The Socialist Party has finally and definitely cut loose from the advocates of brute force, and has taken its place as a great civilizing and constructive buoy."[29]

Eugene Debs

Along with Haywood, Eugene Debs may have taken more risks and scored more victories for organized labor than anyone else in first two decades of the 20th century, beginning with the Pullman Strike of 1894 and gaining worldwide attention with the founding of the Industrial Workers of the World, which later became synonymous with violence and political danger. He ran for president five times, earning close to a million votes twice, with his biggest share at 6 percent of the electorate in 1912 and his most stunning performance in 1920, when his 900,000-plus votes were cast while he was in prison.

Debs took a tour of the Midwestern states in 1918 to measure the mood of the electorate in regions that would eventually wear the ubiquitous label "red states"—code for conservative Republican states, a hundred years later. In 1918, the term "reds" was gaining traction as a popular synonym to label the left wing of American politics—Communist, socialist, anarchist, left–non-conformists and even progressive liberals while nationalist propaganda dominated civic dialogue. Debs was considering another run for the presidency in 1920. His deeper concern was the health of the Socialist Party and the relevancy of the American Left, which could not unify over the acceptance or effectiveness of negotiation, protest, civil disobedience or violence.[30]

Reed, blacklisted from almost every mainstream newspaper and magazine in the nation, traveled to Indiana to interview Debs, who had been threatened by police and vigilantes on his speaking tour. (A sign of the times: a former business manager for *The Masses*, who was Reed's primary journalistic connection to socialists, was now directing publicity for the U.S. War Department.) Debs impressed Reed with his calm, gentle humor that was never far from the surface of his defiance. Anger was difficult, if not impossible, to detect. Reed's profile of Debs, which included Debs' arrest in Cleveland in June of 1918, found a home in the *Liberator* in September 1918 along with a piece about the I.W.W. federal court trial.

The progression from grandstanding, fun-loving journalist to angry revolutionary was under way. Reed never lost sight of the people he considered the true heroes of the revolutionary movement, and he was not shy about pointing fingers at those who did lose perspective, in his view. The former included "lumberjacks, harvest hands, miners" while the latter included liberals "who think Karl Marx wrote good anti-trust law." Nor did he lose his gift for floating outrageous ideas to take meaningful steps towards the most outrageous concept of all—a second American revolution. Elaborate plans to rescue Debs from jail were among those ideas. The scheme had no chance. Debs was serving a ten-year prison term stemming from ten counts of sedition for calling upon the working class to resist the military draft at a speech in Canton, Ohio.[31]

Debs and Reed shared a deep affection for the exploited laborer in America, recognizing that their own education and experiences allowed them to develop conceptual thinking about economics that many tradesman could not develop. Reed sprinkled his language with a salt and pepper mixture of romance and anger. Debs, who dropped out of public school at age 14 and attended a local business school at night at age 20, threw in a dash of spirituality here and a touch of testosterone there.

"The worker," Debs told a Kansas trade union audience in 1908, "has under capitalism nothing but his labor. Capital owns the means of production, and the worker, more dependent than ever, must find a buyer for his labor. But 'can you boast of being a man among men' in this context? Of course not: No man can rightly claim to be a man unless he is free. There is something godlike about manhood. Manhood doesn't admit of ownership. Manhood scores to be regarded as private property."[32]

Debs sounded like a contemporary conservative when he talked about personal responsibility as an issue that the working class must grapple with.

"I am not a Labor Leader," he told an audience in Utah. "I do not want you to follow me or anyone else; if you're looking for Moses to lead you out of this capitalist wilderness, you will stay right where you are. I would not lead you into the promised land if I could because if I could lead you in, someone else would lead out. You must use your heads as well as your hands, and get yourself out of your present condition."[33]

Chapter Nine

You Can't Go Home Again, Part II

John Reed wrote *America 1918* in Russia, where he supported a global communist revolution, and in Sweden, where he was detained by authorities but not charged, and in New York, where he faced charges of sedition. The poem could pass as a letter to a loved one that the writer has mistreated or as a melancholy reflection of America's wasted potential. Historian Robert Rosenstone believed that Reed was trying to make sense of what America actually stands for. He suggested that the power of Reed's love for home overpowered his socialist ideology.[1] Whatever his intent, Reed wasn't ready to distance himself from Lenin's suppression of press freedom or Lenin's insistence that democratic-style compromise on public policy would doom Russia's worker revolution. Having witnessed the cold, hungry and tired in New York, and having lived with the cold, hungry and tired in Petrograd, Reed remained unflinching in his assessment that laborers throughout the world had a better chance for a satisfying life under Soviet-style socialism. Upon yet another return to American soil, on April 28, 1918, he championed the communist cause, seizing opportunities to educate Americans about Russia even as he was under federal indictments while U.S. security agents watched his every move. (The *New York Times*, complying with censors, reported that Reed arrived "at an Atlantic port.")[2] *America 1918* suggests that Reed saw his homeland characterized by brashness and boldness, a fighting spirit, beauty and ugliness, dreamers always moving forward, competitors boasting whether they won or lost. His other writings at this time, along with his speeches, suggest he also saw the United States, not Russia, as a nation that will crush the spirit of those who cannot or will not conform. Reed, who often identified himself as a poet, would not abide by a system that promised dream fulfillment but did nothing to help pick up the pieces of shattered dreams. He was an American in love with Russia, one who knew that America was where he had become fearless and famous. In *America 1918* he ached for fundamental fairness for all to enjoy his homeland's beauty and promise.

In 1918–1919, Reed could still claim a wide circle of friends and associates, but many were increasingly turned off by his radicalism. A new crowd of political radicals consisted of younger immigrants who had grown up in poverty; they hadn't attended Harvard or partied with well-known artists.[3] In the final two years of a decade that changed America forever and defined John Reed, he became a man without a country. He was either slow to recognize that reality or, more likely, he refused to accept it. It began with his journey back home after his nomination as Russian consul to New York. Lenin had rejected the nomination. Reed had left for America in February 1918, assuming he had plenty of time to attend his first court trial—and to spread the gospel of revolutionary socialism. He and other staffers at *The Masses* were charged with obstructing military recruitment and enlistment (the trial ended with a hung jury jury after ten days of debate). He was late for the trial. The U.S. State Department had pulled levers and persuaded the Swedish government to block his departure when he reached Christiania. Louise Bryant and Lincoln Steffens cabled Reed, urging him not to come home just yet. Steffens was convinced the Russians were using Reed more than they were working with him. He was livid over the armistice terms Russia was offering Germany, which many anti-war liberals felt was an invitation for Germany to take Russian territory by force. Steffens even asked Reed to persuade Leon Trotsky and Lenin to withdraw their offer to Germany. Reed's reaction to Steffens' idea: "From my viewpoint [your proposal] looks absolutely ridiculous."[4] By trusting Lenin more than he trusted any American government official, Reed managed to inflict more damage to his reputation among friends, political enemies and government authorities.

The cold shoulder Reed received from friends and professional peers upon his return to America in 1918 began with Edgar Sisson, who had been part of the American social circle of journalists, diplomats, and government officers working in Petrograd during the 1917 tumult in Russia. Sisson, former editor of Hearst's *Cosmopolitan* magazine, worked in Russia for George Creel's Committee of Public Information, delivering President Wilson's speeches and distributing U.S. political propaganda—while spying on the Bolsheviks on behalf of the U.S. government. Sisson, doing his job, focused on Reed with some of his reports to the State Department. He was part of the effort to prevent Reed from leaving Sweden in time to take the witness stand in the first *Masses* trial in April 1918.[5]

Although the United States in 1918 had enough socialists, radicals, and angry or disillusioned liberals to produce another million votes (4 percent of the electorate) for Eugene Debs on the presidential ballot in 1920, associating with these types was now unthinkable for many who had claimed to be free thinkers. Charles Copeland, the Harvard professor who, a few years earlier, had groomed Reed for greatness and pouted when his globe-trotting protégé did not immediately respond to his letters, delivered his former student a shivering reality check when they got together in Boston in the spring of 1918. Copeland was friendly but unambiguous about his distaste for Reed's politics in general and his anti-war rhetoric in particular. Copeland, Reed wrote, was "in a frame of mind that thinks no one is a he-man who hasn't gone into naval aviation." Reed, perhaps sparing his mentor the pain of terminating their relationship, told Copeland that perhaps they should stop corresponding.[6]

Heyward Braun described the Harvard freeze-out of Jack Reed in a *New Yorker* profile of Charles Copeland: "His boys were on every front, in the waters, under the earth and the heavens above. Here was the test of gallantry which was the shibboleth of Copey. They wrote to him, scores of them, and brought the lilt of battle to this little man from Maine up in his room in Hollis. Jack was not one of them. Jack was against the war. Out of the whole Copeland fraternity he was the one who stood out and faced trial for obstruction.... Nobody spoke of John Reed. He had been dropped from the Harvard Club."[7]

Reed's beloved father figure, Lincoln Steffens, took a more direct approach to let Reed know he had gone too far astray. Responding to a letter in which Reed complained about his Russian papers held by the State Department and about his mother declaring he had smudged the family name with his politics, Steffens wrote:

> You do wrong to buck this thing. In the first place, the war was inevitable; in the second place, the consequences of war, its by products, are normal and typical; in the third place, the public mind is sick. This last is what I learned in my experiences with it. I gave pain, I tried to speak, always with consciousness that an audience was in trouble, psychologically, and I was just as tender as I could be. But sometimes I saw that what I said cut like a surgeon's knife into a sore place, and I was sorry. I must wait. You must wait. I know it's hard, but you can't carry conviction. You can't plant ideas. Only feelings exist. I think it is undemocratic to try to do much now. Write, but don't publish.[8]

In the spring of 1918, important relationships established in Reed's early 20s—including Marlen Pew and Max Eastman from the *Masse,* and Julian Street from the *Metropolitan*—suffered from what biographer Granville Hicks described as a bitter, headstrong, harsh and intolerant attitude on Reed's part as he increased the heat of his rhetoric rather than adapt to the political winds. While pressing the government about the fate of his notes and documents, Reed proselytized about the promise of a new Russia in speeches to sympathetic crowds of unionized laborers, European-born workers, socialists and radicals. He was not subtle about his intention to report back to Russia about the state of the American working class as he saw it. He did enjoy his meetings with Eugene Debs and I.W.W. leader Bill Haywood, both of whom were more than willing to serve jail time.[9] Few of Reed's friends in journalism were ready for that kind of martyrdom.

A former business manager for the socialist *Masses*, Marlen Pew was working for the War Department in 1918 when he met with Reed in Washington. Looking out the window of Pew's office, observing marching soldiers, Reed made a comment about how silly sheep looked in uniform. Pew said, in essence, that's life, and that Reed should be well beyond ruining his career trying to change things he could not change.[10]

Even his relationship with Max Eastman suffered, although Eastman never stopped publicly expressing his unqualified and passionate support for Reed. After the federal government shut down *The Masses,* Eastman and his backers produced a more politically palatable version of *The Masses*, called the *Liberator*, which aimed for high-minded public discourse about serious issues without crossing the broad line the government had drawn to eliminate criticism. The *Liberator* published Reed's articles on Eugene Debs and the I.W.W. sedition trial, including a scathing description of Judge Kenesaw Mountain Landis and the conditions under which prisoners had been held, pre-trial, on bail too high for them to pay. But there was much, much more that Reed had to say that the *Liberator* could not publish. Reed and Eastman knew what was coming, and both men handled their parting of ways professionally.

"Dear Max," Reed wrote in a letter published in the *Liberator.*

> I'm going to have to resign as one of the contributing editors of the *Liberator.* I've thought about it for a long time, and I make this decision not without emotion, remembering our long work together on the *Masses.*
>
> But I feel that I must take my name off the editorial page. The reason is, I cannot in these times bring myself to share editorial responsibility for a magazine which exists upon the sufferance of Mr. Burleson. [Postmater A.S. Burleson enforced the federal denial of *The Masses*' mailing privileges.]

Of course, this does not mean that I want to stop contributing to the *Liberator*. And in the happy day when we can call a spade a spade without tying bunting on it, you will find me, as you have in the past, Yours for the Profound Social Change, John Reed.

The *Liberator* also published Eastman's reply, beginning "Dear Jack."

> I haven't a word of protest—only a deep feeling of regret.
>
> In your absence we all weighed the matter and decided it was our duty to the social revolution to keep this instrument we have created alive toward a time of great usefulness. You will help us with your writing and reporting, and that is all we ask.
>
> Personally, I envy you the power to cast loose when not only a good deal of the dramatic beauty, but also the glamor of abstract moral principle, is gone out of the venture, and it remains for us merely the most effective and therefore the right thing to do. Yours as ever, Max Eastman.[11]

Meanwhile, *Metropolitan* magazine had turned it back on the man it had once called the most brilliant writer in America. In a *Saturday Evening Post* article published a decade after Reed's death, Julian Street wrote, "H.J. Whigham, who was editor of the *Metropolitan* magazine, tells me in 1916 he gave Jack up for lost." Aside his refusal to cooperate with censors by curbing his anti-war rhetoric, according to Street, Reed told Whigham: "You and I call ourselves friends, but we are not really friends because we don't believe in the same things and the time will come when we don't speak to each other. You are going to see great things happen in this country pretty soon. It may kill me and it may kill you and all your friends, but it's going to be great!"[12]

Reed made speeches. He kept getting arrested. He talked about how the farmers and factory workers carried the weight of all economies on their backs, only to be neglected by those who make money off the workers' sweat. His audiences were enthralled, but the press, police, State Department and, increasingly, his frightened friends saw a man preaching to a marginalized choir of socialists and Marxists. They saw Reed digging himself deeper into not just a political hole, but a legal trench from which he could not emerge safely. Reed, of course, did himself no favors in this regard. He did not just burn bridges. He bragged about doing it beforehand and boasted about doing it after the burning. And he insisted that this statement he wrote in the *Liberator* (the reconfigured *Masses*) held true for every capitalist society: "That in the last analysis the property owning class is loyal only to its own property. That the property owning class will never readily compromise with the working class. That the masses of the workers are not only capable of great dreams but have in them the power to make dreams come true."[13] He was openly advocating a revolution in America based on the template of the Bolsheviks' success in Russia.

His first speech after the initial *Masses* trial took place in New York as part of a celebration of the verdict (the judge had thrown out the first part of the indictment, conspiracy to promote insubordination in the U.S. military). He then spoke at a meeting of immigrants committed to freedom for Finland. He traveled to Washington in an attempt to get his Russian papers from the State Department, without success. While in town, he spoke to a gathering of the James Connolly Socialist Club. At Carnegie Hall in New York on May 18, 1918, he spoke about the Bolsheviks rejecting compromise from moderate Socialists. On May 23, he gave a lecture to a packed house at the New Star Casino, organized by the Harlem Educational Center to raise funds for the *Liberator* and to rally left-wing activists. Former *Masses* editor Art Young also spoke at the event. More than 5,000 people, well above the casino's capacity, jammed into the venue. After every seat was filled, people crowded shoulder to shoulder in the aisles and back up to the doors while others sat on window sills. Many of them heckled and jeered the speaker, but when it seemed that the uproar might become threatening, Reed—never at a loss for words and loving the attention—let the disrupters know who they were dealing with.

"I addressed the Third National Russian Congress!" he told them. The New Star Casino event produced signatures for resolutions urging President Wilson to authorize financial support for Russia's new government in order to save the country.

The Harlem lecture featured talking points that Reed loved to use before a crowd, including ironies and hypocrisies of capitalist economies. Reed pointed out the United States government used the war as justification for imposing temporary shutdowns of major private-sector industries, implying that our capitalist system needs government planning and intervention more than we'd like to admit. In Petrograd, Reed told his audience, in the middle of a revolution with three-fifths of the mines destroyed by insurgent-backed terrorism, there was no government-imposed suspension of industrial production.

From there Reed moved on to speak at Tremont Temple in Boston, where the loudest Harvard students were not revolutionaries but reactionaries hostile to his message. He didn't win them over, although he tried to outmaneuver them with his wit and command of the subject matter. On June 1, he had a speaking engagement planned in Philadelphia, but when he found the venue closed and padlocked, and 500 people waiting outside, he led the crowd to a quiet street, stood on a box and began his lecture. City police arrested him on charges of disobeying a municipal ordinance, inciting to riot and inciting to seditious remarks. Bail was set at $5,000.

Somehow Reed raised the money for his bail as well as another $5,000 for another man arrested at the scene, a Finnish shipyard worker assaulted by the police.[14]

In the spring of 1918, Reed tried to fill a void for Americans who were hungry for information about the Russian Revolution. The void had two primary sources: the dire conditions of America's working class and a compromised mainstream press unable or unwilling to report on one of world history's most important events as it unfolded. The demand for his speeches validated his assessment. Reed lectured in the Bronx on June 4, in Newark two days later, and in Brooklyn on June 7. He was indefatigable. He would take off his coat, roll up his sleeves and talk non-stop for two hours. At Newark, before he spoke his first words, the crowd rose without prompting and sang "The Marseillaise," the French national anthem often cited as the world's preeminent revolutionary song. In Detroit five days later, Moose Hall was filled with Russian-Americans under the watchful eyes of city police officers and federal officers from the Department of Justice. Members of the crowd kept Reed in the building long after the speech ended, asking him questions. Meanwhile, police took 150 members of the audience and held them overnight in a Municipal Building room with no sleeping quarters and no toilets. Exhausted, Reed told a friend that night that the crowds were great, but Americans on the whole did not understand or care about his message. He saw his country turning its back, closing its eyes and covering its ears as world history turned a page. In the morning he rose from his friend's couch and traveled to New York, Worcester and back to New York for more lectures.

Reed delivered a speech in Cleveland shortly after Eugene Debs had been arrested for making seditious remarks. The city was crawling with spies, not all of them working directly for the government; many of them had connections to private organizations, such as the American Protective League, taking their version of American loyalty and justice into their own hands. Reed made authorities even more nervous than they already had been by showing up earlier than they had expected. When he asked a friend to hold his suitcase, police hunted down the man, took Reed's suitcase and confiscated all the contents. They returned the material, telling Reed it had been a mistake. When he left his hotel following the speech, a police officer told him, "We got this place sewed up. We know everything that's going on about everybody in the place. You can't eat your dinner in a restaurant, you can't go to the theatre, you can't lay down to sleep, without we hear every word you utter."[15]

By mid–September he was under three indictments, with a cumulative bail of $12,000. On the day the second *Masses* trial began, he was indicted for a September 13 speech at Hunt's Point Place, the scene of Emma Goldman's arrest—which he had witnessed firsthand, along with Alexander Berman's arrest.

Reed later admitted to being nervous during jury selection for the second trial. A year of relentless political persecution against tens of thousands of Americans showed no signs of stopping for the white, well-educated editors and writers of a left-wing magazine that had already been forced out of circulation. Again, however, his relentless sense of humor emerged as he wrote notes to himself during jury selection. One selected juror said he did not know what Socialism was but he was against it. A cotton manufacturer who made immense profits during the war insisted he would be an impartial juror. A German passionately defended his American patriotism. And another juror earned four cryptic words written from Reed's hand: "son of a bitch."[16]

Defense attorney Seymour Stedman asked each defendant about their position on the war. Reed became tense. He said he had been in active war battlefields 55 times, including the Mexican Revolution and the European War. He went into great detail about trenches in Germany, then talked about his senses shaken when he returned to the pro-war fervor in the United States, which ranged from hysteria to celebration, with knitting parties for soldiers taking place in the Upper West Side and upper Fifth Avenue—a mirror image of the war lust displayed by the well-off European classes four years earlier, celebrating their own poor, less-educated countrymen leaving home to get slaughtered.

> We were in this trench, up to our waists in running water, in the back of the trenches, where it was slightly drier, were dugouts, where the men lived for five days before they were taken back for rest. And the walls of these dugout were of soft mud, they moved slowly down as the man lay down; and the only sounds were the snores of the exhausted people sleeping, and then next were the screams of rats. As we could look at the people as they lay there in the light of the candle, you could see over their faces where insects were crawling, vermin crawling. From this German trench, I remember, lights were going up at one time; they were flashing the lights, lighting up to the other trenches; and we looked through the port-hole, to the enemy trench, eighty yards away. It had been raining for two weeks, two solid weeks of rain had come down, and in this mud midway between the two trenches.

Reed's voice trailed off. Stedman asked him to speak louder.

> Between these two trenches, in the mud, forty yards from each trench, there lay a heap of bodies, all that was left of the last French charge, and these bodies were slowly sinking in the mud, had been left out there wounded to die. Nobody dared to come out, although they were only forty yards from the French trenches, and forty yards from the Germans. There had been no cessation of fighting; the wounded had lain

out there screaming and dying in the mud, and there were sinking in the mud, and in some cases there wasn't anything left of those bodies but an arm or a leg sticking up out of the soft mud with the flesh rotten on it.[17]

Upon his return to the states in early 1916, Reed recounted, he found sock-knitting parties for soldiers, a circuit of well-heeled galas glorifying systematic carnage about which the well-heeled society types showed little interest. They were participating because it was fashionable. Thus, he explained, the headline he wrote, "Knit a Straight Jacket for Your Soldier Boy"—eight words that earned *The Masses* an indictment on charges of interfering with the military draft.

The descriptions of war scenes that he had witnessed first-hand lasted more than an hour—whereupon Reed was rendered momentarily speechless by the defense attorney's question "Didn't you think it was time we got into it if you saw all that?"

Thrown off his game, Reed struggled in a halting voice, "No, I ... I did not think.... I do not see the analogy. I think it was a reason to keep out." He talked about his lifelong passion for history and how obvious it was that the war's only objective, for all combatants, was to protect commercial interests. Judge Manton redirected Reed and Stedman to focus on Reed's state of mind. The judge declared, from the bench, that if Reed had always been opposed to war and was more so after the United States entered the European conflict, he was, by definition, opposed to "obtaining the necessary forces."

Reed, mindful of the trap (the charges included obstruction of recruitment and enlistment), muttered, "No, I was not opposed."

A few minutes later, Judge Manton took over the questioning from Reed's defense attorney. "Are you a Socialist?" he asked. Reed said he was, in fact, a Socialist, although his work with the party had not resulted in his membership until the previous summer.

Prosecuting attorney Barnes asked about military intervention in Siberia, which Reed opposed, and then asked about Reed's infamous shooting of a rifle from a German trench two years prior. His explanation—that he had shot into the air, not at an Allied trench—ended that line of questioning, whereupon Barnes asked: "Do you agree with the views announced in the *Masses* with regard to the desirability of a proletarian revolution against the capitalists and the bourgeoisie?"

"Yes, sir," Reed responded. "All Socialists do."

"All Socialists do?"

"Yes."

"And that, in your mind, is the only war that is worth fighting for?"

"Well," said Reed, finally breaking into his well-known smile, "it is the only war that interests me."

Barnes ended his questioning. Moments later Max Eastman delivered an impassioned description of the persecution of radicals and pacifists. He also told the jury what prosecutor Barnes was going to say during closing arguments. Barnes delivered the message Eastman had predicted before telling the jury a story of his friend who had died fighting for the Allies.

"Somewhere in France, he lies dead, and he died for you and me," Barnes told the jury. "He died for Max Eastman, he died for John Reed, he died for Merrill Rogers. His voice is but one of a thousand silent voices that demand that these men be punished."

Masses editor Art Young, also on trial, had fallen asleep, but was awakened by Barnes' oratory. He whispered to Reed, "Who's he talking about? Who is this hero who didn't die for me?"

"Cheer up, Art," Reed said. "Jesus died for you."[18]

Eight of the 12 jurors voted for acquittal, and the second *Masses* trial ended, the indictment dropped soon thereafter.

Four months later, in February 1919, Reed's Philadelphia trial date on charges of riot and assault and battery began; the charge of incitement to seditious remarks had been dropped. He handled himself well on the witness stand, with fewer hiccups, more poise and less humor than on his first trial. He certainly had opportunity to emulate his father's "fine slashing wit" as the judge, Raymond MacNeille, claimed to be proud of his ignorance about Socialism. But Reed stuck to the facts and his lawyer, David Wallerstein, turned out to be a great ally. Ironically, Wallerstein had credentials that would often raise Reed's suspicion—he was a corporate lawyer, and he was a liberal. Reed, however, had shown many times throughout his dual careers as a journalist and revolutionary that he loved conversing with people who were intellectually honest with their viewpoints that conflicted with his (including Henry Ford, Woodrow Wilson, Theodore Roosevelt and William Jennings Bryan). Reed and Louise Bryant were overnight guests of Wallerstein during the trial, and they enjoyed each other's company. Reed was deeply moved by Wallerstein's successful closing argument, which focused on the First Amendment as he discussed the Philadelphia police treatment of Reed: "I am not a Socialist, but when the superintendent of police can say who shall or shall not speak, it is better that we stop talking about democracy."[19] The jury delivered an acquittal.

More good news soon followed a month later, when *Ten Days That Shook the World* appeared in bookstores. There were predictably unfavorable reviews as well as grudging respect from some quarters of the mainstream press. Reed saw the power of his work in the letters he received from I.W.W. members imprisoned at Leavenworth and other penitentiaries. He learned of a bookseller in Colorado who bought up a hundred copies of *Ten Days* and distributed them to mining camps for the workers. Walter Whitman's friend Horace Traubel, a revolutionary as well as a U.S. military veteran, told Reed, "I have great respect for all you do—and better still, for all you are." Had he lived into his 50s, Reed may have smiled as he read U.S. diplomat George Kennan's assessment of *Ten Days*. Kennan, the architect of the United States' Cold War policy of "containment" in response to Soviet aggression, wrote that "Reed's account of the events of that time rises above every other contemporary record for its literary power, its penetration, its command of detail." Kennan further described Reed's account as "a reflection of blazing honesty and a purity of idealism that did unintended credit to the American society that produced him, the merits of which he himself understood so poorly."[20]

Still, by the time *Ten Days That Shook the World* had been circulated enough to be widely recognized as great journalism, the die had been cast for Reed's reputation—and for many, his legacy—in the waning months of 1918, between the second *Masses* trial and the Philadelphia trial. Good things happened for Jack Reed in 1918 and 1919, but the impenetrable bond between America's corporate and political culture turned what could have been victorious moments into punishment for a man deemed dangerous by those in the highest ranks of power.

Less than two months before the end of World War I, in September of 1918, a U.S. Senate subcommittee held a hearing on alleged links between German propagandists and the American brewing and liquor industries. Political winds shifted the hearing's focus to the threat of Bolshevism in America. Louise Bryant and Jack Reed were among those who testified after the committee spent hours calling upon fervent anti–Socialists who spoke of, among other things, the Bolsheviks' immorality, which included free love and insinuations of polygamy.

Bryant stunned the senators on the panel with her aggression, her knowledge of international affairs, her skill at avoiding entrapment, and her ability to turn the rhetorical tables on her inquisitors. She was a force to be reckoned with from the outset. Asked about whether she believed in the sanctity of the oath, she replied, "It seems to me as if I were being tried for witchcraft."[21] Then came Reed, who spoke the truth as he saw it, from the heart, and walked away thinking that he had made progress for a new revolutionary America.[22] He gave the senators a tutorial on the

Russian Revolution; such was his command of the topic, his comfort with speaking under pressure, and his humor that the committee could not portray him as an enemy in their midst. Senator Wolcott said, "Your mental agility, is, I confess, too much for me." Reed spoke of factory management in the soviets (local councils), the press, violence from the counter revolutionaries, the dissolution of the Constituent Assembly, food cards, crime and more—concepts illustrated with detail and passion. Searching for a button to push, the senators tried to connect Reed's revolutionary zeal with the prospect of a violent overthrow of the U.S. government.

"Have you in any of your public speeches advocated a revolution in the United States similar to the revolution in Russia?" Senator Humes asked.

"I have always advocated a revolution in the United States," Reed replied.

"You are in favor of a revolution in the United States?"

"Revolution does not necessarily mean a revolution by force," Reed said. "By revolution I mean a profound social change. I do not know how it will be attained."

"Do you not in your speeches leave the impression with your audience that you are talking about a revolution of force?"

"Possibly."

"Do you mean to leave that impression?"

"No. My point is that the will of the people will be done; the will of the great majority of the people will be done."

"That is a sound point."

"That is my point, and if the will of the great majority is not done by law, it will be done some other way. That is all."

"Do you not know, Mr. Reed, that the use of the word revolution in the ordinary meaning carries the idea of force, arms and conflict?"

"Well, as a matter of fact, unfortunately, all these profound social changes have been accompanied by force. There is not one that has not."

The exchange may have been more civil and respectful than either side expected. At the end, Senator Walcott asked Reed, "Suppose you lived in one of these [Soviet] villages. And you had a couple of sons—and they were twins." Reed interjected and bowed. "Thank you, sir," he said.[23]

Newspaper accounts of the hearing were not so civil or respectful. Stanley Frost of the New York *Tribune* called Reed "a man to whom clever phrases are an intoxication and patient study utterly impossible." Frost also called Reed "a soldier of fortune" and "a matinee idol." The Jacksonville (Florida) *Times-Union* editorialized on Reed's testimony with the headline "One Man Who Needs the Rope." By supporting the Bolsheviks and advocating revolution in his own country, the editors asserted, Reed had earned the ultimate punishment. "If a man should be hanged for instigating another to murder one man, he should certainly be hanged for instigating men to kill thousands of men. If the law is defective, why wait until tomorrow to remedy its defects? A law should be passed at once against such utterances as those brazenly made by this man Reed, and then as soon as possible ten thousand hangings should follow."[24]

Reed had always been selective when answering his critics. For all his bombast, he seemed to know that continuously responding to criticism served only to validate the critics.[25] He had, in the past, responded to the *New York Times,* perhaps because he expected the paper to hold itself to a higher level of public discourse. But he did not feel compelled to repeat an autobiographical sketch that he had delivered earlier in the year at a speech in Brooklyn, where he had been warned that any criticism of the government could result in another arrest. His words that night, before a large audience that included one hundred policemen, did not land him in jail. The contrasts and hypocrisies he outlined, and the nuanced explanation of what it means to be an American patriot and a revolutionary at the same time, did not win him any new friends in high places.

"My family came to this country, both branches, in 1607," he began. "One of my ancestors was Patrick Henry, who signed the Declaration of Independence; another of my ancestors was a general under George Washington; and another was a colonel on the northern side in the Civil War. I have a brother, a major in the aviation corps, now in France. I am a voter and a citizen of the United States, and I claim the right to criticize it as much as I please. I criticize the form of it because I claim that it is not a democratic enough government for me. I consider the Soviet government a more democratic government at the present time than our own government."[26]

Reed's writing at this time was confined to radical and socialist publications; he was blackballed from the mainstream press. With his essays shielded from readers who comprised public opinion, he kept hitting the road for more speeches. Subsequently getting lambasted by the editors in the popular periodicals and daily newspapers was better than being ignored, as far as Reed was concerned. When he outlined the shortcomings of liberals and Socialists with regards to making serious changes that America needed, the public saw an un–American zealot. He had, in fact, moved to the furthest left-wing boundaries of the socialism as America knew it.

"Socialism is really Jeffersonian democracy, to intimate that all we want are reasonable reforms, labor legislation and the full dinner pail," he wrote in *Revolutionary Age*. He said Socialists had adopted the strategy of "first make a liberal, and then convert him to Socialism." And this nugget: "Fully a third of the Socialist votes are, in normal times, cast by middle-class persons who think that Karl Marx wrote a good anti-trust law."

"I have no quarrel with that kind of propaganda—except that it does not make Socialists," he wrote. The American left wing, he said, "must find out from the American workers what they want most, and they must explain this in terms of the whole labor movement, and they must make the workers want more—make them want the whole revolution." The last line—"make them want" more—came from a place in Reed's heart that ached. He told friends that the American working class was the least informed about government and economics than any country in which he had lived and worked, including Mexico and Russia.[27]

* * *

Ten Days That Shook the World made the demand for Reed as a public speaker stronger; he could not say no, because at this point the spoken word was a better tool for him than the printed word. The word "Bolshevism" had become a lightning rod in America—for those who knew nothing about it and believed that it was an organization of terrorists and for committed Socialists who believed that working within the current U.S. political system could help make Socialism work. Because Reed proudly cast himself as a Bolshevik, nothing he could say or write would persuade the government, the mainstream press or the public at large that he wanted what was best for Americans.

He understood what was going on, politically, but his message—which conveyed his convictions—did not budge: a workers' revolution was possible in America. It had happened, after all, against all odds in Russia. What was more improbable, changing the course of 300 years of tsarist rule or challenging the capitalist class in America that had set the rules for slightly more than a century? Reed pressed forward even after confiding to a friend that the American working class was the worst informed working class in the world. He wore as a badge of honor the petty slights that branded him as persona non grata among those who held access to power and money. A Fifth Avenue bank that he had been patronizing refused his deposits because he had overdrawn his account. The Harvard Club suspended him for an unpaid bill. Reed laughed, claiming the moral high ground.[28]

He did not always take the high ground. At a March 6, 1919, debate with moderate Socialist Joseph Shaplen (who had spent time in Russia, unlike many American Socialists). Shaplen held that the Bolshevik regime was undemocratic. Reed's retort: the Bolsheviks believe in democracy of the working class and no democracy for anybody else. He quoted Marx and cited statistics showing how productive the worker-owned factories were at that moment. But in the heat of the moment, Reed ignored the debate protocol and verbally attacked Shaplen, saying he had connections to the tsarist regime and that he favored U.S. intervention in Russia. It was not Reed's finest moment.[29]

The relentless 1919 speaking tour—Minneapolis, Cleveland, Detroit, Toledo and Chicago during one ten-day stretch—forced Reed to study Marx and economics with more intensity than ever before. Reed's earlier writings about the working class—from New York, Paterson, Ludlow, Lawrence, Mexico, Europe, Russia and points between—were heavily dependent on what he witnessed and what he heard, his ability to connect with just about anyone, and saturation reporting. Back in America in 1919, he conducted a deep dive into Marx to add weight to his speeches. The added benefit of hitting the books again was that it prepared him to operate within the Socialist Party in the unglamorous, detail-oriented work of a grunt. The working class revolution was no longer about Jack Reed discovering ideas and sharing them. It was more about planting those ideas into the minds of enough people to make a difference in a world of injustice. It was about propaganda, and he was ready to be a propagandist.[30]

Unfortunately for Reed, moving into the inner workings of party politics exposed him to more frailties of human nature than he wanted to see. While he still showed signs of his trademark mischiefness—such as plotting to help Eugene Debs escape from jail, and discrediting moderate Socialists by producing a newspaper that looked exactly like their party publication—Reed spent much of 1919 taking very seriously the hot-blooded rhetorical wars between the so-called right wing of the Socialist Party, the left wing, the splinter group that called itself the American Communist Party, and still another breakaway wing that called itself the Communist Labor Party. To say that an overwhelming majority of Americans didn't know or care about the issues or party conflicts that consumed these groups would be an understatement. And it would not be overstatement to say that a similar number of Americans dismissed all of these left wingers as Bolsheviks.

Journalist Bruce Watson, author of *Sacco and Vanzetti*, described the political climate in post-war America, 1919:

> Scarred by war, devastated by plague, terrorized by bombs, America lashed out against a new scapegoat, one that had surged to prominence during the 1917 Bolshevik

Revolution. Reds had stirred up "the Negroes." Reds had caused all those strikes. Reds had infiltrated the schools, the government, the movies. America's first Red Scare was shorter than its McCarthy-era successor yet far more intense. Teachers were fired for merely mentioning Bolshevism. A Connecticut man was jailed for praising Lenin. Following a shoot-out in central Washington, one of the accused—both a Wobbly and a veteran—was dragged from jail, castrated with a razor, hung from bridge, and riddled with bullets. Then the federal government took over [in the form of raids orchestrated by attorney General Palmer and J. Edgar Hoover]. Just before Christmas, the feds shipped 249 radicals to Russia on a ship nicknamed "the Soviet Ark."[31]

Against that backdrop, Reed briefly earned enough income to help his family for the first time since since the mainstream press blackballed "the best reporter of his generation" for his European War reporting in 1916. Solon Fieldman, president of Press Forum newspaper service syndicate, paid Reed 15 cents a word (more than than many periodicals pay writers a century later) for a series of columns in which he debated former socialist Henry L. Slobodin, who had left the party because of its anti-war position. The topics included internationalism, government, democracy, militarism, industry, agriculture, the family, social welfare, education, religion, culture and scientific progress—all of it in relation to Bolshevism. The forum was called "Bolshevism—Promise or Peril?" Reed made several hundred dollars before Fieldman realized that his client newspapers were publishing only Slobodin's anti–Socialist columns. Reed sent some money to his mother, whose family finances were in ruins. His brother, Harry Reed, could not land a job despite a stellar military record and a Harvard degree. Harry was trying clean up the family's once-robust estate but had difficulty selling their property. Tension rose between the brothers over Jack's unavailability and between mother and oldest son over Reed's politics and the further tarnishing of the family name.[32]

Reed had opportunities to rein in his assault on the America's political, social and economic systems. So many writers and editors had put their boxing gloves on the shelf—including Lincoln Steffens and Upton Sinclair. So many left-wing journalists of the World War I decade, including Max Eastman, had opted to soften their political criticism in order to remain in print. Reed, whose politics had only marginal effect on grudging praise from the mainstream press for *Ten Days That Shook the World*, gave no signals that he was open to compromise or softening his message. Had he walked away from the Bolshevik wing and supported the moderates in the Socialist Party, his strong ideas about a system rigged against laborers may have connected with a larger audience. But he did not want to write for intellectuals. They did not make economies work, as far as he could discern, and they did not, as he could tell, do anything important.[33]

Nine. You Can't Go Home Again, Part II

In the fall of 1918, Upton Sinclair declined to publish an article Reed wrote for *Upton Sinclair's Monthly Magazine for Social Justice by Peaceful Means*. Reed responded with a respectful letter to the editor, saying he understood Sinclair's editorial decision but disagreed with his judgment:

> The war to you seems simple, the Russian revolution complicated. I must confess that it seems the other way round for me; not that the Russian revolution is entirely simple, however. I cannot see how any Socialist can doubt either the integrity of the great majority of the Soviet leaders, or the splendor of the Bolshevik dream, or even the possibility of its practical working out. All intellectuals will criticize and be disappointed with the social revolution when it starts; and if it seems hasty, unprepared for, or based on irrealizable dreams, they will perhaps oppose it. But if the overwhelming masses of the people are going quite consciously somewhere, neither you nor I [will stop it] ... I know it is the facts I tell you that you do not believe; and I must be content to wait for history. But I know that I am right. I have not dreamed, but have studied and investigated as I never did before.[34]

He called the Russian revolution a work in progress, not a dream. It had once been a dream belonging to workers, farmers, peasants and their political leaders, but now it was the proverbial day after, and Reed insisted he was not dreaming. How does one prove that that a vision is not a dream? Reed decided the only way to answer that question was to take one more plunge, in September 1919, into unchartered waters. Instead of waiting for history to prove him right, he chose to help the Bolsheviks create history. His final quest took him back to Russia, with the intent of creating a new beginning from the ashes of tsarist rule and bloody revolution, layered with the indomitable hope of the human spirit. His life would end a year later.

CHAPTER TEN

Revolution: The Day After

The writer and rebel had been part of the national conversation for most of the decade. His actions and words went from attention-grabbing (Paterson) to spectacular (Mexico) to self-inflicted damage (the German front and U.S. labor rallies) to the inconceivable (Russia). By 1919, John Reed stood alone. Nobody fighting the cause for socialism in America— with the exception of Eugene Debs—had the name recognition of John Reed. Nobody among the radicals and revolutionaries within U.S. borders had the pedigree or resume that Reed had. None of them had had the access to power, the fame and or the commercial success that Reed once had before he kept marching leftward, beyond acceptable boundaries, all the way to Russia. By 1919, rebellion had long ceased being a pastime for Reed. It was a personal crusade with roots dating back to 1912, when he realized how much his father had sacrificed to fight for his beliefs. Before he risked a long prison sentence with his public war against the U.S. government, Jack had turned his back on commercial success to keep fighting for social and economic justice (he was one of the nation's highest-paid international correspondents by the time he began covering World War I.)[1] He made a decision to go beyond the war of arm's length rhetoric found in essays and the editorial pages and past the field of political battle. He had been on the front lines of life-and-death fighting, on the military fields of Mexico and France, and in the urban battles of American cities between police and protestors. But he had been there to tell stories. As the decade wobbled perilously to an ending that offered less hope for America's claim to personal liberty, he had moved well past Jack Reed, the flamboyant storyteller. He was making a case, through research, investigation and accounts picked up through his gift for getting people to tell their stories, that America had no authentic claim as the land of liberty. The ideals of the Russian Revolution were exactly what the overwhelming majority of American workers needed, according to Reed. The ideals the Bolsheviks fought for applied to workers in every nation that built economies on the principles of capitalism and the backs of laborers. Reed was not the only person delivering this message. But by picking up newspapers, their primary and often only source of information, most Americans learned that the people delivering this message were labeled radicals, zealots, anarchists, Communists, Socialists, Bolsheviks, terrorists or all of the above—demons ready to steal everything that Americans valued. Eugene Debs and Big Bill Hayward went to prison. America had heard enough from the radicals by 1919. Jack Reed—loud, aggressive, angry, occasionally flashing his hallmark charm and humor—continued to shout from stages and pages when he was not immersing himself in the machinations of left-wing party politics, American-style. In response, government authorities from local police to the U.S. attorney general's office and the State Department made it clear that they considered Reed a dangerous man. They overwhelmed the meetings where he delivered speeches. They did not leave him alone until 1920, when they did nothing to extract him from two months of solitary confinement in a Finnish jail to face his sedition charges in a U.S. court.

In Boston that spring, Reed railed against U.S. support for the Russian White Army (loyal to the tsar) that was trying to take back the country now in the hands of the Bolshevik wing of the Communist Party. "No one who thinks it was wrong to go into Belgium (during the European War) can think it it right to go into Russia," he said. "The Red Terror isn't confined to Russia; we have a little terror here."[2]

History shows he was right about domestic terrorism in the United States. The pushback against socialists, communists, anarchists and outspoken critics of the U.S. government devolved into mob mentality in 1919. The city of Cleveland (which by 1919 already had decades of well-established, organized socialist activity) was the scene of a May Day riot that began when a World War I veteran took offense at red flags held by protestors marching toward the public square. Fist fights morphed into brawls that devolved into a melee leading to a mob ransacking the Socialist Party headquarters on Prospect Avenue. Dozens of people were injured, and two people died. The Cleveland May Day rally had been called to protest the jailing of Eugene Debs, who had been convicted in a Cleveland federal court.[3] The original May Day held for empowerment of workers took place a year before Reed was born, on May 1, 1886, in Chicago, where workers demanded an eight-hour work day. Three years later, in 1889, when Reed was not yet three years old, the International Socialist Conference declared that May 1 would be an international holiday for laborers.

Ten years after the Cleveland May Day violence, the mainstream press was still firing its shots at disruptive left-wing agitators. "To old fashioned people, May Day means flowers, grass, picnics, children, clean frocks. To up and coming socialists and communists it means speechmaking, parading, bombs, brickbats, conscientious violence. This connotation dates back to 1886, when some 200,000 U.S. workmen engineered a nationwide strike for an 8-hour day."[4]

The Boston May Day rally in 1919 led to 12 arrests and jail time for the demonstrators. Among the targets was William James Sidis, a 15-year-old graduate of Harvard. The lead paragraph of a *Boston Herald* story following his sentencing reveals a slice of the tenor of the times: "William James Sidis, who was graduated from Harvard at the age of 15, told Judge Albert F. Hayden in the Roxbury Municipal Court yesterday afternoon that he is a Socialist, a believer in the Soviet form of government, that he believes in evolution, that he does not believe in God, that his god is evolution, and that he believes in our form of government to the extent of the Declaration of Independence."[5]

In Erie, Pennsylvania, that spring, Reed spoke to a group called the Erie Soviet of Workers, which gave him a written testimonial to thank him for "the valuable and faithful services you have unflinchingly rendered the Russian Socialist Republic since your arrival in this country from Russia." In Brooklyn, he referenced World War I, which Americans at the time knew as the European War, the Great War, the War to End All Wars. "Well, the war is finished, comrades, and where the hell is the democracy? Now in New York City, free speech is suppressed; Socialists are not allowed to meet; the red flag is banned; periodicals are barred from the mails; all evidence of Prussianism appear." The Great War was exactly what he had called it from the time he set foot on European soil as a war correspondent in 1914: a war of traders, a war of capitalists trying to win the zero-sum game of capitalism. "Now the war is ended," he said. "But a new war is beginning, and this time it is a war between two ideas."[6]

In fact, there was more than one war and more than two competing ideas within the left-wing organizations in America. Radicals fighting reformists. Left-wingers and right-wingers within the Socialist Party refusing to work with each other. By the summer of 1919, the revolutionary movement in America had splintered into finger-pointing, name-calling factions. The national Socialist Party expelled factions it considered too radical, including the entire Michigan delegation and seven foreign-language federations that contributed 30,000 members to the national party. Soon afterward it expelled the Massachusetts and Ohio chapters for similar reasons. Reed, for the most part, was in step with the radical left wing that had fallen out of favor with the Socialist Party, although this group continued to fight among themselves over tactics, vision and rhetoric.[7]

Reed knew enough about himself at this point to know that his formal American history education had been lacking before enrolling at Harvard (he blamed the "dead rhetoric" of his uninspiring classroom teachers) and that he hadn't been particularly interested in catching up on that subject in college because campus life was far too interesting for that. The history he did know—picked up in pieces as context for the stories he had reported and the essays he had written as a professional journalist—convinced him that revolution was the only path toward the life, liberty and the pursuit of happiness that America promised. His country's willful ignorance about socialism astonished him. By spring of 1919 he had devoted himself to revisiting the works of Karl Marx. Reed had talked to Lenin, learning about his preparation for revolution since 1905. Reed at this point could articulate visions of worker control of industries. This was policy wonk stuff that he need for his public debates with Joseph Shapley to answer his critics and to offer his trade union audiences a glimpse of a future with worker empowerment. Reed had become a more serious man in 1919, although he tried to hold on to his sense of humor. In one article he wrote, he referred to a meeting of right-wing socialists as "The Convention of the Dead." In another instance, he went a step further, mocking the alarmist nature of the *Socialist* newspaper when it warned party members of infiltration by Communists. He produced a near-replica of the *Socialist*, full of what we now refer to as "fake news."[8]

Divisions within the ousted Socialist Party radicals led to a proposal, in June of 1919, for a new American Communist Party. That effort initially failed, but by early July the left wing had agreed to hold a conference in Chicago on August 31, with a plan to rejoin the Socialist Party if they had garnered enough support for their group to take over the organization. If that failed, they would start their own Communist Party. Reed and 80 members of the left wing, without credentials, invaded Machinist Hall in an effort to save the Socialist Party. The tactic led to pushing, shoving and fist fights. Reed, still proposing a new Communist Party, was expelled from the convention along with 30 other left-wing socialists.

Police broke up the convention. Reed and his allies found a meeting room downstairs from the Socialist Party's gathering for an impromptu meeting, where they formed the Communist Party. Reed was not alone believing in revolution and the impossibility of success through the established American political system. History cannot tell us how many people agreed with his vision for the future, but at that point, he had perhaps 29 allies in America—the group that had been kicked out of the Socialist Party convention. Even that group failed to produce a consensus on what to do next. Reed believed they could still align with radicals who remained upstairs with the Socialist Party. The nascent Communist Party could not agree to do that, so the next day Reed led yet another splinter group to the nearby I.W.W. Hall, where they formed the Communist Labor Party. Reed became chairman of a committee charged with drawing up a program. This move authorized him to listen to more arguments over whether the platform should be loyal to the teachings of Marx, the experience of Lenin and the Bolsheviks ... or whether it should back off and negotiate with the left-wing groups that were less radical. Reed, for his part, outlined a plan for training the working class for the seizure of power—a plan based in large part of what he had seen in his reporting for *Ten Days That Shook the World*.[9]

The spectacle of American radicals cannibalizing each other made it easy for authorities to paint the political left as a bunch of disgruntled crazies with dangerous ideas. John Reed was trying to win an argument about the future of the American working class and American ideals, but fewer people were paying attention to the debate in the days, weeks and months following passage of the Espionage and Seditions Acts. Arrest the radicals, lock them up, ship them out, and then play the Star Spangled Banner.

Reed was in deep, long past the stigma of blackballed writer, seemingly off the rails as far as his connection with American politics was concerned. He snatched fleeting moments to revisit pieces of his self-identity that often got tossed aside. A month before the Chicago convention in August 1919, Reed had snuck off to Provincetown with Louise Bryant for time on the beaches. "I wish I could stay here," he told some friends. "Maybe it will surprise you, but what I really want is to write poetry." Asked why he didn't do that, he said, "I've promised too many people." In Chicago, Reed reached out to Sherwood Anderson during the tumult of the Socialist Party convention. They went for a walk. Reed talked about poetry and how much he still daydreamed about being a poet first and letting everything else in his life compete for second and third place. He showed Anderson some of his unpublished poems. Anderson was impressed. Their walk-and-talk lasted about 30 minutes. Then Reed abruptly ended the conversation, explaining that he was needed at the convention.[10]

Ten. Revolution: The Day After

The Communist Labor Party appointed Reed as its international delegate, with his first order of business being a trip to Russia to secure his party's recognition from the Communist International group. Reed spent the next few weeks writing articles for party publications and the few remaining left-wing publications available to the public, including the *Liberator*, run by Max Eastman. He attended an endless series of meetings to solidify his party's platform and to prepare for his Russian trip. He made more speeches, this time to much smaller groups. Whatever he did during this time, he did it while dodging the police. The U.S. government had outlawed the Communist Party and the Communist Labor Party.

Reed had a lot of work to do before he left for Russia in late September 1919. Both the Communist Labor Party and the Communist Party were on the clock; they wanted and needed certification from the Communist International as a first step toward showing commitment to a worldwide workers' revolution. It was simply understood that no nation could put the vision of Karl Marx into application without the help of allies and coalitions, given the power of capitalist countries to impose trade embargoes and military threats—just as Western powers had been doing to the USSR, the reconfigured Russia. The two communist parties in America, at odds with each other, needed to move quickly in order to secure recognition so that the party left behind would be forced to acquiesce to their rivals' platform. Working in secrecy to avoid arrest for being a communist, Reed spent weeks writing articles and speeches for the Communist Labor Party at their headquarters. His bravado emerged occasionally, as when novelist-journalist Don Marquis saw him walking on Fifth Avenue in New York and asked him, essentially, what the hell he was doing out here. "This is a dickens of a place to hide," Marquis said. "None better," Reed replied. "And besides, the red-hunters never catch anybody."[11]

The only way to leave the country for his mission in Russia was to go undercover to avoid arrest. Reed posed as a stoker on a Scandinavian ship, taking the name Jim Gormley. It was his eleventh crossing of the Atlantic since the spring of 1910. While many of his shipmates assumed that his name was fiction, they respected the hard labor that Reed performed. They were not surprised when he sneaked off the ship in Gergen. He reached Christiana in mid–October. He networked in the shadows, seeking and finding radicals. He also managed to get a letter to Louise, expressing his doubts that a revolution could happen in Scandinavia. In Norway, where he crossed the border by foot on October 22, Reed learned about terror and the murders of socialists and suspects carried out by the Russian White Army loyal to the tsar. Within a couple of weeks he was a stowaway on a ship to Finland, beneath the bow in disgusting, unsanitary conditions. He had no doubt that if he were found, he would be murdered. When he got off the ship with the help of sympathetic workers, he briefly walked the streets in a panic after his connections disappeared and he followed the wrong group of workmen. Finally able to sleep in a bed in an apartment belonging to a fellow radical, after he found his connections, Reed learned more about terror targeting communists, socialists and Bolsheviks in Slavic countries, Germany and the United States.[12]

Reed reached Petrograd in November 1919. It had been two years since he had left Russia to write *Ten Days*, publish the book and make speaking tours across America. During those two years, the civil war that followed the Bolshevik victory left Petrograd and many Russian villages with scenes of devastation and horrifying living conditions. Upon his return to Russia, Reed found his way to Moscow to resume his work for the Communist Labor Party recognition. There the Communist International offered him living arrangements, including an apartment and food, that were clearly above those of working class Russians. Reed chose to find his own apartment and cook his own food. When he had the first of many meetings with Vladimir Lenin, the president expressed his approval.[13]

That winter, 1919-1920, was among the worst in Russian history. Food shortages were a way of life. The government took good care of the military but the factory workers were on their own after authorities gave their soviets a structural framework to take care of their own needs. Reed felt the hunger and cold, but he could always use his connections in the Soviet government if he so desired. He rationalized the inequities as the cost of revolution, the aftermath of organized terror on the part of the Red Army to fight off insurgents trying to take back the government, and the devastating blockades that stopped foreign shipments of medical supplies and food to Russia.

It was a society still struggling to enter the 20th century while having skipped much of the world's industrial progress of the 19th century. And yet Reed, as he had done on the streets of New York, in the factory towns of Colorado, Ohio and the northeastern United States, as he had done in Mexico, searched for and found beauty and hope in the human spirit. He did this the way he had always done it—by roaming to places psychically and geographically removed from the urban centers where the professionals, politicians, writers and artists did their thing. He talked to peasants and villagers, authentic and humble, struggling make a living, the masses who were supposed to benefit from economic and social revolution. They were hopeful, but with no history of formal education in these parts, many of the locals could not conceptualize their role in a new Russian society. One peasant told Reed, "This is a poor village.... I do not own my own house. But I did own two horses, and they called me bourgeois, and took one away." Another villager told Reed he didn't understand why he should eat vegetables when there were nice fat dogs running around. A third man told Reed that the Communists were doing good things, but because he had a wife and three children, he could not formally join the party because party membership required considerable sacrifice.[14]

Moshe Lewin, a historian who worked on a collective farm in the USSR, as a soldier in the Soviet army, and as a senior fellow at the Russian Institute of Columbia University, described the scene differently in *Lenin's Last Struggle*, published a half-century later:

> The workers undoubtedly played a major role in the seizure of power by Bolsheviks. Throughout the civil war they continue to provide the Soviet Army and administration with their most dedicated cadres. But this war caused an incalculable loss of lives and installations. Many factories were destroyed and production had come to a standstill. The workers, who had led the struggle in every sphere of activity, suffered particularly heavy losses and many of the survivors had dispersed and taken refuge in the countryside. At the same time the most dedicated and most gifted among them had been mobilized by the governmental services, both local and central. The administrative machine considerably reduced the ranks of the working class.[15]

In the city of Serpukhov, about 60 miles south of Moscow, factory shop-committee delegates walked through deep snow for miles to hear the famous John Reed talk about a new American revolution. One of them said to Reed:

> Tell our brothers in America that for three years the Russian workers have been bleeding and dying for the revolution, and not our own revolution, but the world revolution. Tell our American comrades that we listen day and night for the sound of their footsteps coming to our aid. But tell them, too, that no matter how long it may take them, we shall hold firm. Never shall the Russian workers give up their revolution. We die for Socialism, which perhaps we will never see.[16]

Reed kept moving, has he always had. He visited more Russian villages, where he saw hope. He saw new medical centers, education programs, schools, maternity hospitals, dispensaries and child-care centers—almost all of it free—created in areas that had had none of these basics of community life before.[17]

The Communist International, in December, formalized a plan for the U.S.-based Communist Party and Communist Labor Party to merge in order to move forward with the certification from the CI. The fact that both American parties had been outlawed by U.S. authorities made this problematic. On January 2, 1920, as part of the infamous Palmer raids,

U.S. federal agents working under Attorney General A. Mitchell Palmer, arrested 10,000 Americans across the United States, raiding Communist, Communist Labor and Socialist meeting places. Reed was among those indicted three weeks later. The raids occurred just two weeks after one of the most famous mass deportation episodes in history, when the Department of Labor and law enforcement agents put 249 foreign-born radicals on the ship *Buford* bound for Europe.

Reed, aware that his indictment (for organizing the Communist Labor Party in America) almost guaranteed imprisonment under the climate of hysteria, made plans to return to the United States. He wanted to face to the charges against him, knowing that the court system had ruled on his side in his previous cases. He wanted to be with Louise. He wanted to support his friends and comrades back home who had supported his writing, his politics, even his amateur theater projects. Given what American law enforcement and citizen mobs were doing to radicals at political gatherings, maybe trial publicity could help the communists. He could be of use to the Communist International and the Russian Communist Party to close the deal on the merger of the American communist groups. Emma Goldman, who had been deported to her Russian homeland, and who was losing hope for a true workers' revolution on a global scale, tried to convince Reed the the fight was almost over and that they had lost. He still wanted to go home, yet again. They argued. The old friends were not averse to heated disagreements as a term of their relationship.[18]

For the next two months, from early January to March 1920, Reed lived in a unique kind of hell, trying to leave a country that had been turned upside down and ravaged, a country trying to crawl out of the rubble of revolution, a country for whom he had given his heart and soul, to his homeland, a place that had made him who he was, a place that was crushing dissent and free speech, a land where the criminal justice system was ready to imprison him for his politics. He spent those three months trying to get past armies that were blocking passage for Russians trying to leave the country. On this first failed attempt, he spent a day and a night in Latvia, at a broken-down train station where the windows were broken, the pipes had frozen, the floor was covered with ice, and 300 soldiers lay dead, frozen, outside the building. He was five miles from the nearest village. On second attempt, he hid in the bunker of a Finnish ship. Authorities found him, charged him with smuggling, and placed him in solitary confinement at a small-town police station.

For the following 13 weeks, from early March to early June of 1920, John Reed remained in solitary confinement in Finland, never changing his clothes, eating bad food, hearing nothing from the U.S. State Department or his wife. He was allowed to read, but his letters to Louise and American diplomats produced no response. (Bryant, knowing that he wanted to come back home for the trial, worked from her end to get information about Reed.) With the help of a Finnish liberal who was trying to obtain legal counsel for him, Reed decided to fake his own death. The liberal, Madam Aino Malmburg, had managed to plant a story in New York newspapers on March 17 about Reed's arrest, but the State Department responded that it had no corroboration. A few weeks later, Malmburg planted another story so several American papers reported on April 10 that Reed had been executed in Finland. The State Department, forced to investigate, said no, Reed was very much alive in a Finnish jail and the U.S. government would not interfere with Finland's criminal justice system. The State Department reported that the smuggling charges were based in part on Reed carrying money and jewels worth 880,000 Finnish marks along with moving picture films, photographs, pamphlets, a seaman's card for a man named James Gormley and forged passports and letters made out to Samuel Arnold, Jr.[19]

Reed did not know whether his wife knew of his arrest until late April, when Finnish authorities allowed him to communicate with America. He and Louise exchanged letters over the next few weeks, catching up, writing about his smuggling charges and mysterious new allegations about treason against the Finnish state, about his health and his financial means. From early to mid–May he received information from Louise that gave him hope; she believed that some American officials were reaching out to the Finnish government to secure Reed a passport. But then the information and hope evaporated. Bryant and Reed were unaware that the Russian government had been negotiating for Reed's release as part of a prisoner exchange: two Finnish professors, alleged counter-revolutionaries, to be traded for Reed. (Legend holds that Lenin claimed he would trade a whole college faculty for Reed.)[20] On June 7, Reed informed Louise that his application for a passport to the United States had been rejected and that the Finns were ready to hand him over to the Russians.

The end was ugly. In the spring of 1920 Reed was sent back to Russia, where it was obvious to anyone who saw him that his health had been ravaged by prison conditions. His appearance has been described as gaunt with a sallow complexion, gray-faced, loose skin, flabby, while wearing clothes that appeared shredded like rags. Still, energized by a letter from Louise saying she was leaving for Russia. He dove right back into his work as a revolutionary, now on behalf of the Soviet Union. His preparation for the Second Congress of the Communist International, scheduled for July 19, included arguments that United States trade unions would not be of any help in global revolutionary efforts. The powerful AFL-CIO squashed radicalism and had its own bureaucracy of leaders with capitalistic movitives to preserve the economic status quo. American trade unions, Reed argued, kept the rank and file compliant by negotiating for wage increases that ensured loyalty and discouraged political risks. Reed argued in vain that American trade unions needed to be destroyed before the Russians had any chance to radicalize the American worker. He lost the argument several times during the summer of 1920, and in the process made enemies with serious Comintern officers.

Lenin still admired Reed for his fighting spirit and the recognition his name would bring to a Soviet-backed propaganda program in America. He was particularly impressed by a report Reed delivered on the prospect of radicalizing the American Negro to for the communist cause. He wrote and spoke about lynchings, rape, Jim Crow, and segregation in hotels, schools and churches as well as laws against interracial marriage. Reed suggested that Negro leaders be invited to Russia for a Negro World Congress to forge solidarity with whites, target Southern state capitalism and attack the gap between Southern Negroes and the bourgeois culture.

He was still on the move, heeding the call of duty, at the end of August, when Louise finalized plans to join him in Russia. He was assigned to speak at the Congress of Oriental Nations in Baku, an old port city on the northern shore of the Caspian Sea in front of revolutionary Persians, Armenians and Turks. Baku had been lost by the Soviets during the civil war of 1918 but had been recaptured in the spring of 1920. The objective was to radicalize the Middle East against Great Britain. Reed did not want to go. He wanted to greet Louise when she arrived in Moscow. The Comintern ordered him to attend the conference, which meant a long trip on a government train with party officials and delegates. In the end, Jack Reed was following orders from bureaucrats he did not respect. In Baku, his speech targeted American mistreatment of its immigrant workers from all over the world as he implored the audience to overthrow capitalist systems. His words did not carry the power of a speech by a Comintern leader who, playing to the crowd, called for 800 million Asians to engage in a holy war against European imperialists.

Reed was angry and discouraged before he boarded the train to Baku, but on the train back to Moscow, his once indomitable spirit may have finally run its course, conceding to the sentiment he first expressed in

Ten. Revolution: The Day After

Louise Bryant at husband John Reed's casket, Labor Temple, Moscow, Russia, October 1920 (courtesy Houghton Library, Harvard University, 518431_01).

"Almost Thirty," when he wrote that he didn't care what happens next as long as the love he found was real. On that return journey, Comintern officials and delegates treated themselves to an order of exotic foods, endless supplies of alcohol, and young prostitutes, some of whom may have been 14. Upon reuniting with Louise in Moscow on September 15, Reed told her about the train debauchery and overall disillusion and fear about his possible misreading of history. He also told her of his desire to go home once again. Their reunion was joyous and gentle; she did not tell him what she told a friend back home—that Reed might not be physically able to make the trip home, and that he most certatinly would not survive a probable conviction and prison term that awaited him in the United States. He became gravely ill less than two weeks after his return from Baku. Dizziness, sharp headaches, high temperature, and diagnoses that went from influenza to typhus in five days. Medicine was in scarce supply due to foreign blockades. Reed was fighting with one kidney and was still sapped from the three months in solitary confinement. On October 17, his run was over, eight years after C.J. Reed's abrupt ending, eight years of searching and fighting, laughing and loving, moving and writing, shaking the world with truths about the untapped potential of people. His funeral in Moscow (and burial at the Kremlin) was quiet, dignified and void of religious symbolism. A century later, John Reed's name is attached to a book about a world that shook, a world that still shakes from the same struggles that compelled him to write and fight.

Chapter Notes

Chapter One

1. Richard O'Connor and Dale L. Walker, *The Lost Revolutionary: A Biography of John Reed* (New York: Harcourt, Brace & World, 1967), pp. 20, 58, 59, 63.
2. Richard O'Connor and Dale L. Walker, *The Lost Revolutionary: A Biography of John Reed* (New York: Harcourt, Brace & World, 1967), p. 37.
3. Robert A. Rosenstone, *Romantic Revolutionary* (New York: Alfred A. Knopf, 1975), p. 58.
4. Robert A. Rosenstone, *Romantic Revolutionary* (New York: Alfred A. Knopf, 1975), pp. 56–57.
5. Daniel W. Lehman, *John Reed & the Writing of Revolution* (Athens: Ohio University Press, 2002), p. 23.
6. Bruce Watson, *Sacco & Vanzetti* (New York: Penguin, 2007), p. 11.
7. Robert A. Rosenstone, *Romantic Revolutionary* (New York: Alfred A. Knopf, 1975), p. 97.
8. Richard O'Connor and Dale L. Walker, *The Lost Revolutionary: A Biography of John Reed* (New York: Harcourt, Brace & World, 1967), p. 6.
9. John Reed, "Almost Thirty," unpublished manuscript, John Reed Collection, Houghton Library, Harvard University, Cambridge, MA.
10. Richard O'Connor and Dale L. Walker, *The Lost Revolutionary: A Biography of John Reed* (New York: Harcourt, Brace & World, 1967), pp. 42–43.
11. Robert A. Rosenstone, *Romantic Revolutionary* (New York: Alfred A. Knopf, 1975), p. 97.
12. Richard O'Connor and Dale L. Walker, *The Lost Revolutionary: A Biography of John Reed* (New York: Harcourt, Brace & World, 1967), pp. 30, 32.
13. Granville Hicks, *John Reed: The Making of a Revolutionary* (New York: The Macmillan Company, 1936), pp. 14–15.
14. Letter from Joseph W. Adams, July 1912, John Reed Collection, Houghton Library, Harvard University, Cambridge, MA.
15. Letter from Joseph W. Adams, September 1912, John Reed Collection, Houghton Library, Harvard University, Cambridge, MA.
16. John Reed, "The Day in Bohemia or Life Among Artists," Hillacre Bookhouse, 1913, http://oldsite.english.ucsb.edu, accessed February 2019.
17. John Reed letter to Robert Hallowell, July 1912, John Reed Collection, Houghton Library, Harvard University, Cambridge, MA.
18. John Reed letter to Robert Hallowell, August 1909, John Reed Collection, Houghton Library, Harvard University, Cambridge, MA.
19. John Reed letters to Robert Hallowell, July and October 1912, John Reed Col-

lection, Houghton Library, Harvard University, Cambridge, MA.
20. Howard Zinn, "Discovering John Reed," *Howard Zinn on History* (New York: Seven Stories Press, 2000), http://www.thirdworldtraveler.com/Zinn/JohnReed, accessed February 2019.
21. Michael Munk, "The Portland Years of John Reed and Louise Bryant," https://www.marxists.org/archive/reed/bio/portland, accessed February 2019.
22. Richard O'Connor and Dale L. Walker, *The Lost Revolutionary: A Biography of John Reed* (New York: Harcourt, Brace & World, 1967), p. 48.
23. Kenneth Z. Chutchian, "Labor Day Is a Time for Jack Reed to Resurface," *The Oregonian*, https://www.oregonlive.com, accessed August 2016.
24. E. Kimbark MacColl, *The Shaping of a City: Business and Politics in Portland, Oregon 1885 to 1915* (Portland: The Georgian Press Company, 1976), www.worldcat.org, accessed July 2015.
25. Robert A. Rosenstone, *Romantic Revolutionary* (New York: Alfred A. Knopf, 1975), p. 9.
26. Richard O'Connor and Dale L. Walker, *The Lost Revolutionary: A Biography of John Reed* (New York: Harcourt, Brace & World, 1967), p. 7.
27. Robert A. Rosenstone, *Romantic Revolutionary* (New York: Alfred A. Knopf, 1975), p. 9.
28. Richard O'Connor and Dale L. Walker, *The Lost Revolutionary: A Biography of John Reed* (New York: Harcourt, Brace & World, 1967), p. 6.
29. John Reed, "Almost Thirty," unpublished manuscript, John Reed Collection, Houghton Library, Harvard University, Cambridge, MA.
30. Michael Munk, "The Portland Years of John Reed and Louise Bryant," https://www.marxists.org/archive/reed/bio/portland, accessed February 2019.
31. Barbara Gelb, *So Short a Time: A Biography of John Reed and Louise Bryant* (New York: Norton, 1973), p. 22.
32. John Reed, "Almost Thirty," unpublished manuscript, John Reed Collection, Houghton Library, Harvard University, Cambridge, MA.
33. John Reed, "Almost Thirty," unpublished manuscript, John Reed Collection, Houghton Library, Harvard University, Cambridge, MA.
34. John Reed, "Almost Thirty," unpublished manuscript, John Reed Collection, Houghton Library, Harvard University, Cambridge, MA.
35. Kimbark E. MacColl, *The Shaping of a City: Business and Politics in Portland, Oregon 1885 to 1915* (Portland: The Georgian Press Company, 1976), www.worldcat.org, accessed July 2015.
36. Kimbark E. MacColl, *The Shaping of a City: Business and Politics in Portland, Oregon 1885 to 1915* (Portland: The Georgian Press Company, 1976), www.worldcat.org, accessed July 2015.
37. Barbara Gelb, *So Short a Time: A Biography of John Reed and Louise Bryant* (New York: Norton, 1973), p. 23.
38. John Reed, "Almost Thirty," unpublished manuscript, John Reed Collection, Houghton Library, Harvard University, Cambridge, MA.
39. John Reed, "Almost Thirty," unpublished manuscript, John Reed Collection, Houghton Library, Harvard University, Cambridge, MA.
40. Michael Munk, "The Portland Years of John Reed and Louise Bryant," https://www.marxists.org/archive/reed/bio/portland, accessed February 2019.
41. Robert A. Rosenstone, *Romantic Revolutionary* (New York: Alfred A. Knopf, 1975), p. 14.
42. John Reed, "Almost Thirty," unpublished manuscript, John Reed Collection, Houghton Library, Harvard University, Cambridge, MA.
43. Richard O'Connor and Dale L. Walker, *The Lost Revolutionary: A Biography of John Reed* (New York: Harcourt, Brace & World, 1967), p. 13.
44. John Reed, "Almost Thirty," unpublished manuscript, John Reed Collection, Houghton Library, Harvard University, Cambridge, MA.
45. The Oregon Encyclopedia, "The Oregon Land Fraud Trials(1904–1910)," http://www.oregonencyclopedia.org, accessed July 2015.
46. The Oregon Encyclopedia, "The Oregon Land Fraud Trials(1904–1910),"

http://www.oregonencyclopedia.org, accessed July 2015.

47. The Oregon Encyclopedia, "The Oregon Land Fraud Trials (1904–1910)," http://www.oregonencyclopedia.org, accessed July 2015.

48. Richard O'Connor and Dale L. Walker, *The Lost Revolutionary: A Biography of John Reed* (New York: Harcourt, Brace & World, 1967), p. 13.

49. Robert A. Rosenstone, *Romantic Revolutionary* (New York: Alfred A. Knopf, 1975), pp. 12–13.

50. The Arlington Club, "Honoring Our Fine History: Our Roots Run Deep in Oregon," The Arlington Club, http://www.thearlingtonclub.com, accessed January 23, 2019.

51. Richard O'Connor and Dale L. Walker, *The Lost Revolutionary: A Biography of John Reed* (New York: Harcourt, Brace & World, 1967), p. 148.

52. Lincoln Steffens, *Lincoln Steffens Speaking*, p. 312. Richard O'Connor and Dale L. Walker, The *Lost Revolutionary: A Biography of John Reed* (New York: Harcourt, Brace & World, 1967), p. 24.

53. Robert A. Rosenstone, *Romantic Revolutionary* (New York: Alfred A. Knopf, 1975), p. 62.

54. John Reed, "Almost Thirty," unpublished manuscript, John Reed Collection, Houghton Library, Harvard University, Cambridge, MA.

55. John Reed, personal letters, John Reed Collection, Houghton Library, Harvard University, Cambridge, MA, December 1911, March 1913, October 1915, accessed August 2016.

56. John Reed, personal letters, John Reed Collection, Houghton Library, Harvard University, Cambridge, MA, accessed July 2015.

57. *Boston Post* article, John Reed Collection, Houghton Library, Harvard University, Cambridge, MA, accessed July 2015.

58. Robert A. Rosenstone, *Romantic Revolutionary* (New York: Alfred A. Knopf, 1975), p. 96.

59. John Reed, "The Day in Bohemia or Life Among Artists," Hillacre Bookhouse, 1913, http://oldsite.english.ucsb.edu, accessed February 4, 2019.

60. Robert A. Rosenstone, *Romantic Revolutionary* (New York: Alfred A. Knopf, 1975), p. 92.

61. Howard Zinn, "Discovering John Reed," *Howard Zinn on History* (New York: Seven Stories Press, 2000), http:www.thirdworldtraveler.com, accessed August 2015.

62. Letters and Correspondence, John Reed Collection, Houghton Library, Harvard University, Cambridge, MA, accessed July 2015.

63. Letters and Correspondence, John Reed Collection, Houghton Library, Harvard University, Cambridge, MA, accessed July 2015.

Chapter Two

1. Lincoln Steffens, *The Autobiography of Lincoln Steffens, Volume II* (San Diego: Harcourt Brace Jovanovich, 1931), p. 653.

2. Robert A. Rosenstone, *Romantic Revolutionary* (New York: Alfred A. Knopf, 1975), p. 39.

3. Barbara Gelb, *So Short a Time: A Biography of John Reed and Louise Bryant* (New York: Norton, 1973), p. 32.

4. Stephen C. Clapp, "Charles Townsend Copeland," *The Harvard Crimson* web site, April 16, 1958, http://www.thecrimson.com/article/1958/4/16/charles-townsend-copeland, accessed December 2015.

5. Richard O'Connor and Dale L. Walker, *The Lost Revolutionary: A Biography of John Reed* (New York: Harcourt, Brace & World, 1967), p. 34.

6. John Reed, "Almost Thirty," unpublished manuscript, John Reed Collection, Houghton Library, Harvard University, Cambridge, MA.

7. Robert A. Rosenstone, *Romantic Revolutionary* (New York: Alfred A. Knopf, 1975), p. 188. Richard O'Connor and Dale L. Walker, *The Lost Revolutionary: A Biography of John Reed* (New York: Harcourt, Brace & World, 1967).

8. Charles Copeland letter, John Reed Collection, Houghton Library, Harvard University, Cambridge, MA.

9. Richard O'Connor and Dale L. Walker, *The Lost Revolutionary: A Biogra-*

phy of John Reed (New York: Harcourt, Brace & World, 1967), p. 35.
10. Barbara Gelb, *So Short a Time: A Biography of John Reed and Louise Bryant* (New York: Norton, 1973), p. 45.
11. Barbara Gelb, *So Short a Time: A Biography of John Reed and Louise Bryant* (New York: Norton, 1973), p. 45.
12. Robert A. Rosenstone, *Romantic Revolutionary* (New York: Alfred A. Knopf, 1975), p. 47.
13. Daniel W. Lehman, *John Reed & the Writing of Revolution* (Athens: Ohio University Press, 2002), p. 13.
14. John Reed, "Almost Thirty," unpublished manuscript, John Reed Collection, Houghton Library, Harvard University, Cambridge, MA.
15. Robert A. Rosenstone, *Romantic Revolutionary* (New York: Alfred A. Knopf, 1975), p. 53.
16. John Reed letter to Charles Copeland, 1915, John Reed Collection, Houghton Library, Harvard University, Cambridge, MA.
17. John Reed letter to Charles Copeland, 1915, John Reed Collection, Houghton Library, Harvard University, Cambridge, MA.
18. Richard O'Connor and Dale L. Walker, *The Lost Revolutionary: A Biography of John Reed* (New York: Harcourt, Brace & World, 1967), p. 35.
19. "John Reed," http://spartacus-educational.com/Jreed.htm, accessed February 2019.
20. Robert A. Rosenstone, *Romantic Revolutionary* (New York: Alfred A. Knopf, 1975), p. 83.
21. Richard O'Connor and Dale L. Walker, *The Lost Revolutionary: A Biography of John Reed* (New York: Harcourt, Brace & World, 1967), p. 50.
22. Richard O'Connor and Dale L. Walker, *The Lost Revolutionary: A Biography of John Reed* (New York: Harcourt, Brace & World, 1967), p. 50.
23. Richard O'Connor and Dale L. Walker, *The Lost Revolutionary: A Biography of John Reed* (New York: Harcourt, Brace & World, 1967), pp. 53–54.
24. Lincoln Steffens, *The Autobiography of Lincoln Steffens, Volume II* (San Diego: Harcourt Brace Jovanovich, 1931), p. 654.
25. Richard O'Connor and Dale L. Walker, *The Lost Revolutionary: A Biography of John Reed* (New York: Harcourt, Brace & World, 1967), p. 54.
26. Richard O'Connor and Dale L. Walker, *The Lost Revolutionary: A Biography of John Reed* (New York: Harcourt, Brace & World, 1967), p. 193.
27. Lincoln Steffens letter, 1912, John Reed Collection, Houghton Library, Harvard University, Cambridge, MA.
28. Richard O'Connor and Dale L. Walker, *The Lost Revolutionary: A Biography of John Reed* (New York: Harcourt, Brace & World, 1967), p. 61.
29. John Reed, "Sanger: To Lincoln Steffens," *Poetry Magazine*, July 1912, posted on Poetry Foundation web site, www.poetryfoundation.org, accessed December 2015.
30. Richard O'Connor and Dale L. Walker, *The Lost Revolutionary: A Biography of John Reed* (New York: Harcourt, Brace & World, 1967), p. 147.
31. Robert A. Rosenstone, *Romantic Revolutionary* (New York: Alfred A. Knopf, 1975), p. 335.
32. John Reed, "Almost Thirty," unpublished manuscript, John Reed Collection, Houghton Library, Harvard University, Cambridge, MA.
33. Richard O'Connor and Dale L. Walker, *The Lost Revolutionary: A Biography of John Reed* (New York: Harcourt, Brace & World, 1967), p. 238.
34. Robert A. Rosenstone, *Romantic Revolutionary* (New York: Alfred A. Knopf, 1975), p. 335.
35. Robert A. Rosenstone, *Romantic Revolutionary* (New York: Alfred A. Knopf, 1975), p. 328.
36. "John Reed," http://spartacus-educational.com/Jreed.htm, accessed August 2015.
37. Max Eastman, *Enjoyment of Living* (New York: Harper, 1948), p. 406. Richard O'Connor and Dale L. Walker, *The Lost Revolutionary: A Biography of John Reed* (New York: Harcourt, Brace & World, 1967), p. 68.
38. Max Eastman, *Enjoyment of Living* (New York: Harper, 1948), p. 443. Richard O'Connor and Dale L. Walker, *The Lost Revolutionary: A Biography of John Reed*

(New York: Harcourt, Brace & World, 1967), p. 95.

39. Richard O'Connor and Dale L. Walker, *The Lost Revolutionary: A Biography of John Reed* (New York: Harcourt, Brace & World, 1967), p. 294.

40. Max Eastman, *Heroes I Have Known*, pp. 208–209. Richard O'Connor and Dale L. Walker, *The Lost Revolutionary: A Biography of John Reed* (New York: Harcourt, Brace & World, 1967), p. 124.

41. Max Eastman, *Enjoyment of Living* (New York: Harper, 1948), p. 565. Richard O'Connor and Dale L. Walker, *The Lost Revolutionary: A Biography of John Reed* (New York: Harcourt, Brace & World, 1967), p. 176.

42. Robert A. Rosenstone, *Romantic Revolutionary* (New York: Alfred A. Knopf, 1975), p. 256.

Chapter Three

1. John Reed, letter to *Poetry Magazine*, July 1912, posted on Poetry Foundation web site, www.poetryfoundation.org, accessed December 2015.

2. Robert A. Rosenstone, *Romantic Revolutionary* (New York: Alfred A. Knopf, 1975), p. 39.

3. John Reed, "Almost Thirty," unpublished manuscript, John Reed Collection, Houghton Library, Harvard University, Cambridge, MA.

4. Barbara Gelb, *So Short a Time: A Biography of John Reed and Louise Bryant* (New York: Norton, 1973), p. 29.

5. Richard O'Connor and Dale L. Walker, *The Lost Revolutionary: A Biography of John Reed* (New York: Harcourt, Brace & World, 1967), pp. 29–32.

6. Richard O'Connor and Dale L. Walker, *The Lost Revolutionary: A Biography of John Reed* (New York: Harcourt, Brace & World, 1967), p. 36.

7. Richard O'Connor and Dale L. Walker, *The Lost Revolutionary: A Biography of John Reed* (New York: Harcourt, Brace & World, 1967), p. 27.

8. Richard O'Connor and Dale L. Walker, *The Lost Revolutionary: A Biography of John Reed* (New York: Harcourt, Brace & World, 1967), p. 29.

9. Richard O'Connor and Dale L. Walker, *The Lost Revolutionary: A Biography of John Reed* (New York: Harcourt, Brace & World, 1967), p. 33.

10. Robert A. Rosenstone, *Romantic Revolutionary* (New York: Alfred A. Knopf, 1975), p. 46. Richard O'Connor and Dale L. Walker, *The Lost Revolutionary: A Biography of John Reed* (New York: Harcourt, Brace & World, 1967).

11. H.V. Kaltenborn, *Fifty Fabulous Years*, p. 43. Richard O'Connor and Dale L. Walker, *The Lost Revolutionary: A Biography of John Reed* (New York: Harcourt, Brace & World, 1967), p. 32.

12. John Reed, personal letters, John Reed Collection, Houghton Library, Harvard University, Cambridge, MA.

13. Robert A. Rosenstone, *Romantic Revolutionary* (New York: Alfred A. Knopf, 1975), p. 57.

14. John Reed, personal letters, John Reed Collection, Houghton Library, Harvard University, Cambridge, MA.

15. John Reed, "Almost Thirty," unpublished manuscript, John Reed Collection, Houghton Library, Harvard University, Cambridge, MA.

16. Robert A. Rosenstone, *Romantic Revolutionary* (New York: Alfred A. Knopf, 1975), p. 79.

17. Robert A. Rosenstone, *Romantic Revolutionary* (New York: Alfred A. Knopf, 1975), pp. 108–109.

18. John Reed, as quoted by James C. Wilson, *John Reed for the Masses* (Jefferson, NC: McFarland, 1987), p. 19.

19. Richard O'Connor and Dale L. Walker, *The Lost Revolutionary: A Biography of John Reed* (New York: Harcourt, Brace & World, 1967), pp. 79–80.

20. John Reed, "Almost Thirty," unpublished manuscript, John Reed Collection, Houghton Library, Harvard University, Cambridge, MA.

21. Richard O'Connor and Dale L. Walker, *The Lost Revolutionary: A Biography of John Reed* (New York: Harcourt, Brace & World, 1967), pp. 75–76.

22. John Reed, "War in Paterson," as quoted by James C. Wilson, *John Reed for the Masses* (Jefferson, NC: McFarland, 1987), pp. 26–28.

23. John Reed, "War in Paterson," as quoted by James C. Wilson, *John Reed for*

the Masses (Jefferson, NC: McFarland, 1987), pp. 30–31.

24. Richard O'Connor and Dale L. Walker, *The Lost Revolutionary: A Biography of John Reed* (New York: Harcourt, Brace & World, 1967), p. 95.

25. John Reed, personal letters, John Reed Collection, Houghton Library, Harvard University, Cambridge, MA.

26. Walter Lippmann, "Legendary John Reed," *New Republic*, December 26, 1914, p. 15, www.googlebooks.com, accessed February 5, 2019.

27. Daniel W. Lehman, *John Reed and the Writing of Revolution* (Athens: Ohio University Press, 2002), p. 131.

28. Richard O'Connor and Dale L. Walker, *The Lost Revolutionary: A Biography of John Reed* (New York: Harcourt, Brace & World, 1967), p. 98.

29. Barbara Gelb, *So Short a Time: A Biography of John Reed and Louise Bryant* (New York: Norton, 1973), p. 62.

30. John Reed, *Insurgent Mexico, With Pancho Villa in the Mexican Revolution* (St. Petersburg, Florida: Red and Black, 2009), p. 30.

31. John Reed, *Insurgent Mexico: With Pancho Villa in the Mexican Revolution* (St. Petersburg, FL: Red and Black, 2009), p. 43.

Chapter Four

1. Barbara Gelb, *So Short A Time: A Biography of John Reed and Louise Bryant* (New York: Norton, 1973), p. 140.

2. Robert A. Rosenstone, *Romantic Revolutionary* (New York: Alfred A. Knopf, 1975), p. 135.

3. Robert A. Rosenstone, *Romantic Revolutionary* (New York: Alfred A. Knopf, 1975), p. 135.

4. Robert A. Rosenstone, *Romantic Revolutionary* (New York: Alfred A. Knopf, 1975), p. 151. Richard O'Connor and Dale L. Walker, *Lost Revolutionary*.

5. Barbara Gelb, *So Short A Time: A Biography of John Reed and Louise Bryant* (New York: Norton, 1973), p. 66.

6. Robert A. Rosenstone, *Romantic Revolutionary* (New York: Alfred A. Knopf, 1975), p. 178.

7. Barbara Gelb, *So Short a Time: A Biography of John Reed and Louise Bryant* (New York: Norton, 1973), chapters 1 and 2.

8. Barbara Gelb, *So Short a Time: A Biography of John Reed and Louise Bryant* (New York: Norton, 1973), p. 40.

9. Barbara Gelb, *So Short a Time: A Biography of John Reed and Louise Bryant* (New York: Norton, 1973), pp. 76–101.

10. Barbara Gelb, *So Short a Time: A Biography of John Reed and Louise Bryant* (New York: Norton, 1973), pp. 107–117.

11. Barbara Gelb, *So Short a Time: A Biography of John Reed and Louise Bryant* (New York: Norton, 1973), pp. 121–122.

12. Barbara Gelb, *So Short a Time: A Biography of John Reed and Louise Bryant* (New York: Norton, 1973), pp. 123–124.

13. Barbara Gelb, *So Short a Time: A Biography of John Reed and Louise Bryant* (New York: Norton, 1973), p. 135.

14. Barbara Gelb, *So Short a Time: A Biography of John Reed and Louise Bryant* (New York: Norton, 1973), pp. 139–140.

15. John Reed, "Almost Thirty," unpublished manuscript, John Reed Collection, Houghton Library, Harvard University, Cambridge, MA.

16. Barbara Gelb, *So Short a Time: A Biography of John Reed and Louise Bryant* (New York: Norton, 1973), pp. 170–183.

17. Barbara Gelb, *So Short a Time: A Biography of John Reed and Louise Bryant* (New York: Norton, 1973), pp. 184–192.

18. Barbara Gelb, *So Short a Time: A Biography of John Reed and Louise Bryant* (New York: Norton, 1973), chapter 12.

19. Richard O'Connor and Dale L. Walker, *The Lost Revolutionary: A Biography of John Reed* (New York: Harcourt, Brace & World, 1967), p. 303.

20. Barbara Gelb, *So Short a Time: A Biography of John Reed and Louise Bryant* (New York: Norton, 1973), pp. 303–304.

21. John Reed, "Almost Thirty," unpublished manuscript, John Reed Collection, Houghton Library, Harvard University, Cambridge, MA.

Chapter Five

1. John Reed, personal letters, John Reed Collection, Houghton Library, Harvard University, Cambridge, MA.

2. Bernard M. Gwertzman, "John Reed: The Eternal Cheerleader," *The Harvard Crimson* web site, original print publication October 24, 1958, www.thecrimson.com, accessed May 2016.

3. Robert A. Rosenstone, *Romantic Revolutionary* (New York: Alfred A. Knopf, 1975), p. 166.

4. Robert A. Rosenstone, *Romantic Revolutionary* (New York: Alfred A. Knopf, 1975), p. 167. Granville Hicks, *John Reed: The Making of a Revolutionary* (New York: The Macmillan Company, 1936), p. 134.

5. Robert A. Rosenstone, *Romantic Revolutionary* (New York: Alfred A. Knopf, 1975), p. 210.

6. Walter Lippmann, "Legendary John Reed," *New Republic*, December 16, 1914.

7. John Reed, *Insurgent Mexico* (New York: D. Appleton, 1914), p. 111.

8. John Reed, *Insurgent Mexico* (New York: D. Appleton, 1914), p. 133.

9. Granville Hicks, *John Reed: The Making of a Revolutionary* (New York: The Macmillan Company, 1936), p. 139.

10. Thai Jones, *More Powerful Than Dynamite: Radicals, Plutocrats, Progressives and New York's Year of Anarchy* (New York: Bloomsbury, 2012), p. 165.

11. "John Reed on Ludlow," excerpt from Reed's article "The Colorado War" in the *Metropolitan*, http://m.dailykos.com, accessed May 2016.

12. Robert Rosenstone, *Romantic Revolutionary* (New York: Alfred A. Knopf, 1975), pp. 198–199.

13. Robert A. Rosenstone, *Romantic Revolutionary* (New York: Alfred A. Knopf, 1975), p. 172.

14. Richard O'Connor and Dale L. Walker, *The Lost Revolutionary: A Biography of John Reed* (New York: Harcourt, Brace & World, 1967), p. 142.

15. Richard O'Connor and Dale L. Walker, *The Lost Revolutionary: A Biography of John Reed* (New York: Harcourt, Brace & World, 1967), p. 143.

16. Richard O'Connor and Dale L. Walker, *The Lost Revolutionary: A Biography of John Reed* (New York: Harcourt, Brace & World, 1967), p. 143.

17. Richard O'Connor and Dale L. Walker, *The Lost Revolutionary: A Biography of John Reed* (New York: Harcourt, Brace & World, 1967), p. 143.

18. Robert Rosenstone, *Romantic Revolutionary* (New York Alfred A. Knopf, 1975), pp. 197–198.

19. Richard O'Connor and Dale L. Walker, *The Lost Revolutionary: A Biography of John Reed* (New York: Harcourt, Brace & World, 1967), p. 43.

20. Robert Rosenstone, *Romantic Revolutionary* (New York Alfred A. Knopf, 1975), p. 211.

21. Daniel W. Lehman, *John Reed & the Writing of Revolution* (Athens: Ohio University Press, 2002), p. 23.

22. Robert Rosenstone, *Romantic Revolutionary* (New York: Alfred A. Knopf, 1975), p. 211. Richard O'Connor and Dale L. Walker, *The Lost Revolutionary: A Biography of John Reed* (New York: Harcourt, Brace & World, 1967), p. 148.

23. Walter Lippman, "Legendary John Reed," *New Republic*, December 16, 1914.

24. John Reed, *The War in Eastern Europe* (Memphis: General Books, 2012), pp. 9 and 10.

25. John Reed, *The War in Eastern Europe* (Memphis: General Books, 2012), p. 9.

26. John Reed, *The War in Eastern Europe* (Memphis: General Books, 2012), p. 28.

27. John Reed, *The War in Eastern Europe* (Memphis: General Books, 2012), p. 37.

28. John Reed, *The War in Eastern Europe* (Memphis: General Books, 2012), p. 40.

29. John Reed, *The War in Eastern Europe* (Memphis: General Books, 2012), p. 48

30. John Reed, unpublished manuscript, September 1914, John Reed Collection, Houghton Library, Harvard University, Cambridge, MA.

31. John Reed, unpublished manuscript, John Reed Collection, Houghton Library, Harvard University, Cambridge, MA.

32. John Reed, as quoted by James C. Wilson, *John Reed for the Masses* (Jefferson, NC: McFarland, 1987), pp. 134–135.

33. John Reed, as quoted by James C. Wilson, *John Reed for the Masses* (Jefferson, NC: McFarland, 1987), p. 156.

34. Richard O'Connor and Dale L. Walker, *The Lost Revolutionary: A Biography of John Reed* (New York: Harcourt, Brace & World, 1967), p. 181.

Chapter Six

1. Daniel W. Lehman, *John Reed & the Writing of Revolution* (Athens: Ohio University Press, 2002), pp. 131–132.
2. C.C. Regier, *The Era of the Muckrakers* (Chapel Hill: University of North Carolina Press, 1932), p. 1.
3. John Simkin, "Muckraking Journalism," https://spartacus-educational.com/Jmuckraking.htm, August 2014, accessed February 7, 2019.
4. John Simkin, "Muckraking Journalism," https://spartacus-educational.com/Jmuckraking.htm, August 2014, accessed February 7, 2019.
5. C.C. Regier, *The Era of the Muckrakers* (Chapel Hill: University of North Carolina Press, 1932), p. 203.
6. Rick Musser, "History of American Journalism," history.journalism.Ku.edu, December 31, 2007, accessed February 7, 2019.
7. Doris Kearns Goodwin, *Bully Pulpit: Theodore Roosevelt, William Howard Taft, and the Golden Age of Journalism* (New York: Simon & Schuster), p. 482.
8. Doris Kearns Goodwin, *Bully Pulpit: Theodore Roosevelt, William Howard Taft, and the Golden Age of Journalism* (New York: Simon & Schuster), p. 483.
9. Doris Kearns Goodwin, *Bully Pulpit: Theodore Roosevelt, William Howard Taft, and the Golden Age of Journalism* (New York: Simon & Schuster), p. 483.
10. C.C. Regier, *The Era of the Muckrakers* (Chapel Hill: University of North Carolina Press, 1932), p. 207.
11. Doris Kearns Goodwin, *Bully Pulpit: Theodore Roosevelt, William Howard Taft, and the Golden Age of Journalism* (New York: Simon & Schuster), p. 486.
12. Doris Kearns Goodwin, *Bully Pulpit: Theodore Roosevelt, William Howard Taft, and the Golden Age of Journalism* (New York: Simon & Schuster), p. 479.
13. Doris Kearns Goodwin, *Bully Pulpit: Theodore Roosevelt, William Howard Taft, and the Golden Age of Journalism* (New York: Simon & Schuster), p. 489.
14. C.C. Regier, *The Era of the Muckrakers* (Chapel Hill: University of North Carolina Press, 1932), pp. 205–206.
15. Robert A. Rosenstone, *Romantic Revolutionary* (New York: Alfred A. Knopf, 1975), p. 347.
16. Doris Kearns Goodwin, *Bully Pulpit: Theodore Roosevelt, William Howard Taft, and the Golden Age of Journalism* (New York: Simon & Schuster), p. 495.

Chapter Seven

1. John Reed, "Almost Thirty," unpublished manuscript, John Reed Collection, Houghton Library, Harvard University, Cambridge, MA.
2. Richard O'Connor and Dale L. Walker, *The Lost Revolutionary: A Biography of John Reed* (New York: Harcourt, Brace & World, 1967), p. 197.
3. Robert A. Rosenstone, *Romantic Revolutionary* (New York: Alfred A. Knopf, 1975), p. 282.
4. Robert Rosenstone, *Romantic Revolutionary* (New York: Alfred A. Knopf, 1975), p. 282.
5. Richard O'Connor and Dale L. Walker, *The Lost Revolutionary: A Biography of John Reed* (New York: Harcourt, Brace & World, 1967), p. 201.
6. Granville Hicks, *John Reed: The Making of a Revolutionary* (New York: The Macmillan Company, 1936), p. 259.
7. John Reed, *Ten Days That Shook the World* (New York: Penguin, 1919), pp. 32–34.
8. John Reed, *Ten Days That Shook the World* (New York: Penguin, 1919), p. 35.
9. John Reed, *Ten Days That Shook the World* (New York: Penguin, 1919), p. 34.
10. Granville Hicks, *John Reed: The Making of a Revolutionary* (New York: The Macmillan Company, 1936), p. 260.
11. Robert A. Rosenstone, *Romantic Revolutionary* (New York: Alfred A. Knopf, 1975), p. 335.
12. Richard O'Connor and Dale L. Walker, *The Lost Revolutionary: A Biography of John Reed* (New York: Harcourt, Brace & World, 1967), p. 202.
13. John Reed, *Ten Days That Shook the World* (New York: Penguin, 1919), p. 39.

14. John Reed, *Ten Days That Shook the World* (New York: Penguin, 1919), p. 117.
15. John Reed, *Ten Days That Shook the World* (New York: Penguin, 1919), p. 123.
16. John Reed, *Ten Days That Shook the World* (New York: Penguin, 1919), p. 128.
17. John Reed, *Ten Days That Shook the World* (New York: Penguin, 1919), p. 124.
18. John Reed, *Ten Days That Shook the World* (New York: Penguin, 1919), p. 125.
19. John Reed, *Ten Days That Shook the World* (New York: Penguin, 1919), p. 135.
20. John Reed, *Ten Days That Shook the World* (New York: Penguin, 1919), p. 238.
21. John Reed, *Ten Days That Shook the World* (New York: Penguin, 1919), p. 239.
22. Granville Hicks, *John Reed: The Making of a Revolutionary* (New York: The Macmillan Company, 1936), pp. 295–296.
23. Max Eastman, *The Evening Call*, vol. 11, no. 9 (February 3, 1918), p. 3, transcribed and edited by Tim Davenport, 2007, https://www.marxist.org.
24. John Reed, "America 1918," as quoted in *Romantic Revolutionary* (New York: Alfred A. Knopf, 1975), pp. 302–305. Granville Hicks, *John Reed: The Making of a Revolutionary* (New York: The Macmillan Company, 1936), p. 302. Richard O'Connor and Dale L. Walker, *The Lost Revolutionary: A Biography of John Reed* (New York: Harcourt, Brace & World, 1967), p. 226.

Chapter Eight

1. Thai Jones, *More Powerful Than Dynamite: Radicals, Plutocrats, Progressives and New York's Year of Anarchy* (New York: Bloomsbury, 2012), p. 63.
2. Thai Jones, *More Powerful Than Dynamite: Radicals, Plutocrats, Progressives and New York's Year of Anarchy* (New York: Bloomsbury, 2012), p. 61.
3. Thai Jones, *More Powerful Than Dynamite: Radicals, Plutocrats, Progressives and New York's Year of Anarchy* (New York: Bloomsbury, 2012), p. 63.
4. Bruce Watson, *Sacco & Vanzetti* (New York: Penguin, 2007), p. 8.
5. Thai Jones, *More Powerful Than Dynamite: Radicals, Plutocrats, Progressives and New York's Year of Anarchy* (New York: Bloomsbury, 2012), p. 37.
6. Thai Jones, *More Powerful Than Dynamite: Radicals, Plutocrats, Progressives and New York's Year of Anarchy* (New York: Bloomsbury, 2012), p. 33.
7. Thai Jones, *More Powerful Than Dynamite: Radicals, Plutocrats, Progressives and New York's Year of Anarchy* (New York: Bloomsbury, 2012), 33.
8. Thai Jones, *More Powerful Than Dynamite: Radicals, Plutocrats, Progressives and New York's Year of Anarchy* (New York: Bloomsbury, 2012), p. 34.
9. Thai Jones, *More Powerful Than Dynamite: Radicals, Plutocrats, Progressives and New York's Year of Anarchy* (New York: Bloomsbury, 2012), p. 35.
10. Thai Jones, *More Powerful Than Dynamite: Radicals, Plutocrats, Progressives and New York's Year of Anarchy* (New York: Bloomsbury, 2012), p. 36.
11. Bruce Watson, *Sacco & Vanzetti* (New York: Penguin, 2007), p. 11.
12. Thai Jones, *More Powerful Than Dynamite: Radicals, Plutocrats, Progressives and New York's Year of Anarchy* (New York: Bloomsbury, 2012), p. 294.
13. Richard O'Connor and Dale L. Walker, *The Lost Revolutionary: A Biography of John Reed* (New York: Harcourt, Brace & World, 1967), p. 303.
14. Emma Goldman, *Living My Life*, The Anarchist Library, https://theanarchistlibrary.org, accessed February 7, 2019. Original print publication by Alfred A. Knopf, 1931.
15. Emma Goldman, *Living My Life*, The Anarchist Library, https://theanarchistlibrary.org, accessed February 7, 2019. Original print publication by Alfred A. Knopf, 1931.
16. Emma Goldman, *Living My Life*, The Anarchist Library, https://theanarchistlibrary.org, accessed February 7, 2019. Original print publication by Alfred A. Knopf, 1931.
17. Granville Hicks, *John Reed: The Making of a Revolutionary* (New York: The Macmillan Company, 1936), p. 71.
18. Granville Hicks, *John Reed: The Making of a Revolutionary* (New York: The Macmillan Company, 1936), p. 207.
19. Granville Hicks, *John Reed: The Making of a Revolutionary* (New York: The Macmillan Company, 1936), pp. 206–207.
20. Granville Hicks, *John Reed: The*

Making of a Revolutionary (New York: The Macmillan Company, 1936), pp. 237–238.
21. Granville Hicks, *John Reed: The Making of a Revolutionary* (New York: The Macmillan Company, 1936), p. 244.
22. Granville Hicks, *John Reed: The Making of a Revolutionary* (New York: The Macmillan Company, 1936), p. 378.
23. Granville Hicks, *John Reed: The Making of a Revolutionary* (New York: The Macmillan Company, 1936), pp. 96–97.
24. Granville Hicks, *John Reed: The Making of a Revolutionary* (New York: The Macmillan Company, 1936), p. 100.
25. Peter Carlson, *Roughneck: The Life and Times of Big Bill Hayward* (New York: Norton, 1983), p. 16.
26. Peter Carlson, *Roughneck: The Life and Times of Big Bill Hayward* (New York: Norton, 1983), p. 16.
27. Peter Carlson, *Roughneck: The Life and Times of Big Bill Hayward* (New York: Norton, 1983), p. 17.
28. Peter Carlson, *Roughneck: The Life and Times of Big Bill Hayward* (New York: Norton, 1983), p. 17.
29. Granville Hicks, *John Reed: The Making of a Revolutionary* (New York: The Macmillan Company, 1936), p. 177.
30. Granville Hicks, *John Reed: The Making of a Revolutionary* (New York: The Macmillan Company, 1936), p. 309.
31. Granville Hicks, *John Reed: The Making of a Revolutionary* (New York: The Macmillan Company, 1936), pp. 327–345.
32. Nick Salvatore, *Eugene V. Debs: Citizen and Socialist* (Urbana: University of Illinois Press, 2007), pp. 228–229.
33. Nick Salvatore, *Eugene V. Debs: Citizen and Socialist* (Urbana: University of Illinois Press, 2007), p. 230.

Chapter Nine

1. Robert Rosenstone, *Romantic Revolutionary: A Biography of John Reed* (New York: Alfred A. Knopf, 1975), pp. 302–303.
2. Granville Hicks, *John Reed: The Making of a Revolutionary* (New York: The Macmillan Company, 1936), p. 303.
3. Robert Rosenstone, *Romantic Revolutionary: A Biography of John Reed* (New York: Alfred A. Knopf), p. 339.
4. Granville Hicks, *John Reed: The Making of a Revolutionary* (New York: The Macmillan Company, 1936), p. 298.
5. Granville Hicks, *John Reed: The Making of a Revolutionary* (New York: The Macmillan Company, 1936), p. 304.
6. Granville Hicks, *John Reed: The Making of a Revolutionary* (New York: The Macmillan Company, 1936), p. 308.
7. Daniel W. Lehman, *John Reed & the Writing of Revolution* (Athens: Athens University Press, 2002), p. 165.
8. Granville Hicks, *John Reed: The Making of a Revolutionary* (New York: The Macmillan Company, 1936), p. 308–309; and Richard O'Connor, *Lost Revolutionary*, p. 188.
9. Granville Hicks, *John Reed: The Making of a Revolutionary* (New York: The Macmillan Company, 1936), p. 309–311.
10. Granville Hicks, *John Reed: The Making of a Revolutionary* (New York: The Macmillan Company, 1936), p. 308.
11. Granville Hicks, *John Reed: The Making of a Revolutionary.* (New York: The Macmillan Company, 1936), p. 312. Robert Rosenstone, *Romantic Revolutionary* (New York: Alfred A. Knopf, 1975), p. 329.
12. Daniel W. Lehman, *John Reed & the Writing of Revolution* (Athens, Ohio: Athens University Press, 2002), p. 165.
13. Granville Hicks, *John Reed: The Making of a Revolutionary* (New York: The Macmillan Company, 1936), p. 305.
14. Granville Hicks, *John Reed: The Making of a Revolutionary.* (New York: The Macmillan Company, 1936), p. 306.
15. Granville Hicks, *John Reed: The Making of a Revolutionary* (New York: The Macmillan Company, 1936), p. 310.
16. Robert Rosenstone, *Romantic Revolutionary: A Biography of John Reed* (New York: Alfred A. Knopf), p. 331.
17. Granville Hicks, *John Reed: The Making of a Revolutionary* (New York: The Macmillan Company, 1936), p. 317; and Richard O'Connor and Dale L. Walker, *The Lost Revolutionary: A Biography of John Reed* (New York: Harcourt, Brace & World, 1967), p. 237.
18. Richard O'Connor and Dale L. Walker, *The Lost Revolutionary: A Biography of John Reed* (New York: Harcourt, Brace & World, 1967), p. 236–239. Robert

Rosenstone, *Romantic Revolutionary : A Biography of John Reed* (New York: Alfred A. Knopf, 1975), pp. 330–335.

19. Granville Hicks, *John Reed: The Making of a Revolutionary* (New York: The Macmillan Company, 1936), p. 340; also Robert Rosenstone, *Romantic Revolutionary : A Biography of John Reed* (New York: Alfred A. Knopf, 1975), p. 331.

20. *Ten Days That Shook the World*, 2015 Andras M. Nagy reprint, cover.

21. Robert Rosenstone, *Romantic Revolutionary: A Biography of John Reed* (New York: Alfred A. Knopf, 1975), p. 344.

22. Granville Hicks, *John Reed: The Making of a Revolutionary* (New York: The Macmillan Company, 1936), p. 338. Richard O'Connor and Dale L. Walker, *The Lost Revolutionary: A Biography of John Reed* (New York: Harcourt, Brace & World, 1967), p. 243.

23. Granville Hicks, *John Reed: The Making of a Revolutionary* (New York: The Macmillan Company, 1936), pp. 336–337. Robert Rosenstone, *Romantic Revolutionary : A Biography of John Reed* (New York: Alfred A. Knopf, 1975), pp. 344–345. Richard O'Connor and Dale L. Walker, *The Lost Revolutionary: A Biography of John Reed* (New York: Harcourt, Brace & World, 1967), p. 245.

24. Granville Hicks, *John Reed: The Making of a Revolutionary* (New York: The Macmillan Company, 1936), pp. 338, 419. Robert Rosenstone, *Romantic Revolutionary: A Biography of John Reed* (New York: Alfred A. Knopf, 1975), pp. 344–345.

25. Granville Hicks, *John Reed: The Making of a Revolutionary* (New York: The Macmillan Company, 1936), p. 315.

26. Granville Hicks, *John Reed: The Making of a Revolutionary* (New York: The Macmillan Company, 1936), p. 326. Richard O'Connor and Dale L. Walker, *The Lost Revolutionary: A Biography of John Reed* (New York: Harcourt, Brace & World, 1967), p. 241.

27. Granville Hicks, *John Reed: The Making of a Revolutionary* (New York: The Macmillan Company, 1936), pp. 327–328.

28. Granville Hicks, *John Reed: The Making of a Revolutionary* (New York: The Macmillan Company, 1936), p. 329.

29. Granville Hicks, *John Reed: The Making of a Revolutionary* (New York: The Macmillan Company, 1936), pp. 342–343.

30. Robert Rosenstone, *Romantic Revolutionary: A Biography of John Reed* (New York: Alfred A. Knopf), p. 372.

31. Bruce Watson, *Sacco & Venzetti* (New York: Penguin, 2008), p. 11.

32. Granville Hicks, *John Reed: The Making of a Revolutionary* (New York: The Macmillan Company, 1936), p. 348.

33. Robert Rosenstone, *Romantic Revolutionary: A Biography of John Reed* (New York: Alfred A. Knopf, 1975), p. 337.

34. John Reed, *Upton Sinclair's Magazine for Social Justice by Peaceful Means*, published December 1918, http://books.google.com.

Chapter Ten

1. Daniel W. Lehman, *John Reed & the Writing of Revolution* (Athens: Ohio University Press, 2002), p. 129.

2. Granville Hicks, *John Reed: The Making of a Revolutionary* (New York: The Macmillan Company, 1936), p. 326.

3. "May Day Riot," https://Clevelandhistorical.org, September 16, 2010, accessed February 8, 2019.

4. Lily Rothman, "The Bloody Story of How May Day Became a Holiday for Workers," Time.com, May 1, 1929, accessed February 8, 2019.

5. "Sidis Gets Year and Half in Jail," *Boston Herald*, May 14, 1919, https://www.sidis.net/herald1919.htm, accessed February 8, 2019.

6. Granville Hicks, *John Reed: The Making of a Revolutionary* (New York: The Macmillan Company, 1936), pp. 326–327.

7. Robert Rosenstone, *Romantic Revolutionary : A Biography of John Reed* (New York: Alfred A. Knopf, 1975), p. 341.

8. Granville Hicks, *John Reed: The Making of a Revolutionary* (New York: The Macmillan Company, 1936), p. 350.

9. Robert Rosenstone, *Romantic Revolutionary: A Biography of John Reed* (New York: Alfred A. Knopf, 1975), pp. 354–359.

10. Granville Hicks, *John Reed: The Making of a Revolutionary* (New York: The Macmillan Company, 1936), p. 366.

11. Granville Hicks, *John Reed: The*

Making of a Revolutionary (New York: The Macmillan Company, 1936), p. 369.

12. Robert Rosenstone, *Romantic Revolutionary: A Biography of John Reed* (New York: Alfred A. Knopf, 1975), p. 360.

13. Granville Hicks, *John Reed: The Making of a Revolutionary* (New York: The Macmillan Company, 1936), pp. 373–374.

14. Granville Hicks, *John Reed: The Making of a Revolutionary* (New York: The Macmillan Company, 1936), p. 376.

15. Moshe Lewin, *Lenin's Last Struggle* (New York: Monthly Review Press, 1968), p. 5.

16. Granville Hicks, *John Reed: The Making of a Revolutionary* (New York: The Macmillan Company, 1936), p. 374.

17. Granville Hicks, *John Reed: The Making of a Revolutionary* (New York: The Macmillan Company, 1936), p. 374.

18. Robert Rosenstone, *Romantic Revolutionary: A Biography of John Reed* (New York: Alfred A. Knopf, 1975), p. 370.

19. Granville Hicks, *John Reed: The Making of a Revolutionary* (New York: The Macmillan Company, 1936), p. 379.

20. Granville Hicks, *John Reed: The Making of a Revolutionary* (New York: The Macmillan Company, 1936), p. 385.

Bibliography

Adams, Joseph W., letter to John Reed, July 1912 (John Reed Collection, Houghton Library, Harvard University, Cambridge, MA).
Arlington Club, "Honoring Our Fine History: Our Roots Run Deep in Oregon," The Arlington Club, http://www.thearlingtonclub.com.
Carlson, Peter, *Roughneck: The Life and Times of Big Bill Haywood* (New York: Norton, 1983).
Clapp, Stephen C., "Charles Townsend Copeland," *The Harvard Crimson* web site, April 16, 1958.
Cleveland Historical, "May Day Riot," https://clevelandhistorical.org, September 16, 2010.
Copeland, Charles, letter to John Reed (John Reed Collection, Houghton Library, Harvard University, Cambridge, MA).
Eastman, Max, *Enjoyment of Living* (New York: Harper, 1948).
Eastman, Max, *Heroes I Have Known* (New York: Simon & Schuster, 1942).
Gelb, Barbara, *So Short a Time: A Biography of John Reed and Louise Bryant* (New York: Norton, 1973).
Goldman, Emma, *Living My Life*, The Anarchist Library, https://theanarchistlibrary.org.
Goodwin, Doris Kearns, *Bully Pulpit: Theodore Roosevelt, William Howard Taft, and the Golden Age of Journalism* (New York: Simon & Schuster, 2013).
Gwertzman, Bernard M., "John Reed: The Eternal Cheerleader," *The Harvard Crimson* web site, original print publication October 24, 1958, www.thecrimson.com.
Hicks, Granville, *John Reed: The Making of a Revolutionary* (New York: The Macmillan Company, 1936).
Homberger, Eric, and Biggard, John, *John Reed and the Russian Revolution: Uncollected Articles, Letters and Speeches on Russia, 1917–1920* (New York: St. Martin's Press, 1992).
Kaltenborn, H.V., *Fifty Fabulous Years* (New York: G.P. Putnam's Sons, 1950).
Lehman, Daniel W., *John Reed & the Writing of Revolution* (Athens: Ohio University Press, 2002).
Lewin, Moshe, *Lenin's Last Struggle* (New York: Monthly Review Press, 1968).
Lippman, Walter, "Legendary John Reed," *The New Republic*, December 26, 1914, p. 15, www.googlebooks.com.
MacColl, Kimbark E. *The Shaping of a City: Business and Politics in Portland, Oregon 1885 to 1915* (Portland: The Georgian Press Company, 1976), www.worldcat.org.
Munk, Michael, "The Portland Years of John Reed and Louise Bryant," https://www.marxists.org/archive/reed/bio/portland.

Musser, Rick, "History of American Journalism." history.journalism.Ku.edu, December 31, 2007.
O'Connor, Richard, and Walker, Dale L., *The Lost Revolutionary: A Biography of John Reed* (New York: Harcourt, Brace & World, 1967).
Oregon Encyclopedia, "The Oregon Land Fraud Trials (1904–1910)," http://www.oregonencyclopedia.org.
Reed, Harry, letter to John Reed (John Reed Collection, Houghton Library, Harvard University, Cambridge, MA).
Reed, John, "Almost Thirty," unpublished manuscript, John Reed Collection, Houghton Library, Harvard University, Cambridge, MA).
Reed, John, "The Colorado War," *Metropolitan Magazine*, http://m.dailykos.com.
Reed, John, "The Day in Bohemia or Life Among Artists," Hillacre Bookhouse, 1913, http://oldsite.english.ucsb.edu.
Reed, John, *Insurgent Mexico* (St. Petersburg, FL: Red and Black, 2009 first published in New York, 1914).
Reed, John, letter to *Poetry Magazine*, July 1912, posted on Poetry Foundation web site, www.poetryfoundation.org.
Reed, John, letter to Robert Hallowell, July 1912 (John Reed Collection, Houghton Library, Harvard University, Cambridge, MA).
Reed, John, "Sanger: To Lincoln Steffens," *Poetry Magazine*, July 1912, posted on Poetry Foundation web site, www.poetryfoundation.org.
Reed, John, *Ten Days That Shook the World* (New York: Penguin, 1966; first published in New York by Boni and Liveright, 1919).
Reed, John, *The War in Eastern Europe* (Memphis: General Books, 2012, first published by Charles Scribner's Sons, 1916).
Rosenstone, Robert A., *Romantic Revolutionary* (New York: Alfred A. Knopf, 1975).
Rothman, Lily, "The Bloody Story of How May Day Became a Holiday for Workers," Time.com, May 1, 1929.
Salvatore, Nick, *Eugene V. Debs: Citizen and Socialist* (Urbana: University of Illinois Press, 2007).
"Sidis Gets Year and Half in Jail," *Boston Herald*, May 14, 1919, https://www.sidis.net/herald1919.htm.
Simlin, John, "Muckraking Journalism," https://spartacus-educational.com/Jmuckraking.htm, August 2014.
Steffens, Lincoln, *The Autobiography of Lincoln Steffens, Volume II* (San Diego: Harcourt Brace Jovanovich, 1931).
Watson, Bruce, *Sacco & Vanzetti* (New York: Penguin, 2007).
Wilson, James C., *John Reed for the Masses* (Jefferson, NC: McFarland, 1987).
Zinn, Howard. "Discovering John Reed," *Howard Zinn on History* (New York: Seven Stories Press, 2000).

Index

Adams, Joseph W. 9
Afghanistan 78
AFL-CIO 162
Alien and Sedition Acts 75
"Almost Thirty" 8, 10–11, 13, 16, 18, 28, 30, 46, 72, 100, 105–107, 111, 163
America 1918 135–136
The American Century: People, Power and Politics 100
American Communist Labor Party 149, 156–157, 159
American Communist Party 155
American Dream 8, 101
American Magazine 29–31, 39, 64, 104
American Protective League 141
anarchists 75–76, 95, 125, 129, 133, 153
Anderson, Sherwood 156
Arlington Club 20
Asia 162
Atlantic Monthly 100, 103
Austria, Austria-Hungary 94, 107

Baker, Ray Stannard 101, 103
Baku 162
Balkan wars 91
Balkans 31, 78, 90
Baltic region 24
Baltimore 70
Bavaria 104
Belgium 51, 87, 153
Bell Syndicate 71
Berger, Victor 57
Berkman, Alex 124–127, 129, 130, 142
Berlin 95
Bohemians 33, 43, 67, 69, 127, 131

Boissevain, Eugene 108
Bolsheviks 12, 25, 32–33, 37–38, 40, 73, 78, 107, 110, 114–120, 125, 127, 130, 137, 139, 145, 148–51, 153, 156, 158–159
Boston 48, 64, 124, 136, 140, 153–154
Boston Herald 154
Boston Post 22
Broadway 61, 64
Broun, Heyward 32, 136
Brussels 51
Bryan, William Jennings 144
Bryant, Louise 35, 63–64, 66–71, 73, 107–110, 127, 136, 144, 156–157, 160, 162
Bucharest 31
Budapest 104
Buffalo 64
Buford 127, 130, 160
The Bully Pulpit: Theodore Roosevelt, William Taft and the Golden Age of Journalism 102
Bunyan, John 98, 102
Burleson, A.S. 138
Burns, William J. 18

California 18–19
The Call 08
Canton, Ohio 134
capitalism and capitalists 39, 70–71, 107–109, 118, 126, 130, 132, 139, 140, 143, 148
Carlson, Peter 132
Carnegie Corporation 126
Carnegie Hall 140

179

Cedar Hills (Portland) 13
Central Powers 71
Century magazine 5
Chicago 65, 87, 124, 153, 155–156
Chicago Tribune 100
China 70
Christiana 136, 157
civil rights 100, 105
Civil War 147
Clapp, Stephen C. 27
Cleveland 133, 141, 153, 154
Cobb, Ty 7
Cold War 39, 75, 145
Collier's 5
Colorado 24, 83, 145
Colorado Fuel and Iron Company 81–82, 83, 85–86
Columbia River 13
Columbia University 159
Committee for Salvation 115, 117
Communism, Communists 7, 12, 37, 39, 75–76, 96, 107, 119, 124–125, 133, 135, 153–154, 156, 158, 162
Communist International 157–159
Concord, Massachusetts 46
Coney Island 50–51
Congress of Oriental Nations 162
Congress of the Soviets 115
Conrad, Joseph 89
Constantinople 48
Copeland, Charles 8, 26–33, 38, 44, 49, 94
Cosmopolitan magazine 99, 119, 136
Cossacks 93, 118
Crane, Stephen 5
Creel, George 136
Croton-on-Hudson 69
Crowder, General 108
Cuba 78–79

Davis, Richard Harding 89
The Day in Bohemia or Life Among Artists 10, 22
Debs, Eugene 76–77, 83, 125–126, 134, 137–138, 141, 148, 152, 153
Declaration of Independence 154
Dempsey, Jack 7
Detroit 141
Dodge, Edwin 64, 65
Dodge, Mabel 33, 35, 54, 57, 64–66, 68, 87–88, 127, 129, 131
Dunn, Robert 89
Dunne, Finley Peter 96, 102

East Prussia 94
Eastman, Max 25–26, 33, 37–41, 52, 56, 76, 83, 94, 106, 108, 111–112, 119–120, 138–139, 144, 150
Ellis Island 50
El Paso 65, 87
England 21, 87, 92
Eliot, T.S. 5
The Era of Muckrakers 101, 102
Erickson, Mary E. 123
Erie, Pennsylvania 154
Espionage Act 75
Europe 23, 25, 30–31, 35, 39, 43, 48–49, 64–65, 72, 80, 83, 86–87, 94, 116, 142–143, 162
Evans, Harold 100
The Evening Call 120

Federal Meat Inspection Act 99
Fieldman, Scott 150
Fifty Fabulous Years 28
Filon, Madeleine 35
Finland 140, 153, 156, 158, 160
Fitzgerald, F. Scott 5
Ford, Henry 95, 144
Forum 5
Foster, William T. 12
Foster, William Z. 12
France 22, 24, 37, 48, 71, 87, 89, 108, 142, 147
Frank, Waldo 71
Frick, Henry Clay 126, 129
Frost, Stanley 146

Gelb, Barbara 29, 60, 67, 69
General Electric Company 123
Geneva 93
Germany 24, 37, 48, 51, 70–71, 87–89, 92, 95, 98, 107, 110, 114–115, 117, 136, 142–143, 145, 158
Glaspell, Susan 89
Gold Rush 13, 15
Goldman, Emma 83, 125–130, 142, 160
Goodwin, Doris Kearns 102
Great Britain 162
Green, Charlotte 14
Green, Henry 8, 14
Green, Ray 14, 17, 22, 116
Green family 21
Greenwich Village 9, 32–33, 35, 39, 49, 64, 67, 80, 113
Greenwich Village Inn 111
Gridiron Club 102
Gwertzman, Bernard W. 76

Hague 51
Halifax 108
Hall, John Hicklin 19

Hallowell, Robert Canby 10–11, 22, 47
Harriman, Edward 18
Harvard College 5–11, 14, 21- 23, 26–30, 35–36, 40, 43–50, 53, 56, 60–61, 76, 106, 113, 116, 124, 129, 132, 136, 154–155
Harvard Crimson 27, 76
Harvard Lampoon 10, 22, 45
Harvard Monthly 35, 45
Harvard University 105
Hasting College of Law 19
Hasty Pudding Club 46
The Haymarket 51
Hayward, Bill 34, 53–55, 64, 125, 131–133, 138, 153
Hemingway, Ernest 5
Heney, Francis 18–19
Henry, Patrick 147
Hibben, John 89
Hicks, Granville 9, 130, 138
The History of Standard Oil Company 101
Holland 51
Hook, Sidney 39
House, Colonel 111
Hovey, Carl 77, 86
Hunt, Edward E. 46
Hunt's Point Place 142

immigrants 50
India 48
Indiana 133
Industrial Revolution 8
Industrial Workers of the World 34, 55, 57, 61, 64, 76, 82, 129, 132–133, 138, 145, 156
Insurgent Mexico 28, 31, 35, 59, 61, 77, 79, 90, 95
International Socialist Conference 154
Iraq 78
Italy 64–65, 87, 91, 93

Jews 92–93, 110
Jim Crow 11
Joffre, Marshal 89
Jones Thai 84, 123, 125
The Jungle 4, 54, 99

Kalamazoo, Michigan 123
Kaltenborn, Hans V. 5, 28, 47
Kansas 134
Kennan, George 120, 145
Kerensky 117
Kerouac, Jack 49
Kipling, Rudyard 89
Kropotkin, Peter 125

Land Decree (Russia) 117
Landis, Kenesaw Mountain 138
Larson, Thomas W. 101
Latvia 160
Lawrence, D.H. 89
Lawrence, Massachusetts 8, 107
Leavenworth 145
Lehigh Navigational Company 123
Lehman, Daniel 7, 89, 98
Lenin, Vladimir 76, 116, 119, 135–136, 150, 155–156, 158, 161–162
Lewin, Moshe 159
Lianozov, Stepan Georgerish 110
Liberator magazine 38, 133, 138–139, 157
Life Magazine 103
Lincoln, Abraham 41, 103
Lippmann, Walter 5, 24, 46, 52, 57, 76–77, 79, 88, 90
Little, Frank 132
London, Jack 5, 59, 62
London, England 48, 52
Los Angeles 123
Los Angeles Times 36, 82
Lost Generation 72
Lost Revolutionary 28
Lovejoy, Asa 15
Lownsdale, Daniel H. 15
Loyd, Henry Demaest 100
Ludlow, Colorado 44, 59, 81, 83, 85, 87, 104, 107

MacColl, Kimbark E. 15
Machinist Hall (Chicago) 155
Macmillan publishing 111
Madison Square Garden 54, 59, 64
Mail (New York) 70
Malmbury, Madam Aine 161
Marquis, Don 157
The Marseillaise 141
Marx, Karl (Marxism) 40, 97, 107, 120, 134, 139, 148–149, 155–157
The Masses 38–41, 52, 54, 56, 66, 73, 94, 108, 120, 130, 133, 136–138, 140, 142–145
May Day 153–154
McCarthy, Joseph 39, 150
McClure, Sam 103
McClure's Magazine 101, 103–104
McNamara, J.B. 36
McSorley's tavern 33
Mensheviks 114–117
Metropolitan Magazine 5, 59, 65–66, 70, 71, 77–79, 81, 83–89, 95, 98, 139
Mexican Revolution 28, 44, 59, 87, 89, 142

Mexico 12, 24, 44, 59, 62, 65, 77–78, 80–81, 83, 88–89, 94, 95, 107, 116, 124, 132, 138, 148
Middle East 7, 25, 162
Mitchell, John N. 19
monopolies 103
Moscow 24, 44, 52, 158–159, 162, 164
Mother Earth 126
muckraking journalism 54, 56, 98–104
Munk, Michael 12
Musser, Rick 102

Napoleon 80
National Guard (U.S. and Colorado) 81, 82, 84
nationalism 76, 100, 132
Nevada 66
New England 13, 47
New Republic 47, 57, 90
New Star Casino 140
New York 73, 77–79, 87, 88, 89, 90, 95, 98, 100, 106, 111, 116, 125, 127, 129, 135, 140–141, 154, 161
New York Age 100
New York state 39, 69
New York Times 75, 78, 107, 132, 135, 147
New York Tribune 90
New Yorker 137
Newark 141
North American Review 100
Norway 157
Nye, Bill 17

Obama, Barack 12
O'Connor, Richard 12–13, 15, 28, 32, 46, 97
O'Neill, Eugene 24, 66–71, 73
Oregon 6, 11, 14–15, 18–19, 39, 46–47, 115
Oregon and California Railroad Company 18
Oregon General Land Office 18
Oregon Land Fraud Ring 18–19, 34, 99
The Oregonian 12, 15
Overton, William 15

Pacific Northwest 16
Palmer raids 33, 159, 160
Panama Canal 123
Paris 31, 48, 51
Paterson, New Jersey 44, 53, 54–57, 59, 64, 80, 88, 107, 124, 131
Patriot Act 75
Peirce, Waldo 22, 48, 88
Pendleton, Oregon 123

Persia 48
Petrograd 106,109, 110, 112, 114–115, 135–136, 140, 158
Pettygrove, Francisco 15
Pew, Matthew 138
Philadelphia 140, 144–145
Phillips, David Graham 99, 101
Phillips, John S. 102
Pitter, Stephen A. Douglas 18
Pittsburgh 126
Portland, Oregon 6, 9–18, 20, 23, 30, 35–36, 40, 66, 76, 96, 107, 116
Portland Academy 16, 20
Pottsville, Pennsylvania 123
Progressives, progressivism 7, 18–19, 33, 54, 75, 85, 99, 101, 124, 125
Provincetown 67, 69, 156
Provincetown Players 67–69, 124
Provisional Government, Russia 107, 110, 112,1 14
Prussianism 154
Puget Sound 66
Pullman Strike 133
Puram, Walter 12
Pure Food and Drug Act 99
Puter, Stephen A. Douglas 19

Reconstruction 13
Red Army 158
Red Cross 109
Red Guard 117
Red Scare 75, 150, 153
Reed, Charles Jerome 7–9, 12, 14, 17–21, 23–24, 26, 32, 34, 36, 56, 62, 87, 89, 99, 107, 163
Reed, Charlotte 14
Reed, Harry 21, 22, 23, 56, 150
Reed, Henry 14, 24
Reed, Margaret 6, 9, 12–4, 16, 24, 25, 116
Reed, Simeon C. 12, 34
Reed College 12
Reiger, C.C. 101–103
Reuf, Abe 19
Revolutionary Age 148
Revolutionary Socialists 115
Rio Grande 78
Robbins, Col. Raymond 109
Robinson, Boardman 90, 91
Rochester, N.Y. 86, 107, 128
Rockefeller, John D., Jr. 82–86
Roosevelt, Theodore 8, 17–20, 32, 78–79, 89, 98–99, 101–102, 104, 116, 144
Rosenstone, Robert 13, 15, 23, 31, 48–50, 65, 135
Roumania (Romania) 31

Index 183

Russell, Charles Edward 101
Russia, Russians 7, 37, 40–41, 59, 61, 72–73, 78, 91–94, 106–108, 111–115, 120, 127, 136, 138–139, 148, 151–152, 154, 157–158
Russian Revolution 59, 110, 114, 119, 135, 141, 151, 153

St. Petersburg 24, 44, 128
San Francisco 15, 19, 48
"Sangar" 36–37
Saturday Evening Post 5, 89, 139
Scandinavia 157
Schenectady, New York 123
Schmitz, Eugene 19
Seattle 15
Sedgwick 103
Serbia 91
Serpukov 159
Seven Arts 70–71
Shame of the Cities 34, 54, 101
Shapley, Joseph 148, 155
Shaw, George Barnard 89
Sidis, William James 154
Simkin, John 100
Sinclair, Upton 34, 54, 99, 150, 151
Sisson, George 119, 136, 137
Six Red Months in Russia 73
Slobodin, Henry L. 150
Smart Set 5
Smolny 115
Snow, MacCormac 12
So Short a Time 60
Socialism, Socialist Party 7, 12, 34–37, 39, 57, 59, 61, 70–71, 75, 76, 82–83, 94–96, 98, 107–108, 110, 114, 116–117, 124–126, 129, 132–133, 135–137, 140, 142–145, 147–149, 153, 154, 155–156, 158
Socialist Club (Harvard) 8, 61, 129, 133
Sosson, Edwin E. 102
South America 39
Soviet Ark 7, 127, 150
Soviet Union, Soviets 33, 39, 56–57, 76, 110, 118–119, 135, 145, 147, 154, 157, 159–161
Spain 22, 46
Stalin, Joseph 12
Stedman, Seymour 142–143
Steffens, Josephine 104, 137
Steffens, Lincoln 8, 17–18, 20, 21, 25–26, 28–29, 32–38, 44, 48–49, 54, 76, 83, 87, 94, 99–101, 103, 104, 111, 130, 136–137, 150
Stein, Gertrude 64
Stockholm Socialists 108

Street, Julian 53, 76, 89, 97, 138
Sunday, Billy 95
Sweden 108, 120, 135–137
Switzerland 87

Taft, Prescott 18
Tammany Hall 50, 109
Tannenbaum, Frank 127
Tarbell, Ida M. 101, 103
Ten Days That Shook the World 12, 35, 37–38, 90, 95, 104–106, 111, 113, 116, 118, 120, 144–145, 148, 150, 156, 158
Times Union, Jacksonville, Florida 146
Tribune, New York 146
Trinidad, Colorado 85
Tripoli Volunteer Force 93
Trotsky, Leon 116, 118–119, 136
tsar of Russia 72, 92, 107, 112, 114, 115, 119, 128, 148–149, 151, 157
Turkey 104
Twain, Mark 8, 17, 41

United Mine Workers of America 82, 83
United States (America, Americans, U.S.) 8, 12, 33, 37-38, 40, 47, 49, 51, 52–54, 56, 59, 60–64, 70, 73, 75, 77–78, 86, 92, 94, 96, 98, 105, 107, 110–111, 119, 124–127, 135, 136, 137, 139, 140, 142–147, 158
United States (Danish steamer) 108
United States Committee on Public Information in Russia 119, 136
U.S. Constitution 101
U.S. Department of Labor 160
U.S. House of Representatives 98, 102
U.S. Senate 73, 99, 145
U.S. State Department 71, 108, 136–139, 153, 156, 161
United States Supreme Court 19
United States War Department 133, 138
University of Kansas 102
Utah 134

Vanity Fair 102
Vietnam 78
Villa, Pancho 12, 59, 60, 61, 62, 65, 77, 78, 79, 80, 116
Vogue 102

Walker, Dale 46
Wallerstein, David 144
The War in Eastern Europe 87, 90, 92–93, 95
Washington, George 147
Washington, D.C. 71–73, 89, 124, 132, 140, 150

Washington Square (NYC) 33, 49, 72
Watson, Bruce 149
Wells, Ida B. 100
"Where the Heart Is" 39–40, 50, 52, 61
White Army 153, 157
White Palace (Russia) 114
Whitlock, Brand 101
Whitman, Walt 71, 145
Williams College 39
Williamson, John N. 19
Wilson, Woodrow 37, 74, 86, 103, 111, 116, 136, 140, 144
Wolfe, Thomas 5

women's rights 100
Worcester, Massachusetts 141
World Almanac 12
World War I (also the European War, the Great War, the War to End All Wars) 28, 31–32, 37, 38, 43–44, 59, 65, 72, 78–79, 93–95, 98, 100, 105, 106, 108, 124–125, 132, 142, 145, 150, 152, 154

Young, Art 73

Zinn, Howard 17, 23, 24, 97